"*The Indispensable Electoral College* is an essential primer on presidential elections in the United States. Tara Ross offers a sweeping and nuanced examination of the Electoral College and provides a compelling defense for our oft-misunderstood election system. Her easy narrative style deftly navigates a deep body of history, politics, and law."

—**DEREK T. MULLER**, associate professor of law, Pepperdine University School of Law

THE INDISPENSABLE ELECTORAL COLLEGE

THE
INDISPENSABLE
ELECTORAL
COLLEGE

How the Founders' Plan Saves
Our Country from Mob Rule

★ ★ ★

TARA ROSS

REGNERY GATEWAY

Regnery Gateway™ is a trademark of Salem Communications Holding Corporation
Regnery® is a registered trademark of Salem Communications Holding Corporation

Cataloging-in-Publication data on file with the Library of Congress

ISBN 978-1-62157-674-7

Published in the United States by
Regnery Gateway
An imprint of Regnery Publishing
A Division of Salem Media Group
300 New Jersey Ave NW
Washington, DC 20001
www.Regnery.com

Manufactured in the United States of America

10 9 8 7 6 5 4 3 2 1

Books are available in quantity for promotional or premium use. For information on discounts and terms, please visit our website: www.Regnery.com.

Distributed to the trade by
Perseus Distribution
www.perseusdistribution.com

For Adam, Emma, and Grant,

with much love

CONTENTS

PREFACE

I am often asked if I would change anything about the Electoral College. My answer has changed over time. Perhaps that is unsurprising. I am older and have seen more of life than that third-year law student who started studying the Electoral College in 2001.

As a thirty-something lawyer, I was a firm believer in the system, but I also wavered a bit on the margins: should we fix perceived problems with the House contingent election? Should we work harder to prevent faithless electors? Or should we just leave the system alone? In *Enlightened Democracy: The Case for the Electoral College*, I joked that perhaps the best approach was "if it ain't broke, don't fix it." Yet I think I was afraid to trust that sentiment fully, and I still offered a few small "fixes" for readers to consider.

Those who read both *Enlightened Democracy* and *The Indispensable Electoral College* will doubtless see that my approach has solidified over time. The older I get, the more I think that "if it ain't broke, don't fix it" is always the best approach to the Electoral College. Yes, some aspects of the system sound odd in our democratic-minded society. But making the system more democratic to accommodate modern sensibilities is not the answer. We serve ourselves best if we educate voters about the reasons that our Founders established checks and balances in our Constitution—and in our presidential election system. The Founders created checks and balances in 1787 to protect American liberty from the imperfections of human nature. Humans are still imperfect. Safeguards are still needed.

To some degree, this book is a compilation of things that I've been writing and saying for years, either in books, blog posts, or in testimony before state legislators. But it is also far more than that. How could it be anything else in the wake of the 2016 election? If nothing else, that election showed us that *anything* can happen. We are blessed to have a system with so many checks and balances; it gives us the flexibility that we need, no matter what crazy circumstance heads our way. But we, as a country, need to understand the Electoral College better if it is to serve us with maximum effectiveness. The 2016 election demonstrated that most voters do not understand the intricacies of their system. Thus, they often felt trapped. I spent much of the 2016 election year being sad about the situation. How could so many feel so trapped when the system is actually quite accommodating? If knowledge is power, then I hope this book empowers voters.

This book is neither pro-Trump nor anti-Trump. It is neither pro-Clinton nor anti-Clinton. I ran early drafts of the manuscript by a variety of people, hoping to drive out anything that seemed to fall too much on one side or the other. I asked Donald Trump voters, reluctant Trump voters, Evan McMullin voters, Gary Johnson voters, and Hillary Clinton voters to review this book. I owe many thanks to those who helped in that effort, but I've also decided not to list them individually here. I know how each of these reviewers ultimately cast his or her ballot, but I also know that many of them would rather not take a side publicly. Suffice it to say that they came from many walks of life and several had quite strong opinions about the 2016 election and the candidates. You know who you are. I so much appreciated your input and adjusted the book in several places in response to your comments. Ultimately, I hope we've worked together to create a book that will help voters of any persuasion to better understand those on the other side of the political aisle—or perhaps even those within their own party.

Besides my anonymous readers, I owe many thanks to a few lawyers and academics who reviewed early drafts of this manuscript: Professor Derek Muller, Mr. Sean Parnell, and Mr. Peter Robinson. Thank you for your time and helpful comments. Perhaps I owe an extra big thank you to Mr. Patrick O'Daniel, a lawyer in Texas who has reviewed both of my Electoral College books in advance—and his kids also served as helpful reviewers for *We Elect a President: The Story of Our Electoral College*. A big thank you to the O'Daniel family. Two University of Texas law students performed extra footnote checks on the manuscript during the spring of 2017: Ashley Terrazas and Joshua Kelly. Thank you for taking time out of your studies to help me. Finally, I very much appreciated two Texas electors who answered questions that I had about the behind-the-scenes logistics in our state: Matthew Stringer and Bill Greene. I am grateful for your help.

America's presidential election system was designed to serve a large, diverse country. Some commentators today seem to think that the Electoral College is outdated because of improved technology or greater ease of communications. I would argue the opposite: our country has grown even bigger and more diverse than our Founders could have imagined. The Electoral College is, if anything, needed even more today than it was in 1787.

I hope everyone enjoys the book.

INTRODUCTION

A presidential candidate once wrote that "the choice of a President is a matter for the people:—to be installed against their will no man could calculate upon a happy or beneficial administration."[1]

Just a few weeks later, that candidate would lose the presidential election, despite winning the reported national popular vote.

The campaign had been a rough one, and its conclusion was no easier.[2] Would so-called "faithless electors" influence the outcome? Would someone be deprived of a majority of electors, prompting a back-up election in the House? "I consider whatever choice we may make will be only a choice of evils," one candidate moaned.[3] He was no longer a contender, but many believed that he would take a spot in the new administration if it were offered.

Would the nation accept a president who was not the popular vote winner? Was the election rigged? Was there a "corrupt coalition" arrayed against one of the candidates? One congressman blasted, "The force of public opinion must prevail, or there is an end of Liberty."[4]

The losing candidate in this story wasn't Hillary Clinton. It was Andrew Jackson.[5] The celebrated war hero was one of four serious contenders in the 1824 campaign. As vote totals trickled in from the states, it became clear that Jackson would ultimately win the national popular vote. Of course, that tally was incomplete, and there is reason to believe that a more complete count would have favored John Quincy Adams. But Jackson didn't seem to care about any of that! He'd won a plurality of the individual votes cast and recorded that year. When the presidential electors met, he won the votes of ninety-nine of them. Ninety-nine was more than anyone else had won, but it still fell short of the required 131 majority.[6]

Nevertheless, Jackson believed he had the support of the people. Surely he was on the road to victory. Why would one of the other contenders want to be president without such support? "I should prefer to remain a plain cultivator of the soil as I am," Jackson concluded, "than occupy that which is truly the first office in the world, if the voice of the nation was against it."[7]

Interestingly, Jackson may have received the votes of a few electors who were supposed to vote for someone else. The North Carolina slate of fifteen electors ended up voting en bloc for Andrew Jackson, although as many as five of them may have been pledged to vote for Adams. In New York, three electors who were expected to vote for Henry Clay also defected.[8] One voted for Jackson; another voted for Adams; the third voted for William Crawford.

Whatever Jackson thought about it, his popular vote lead was not enough. American presidential elections are a battle to win the most state votes (called electoral votes), rather than the most individual popular votes nationwide. If no one wins a majority, then the election is decided in the House of Representatives.

Jackson had only a plurality of electors, not a majority, so the election moved to the House. That body selected Adams as the next president.[9] Jackson was irate. He spent the next four years complaining that the will of the people had been thwarted and the election stolen from him. Many voters agreed, and the outrage propelled him to a relatively easy victory in 1828.

Since Jackson's time, as many as four more candidates may have lost the presidency despite winning the national popular vote. These elections occurred, curiously enough, in pairs. In only a twelve-year span, two candidates in the late 1800s won the recorded national popular vote but lost the electoral vote: Samuel Tilden may have won the popular vote in 1876; Grover Cleveland won it in 1888.[10] More than one hundred years later, there was another pair of such elections: Al Gore lost to George W. Bush in 2000, and Hillary Clinton lost to Donald Trump in 2016.

Such outcomes remain relatively rare, but recent elections have resurrected old concerns about the Electoral College. Perhaps making matters worse, throughout the 2016 presidential campaign, polls showed that Donald Trump was one of the least-liked candidates in recent memory.[11] Did the Electoral College fail America? Has it outlived its usefulness? Should it be replaced?

Emphatically, *no*. But the system can and should be better understood by the nation that it serves.

A SYSTEM BIASED AGAINST DEMOCRATS?

In 1824, Andrew Jackson and John Quincy Adams were both members of the same political party. But in every other election with a discrepancy between the electoral and popular votes, the losing candidate has been the Democrat. Odd coincidence? Or is the Electoral College biased against the Democratic Party?

Democratic President Barack Obama seemed to imply just that in a December 2016 press conference: "The Electoral College is a vestige," he told reporters.[12] "It's a carry-over . . . . [T]here are some structures in our political system, as envisioned by the Founders, that sometimes are going to disadvantage Democrats."[13]

It's a funny thing to say, of course. Republicans have spent years bemoaning the huge lead that Democrats have enjoyed in the Electoral College. The so-called "Blue Wall" was thought to be impenetrable, apparently giving Democrats an advantage before voting even started. Pundits claimed that Democrats would begin 2016 with a head start of at least 217 electoral votes—and perhaps as many as 249. "No matter whom Republicans nominate to face Hillary Rodham Clinton in November 2016," one columnist at the *Washington Post* wrote, "that candidate will start at a disadvantage. It's not polling, Clinton's deep résumé or the improving state of the economy. It's the electoral college."[14]

Another political scientist made a similar prediction in 2014. Benjamin Highton, a professor at the University of California, Davis, claimed that the Democratic tilt in the Electoral College was so heavy that a Republican would be unlikely to win the 2016 election unless that Republican first won the national popular vote by at least one or two percentage points.[15] The actual results flipped this expectation on its head: Donald Trump won the electoral vote fairly easily, even as Hillary Clinton won the nationwide popular tally by more than two percentage points.[16]

Such results naturally resurrect the question: Is the Electoral College biased against Democrats? Or did Democrats simply blow their lead by taking voters for granted? If Democrats did indeed blow their lead, then they were merely repeating a mistake that the Republican Party made in the 1990s. After the Ronald Reagan years, it was said that Republicans had a "lock" on the Electoral College. At least twenty-one states, including California, were consistently voting Republican. How could Democrats hope to compete?[17]

Bill Clinton soon found a way, of course. He turned California and eight other states blue for the first time since 1964.[18] Other presidents have accomplished similar feats. In 1952, Republican Dwight D. Eisenhower won sixteen states that hadn't voted Republican since 1928 and two others that hadn't voted Republican since 1924.[19] Democrat Franklin Delano Roosevelt, of course, demolished a North-South divide that had persisted, for the most part, since the Civil War. In 1936, he won every state except Maine and Vermont.

The reality is that any "bias" in the Electoral College does not consistently favor or disfavor either of the political parties. To the degree that there are biases, they are short-lived. States change their allegiances fairly consistently. Party allegiance is like a pendulum, slowly swinging back and forth, first appearing to favor the one party, and then appearing to favor the other. The tension in the system reflects the constant, healthy competition between the two parties: each is always trying to outperform the other by capturing the large bloc of voters in the middle of American politics.

A careful study of history reveals that the Electoral College is neither pro-Democrat nor pro-Republican. It simply rewards the candidate who appears to be listening to the greatest cross-section of people at any given time. President Obama complained that the system put Democrats at a disadvantage, but he came closer to the truth when he concluded, "[I]f we have a strong message, if we're speaking to what the American people care about, typically the popular vote and the Electoral College vote will align."[20]

PUTTING 2016 INTO PERSPECTIVE

The 2016 election results shocked the nation. For most of the year, polls had indicated that Democrat Hillary Clinton would soundly defeat Republican Donald Trump.[21] The business mogul's best-case scenario was believed to be a narrow victory built on swing states like Florida, North Carolina, and Ohio.[22] Pundits never seriously considered the possibility that several states behind the Blue Wall—Wisconsin, Michigan, and Pennsylvania—could go red for the first time since the 1980s. But then they did. Republicans also won three other swing states that voted for Obama in 2012: Iowa, Florida, and Ohio.

The election year was an odd one, right from the beginning. The Electoral College requires coalition building. Historically, the candidate who builds the most diverse coalition will also win the states needed for an electoral majority. So what happens when both political parties nominate candidates who have high unfavorable ratings and aren't especially good at coalition building? Polls showed that most voters wished for a third choice.[23] On social media, users joked that they would vote for the "Sweet Meteor O'Death" instead of Clinton or Trump.[24] Yard signs popped up in some parts of the country: "Anyone Else 2016."[25]

The situation was so bad that Libertarian candidates Gary Johnson and Bill Weld felt that they had an opening. They ran an ad encouraging voters to consider them as a "credible alternative to ClinTrump."[26] In the end, more than eight million voters would cast a ballot for an alternative candidate, far more than the roughly two million voters who had cast third-party ballots in 2012.[27]

The division started in the political primaries, long before Election Day. Remember, the nomination processes are distinct from the Electoral College. The primaries are a creation of political parties and the states. By contrast, the Electoral College has its roots in the Constitution. America's unique presidential system has served the nation well for centuries because it encourages compromise, moderation, and coalition building. In 2016, the primaries seemed to do the precise opposite.

The Democratic primaries had at least one glaring problem: the superdelegates, which the party created in the wake of the disastrous 1972 election.[28] George McGovern lost to Richard Nixon in a massive landslide that year, largely because he was perceived as an extremist. As if that weren't bad enough, the party soon suffered another embarrassing loss when Ronald Reagan trounced Jimmy Carter in 1980. The Democratic Party became determined to create something new—and better. Their new superdelegates would act as a check on voters' emotions, steering the party toward a person with mainstream appeal and away from someone who satisfies only one segment of the party.[29]

In 2016, the superdelegates should have steered the party away from a candidate who was so distrusted by most Americans. Instead, they marched in lockstep, supporting a woman who had high unfavorable ratings and who was being investigated by the FBI.[30] In fact, they backed her so early in the process that she had no serious challenger for the nomination except the self-proclaimed socialist Bernie Sanders—hardly a coalition-building figure himself. The Democratic Party shouldn't have been surprised when things went awry. Open legal questions hung over Hillary Clinton's head throughout the campaign, undermining her efforts to gain the trust of the American people.

The Republican nomination process had its own problems, of course. Those primaries were more purely populist, at least in part because there were no superdelegates. Yet the process that emerged was broken. No one had any incentive to work with anyone else. Coalition building was unnecessary to win the nomination—indeed, it was frequently scorned. Divisiveness, anger, and single-issue voting were rewarded. Each candidate and his supporters effectively hunkered down, hoping to outlast everyone else. No majority was required to win. The only goal was to get a larger plurality than the second-place winner.[31] A bare win of 20 percent over 19 percent would have been sufficient. Voters got swept up in their anger or cynicism and forgot the real goal: to find a presidential candidate who could unify as many people as possible.

The question isn't whether one did or didn't like the nominees who ultimately emerged. Instead, the question is about the process itself. What incentives were created by the primaries? Can such processes reliably produce nominees who know how to unify voters and build coalitions, as the Electoral College requires?

In the end, a coalition was built, but it was based more on policies than people.[32] The winning coalition was composed of voters who were fed up with the establishment in Washington. They disliked many of President Obama's big-government, progressive policies and were suffering under skyrocketing health care costs. They wanted to make a statement against politicians who play by one set of rules while everyone else plays by another. They felt left behind by their government. These voters wanted to shake up the status quo on both sides of the political aisle and felt that voting for Trump was the best way to make that happen.

There was another, quieter coalition in 2016, but it never figured out how to express its voice: it was that group of people who had hoped for a third choice. These voters felt stuck. Should they vote for the "crude" candidate, as Trump supporter Laura Ingraham once described him?[33] Or should they vote for the "corrupt" candidate, as many perceived Clinton?[34] These voters were afraid that a vote for a third-party candidate would be wasted. On Election Day, many held their noses and voted for the candidate they deemed the "lesser of two evils."

These voters might be surprised to learn that they were never as stuck as they thought they were. Instead, the problem can be traced back to state legislatures, which largely refused to intervene in 2016. State officials repeatedly deferred to the Republican National Committee, the Democratic National Committee, and even the mainstream media. They forgot that the Constitution deliberately avoids putting the presidential election in the hands of a select few at the national level. The Constitution instead disperses this power among the various state legislatures. If voters in a state did not like the choice of candidates, their state legislatures had the power to step in and correct the situation, although no one seems to have realized it.

A little education shows that the Electoral College is more adaptable than is generally recognized. The states are ultimately in charge of any presidential election. If they feel that things are going off track, they have many tools to make their voices heard.

**

Should Americans be worried that two elections in sixteen years have shown a discrepancy between the popular and electoral votes? Perhaps, but their worry should not be directed at the Electoral College. The Constitution's presidential election system is one of the few remaining marks of sanity in a political system that has gone awry in many other ways. It should be protected at all costs. Indeed, the Electoral College, which fosters coalitions and consensus, can even be a model for reforming the rest of our election system.

PART ONE

THE FOUNDERS' INVENTION

CHAPTER ONE

A REPUBLIC, IF YOU CAN KEEP IT

As Benjamin Franklin left the Constitutional Convention, he was spotted by a Philadelphia matron. She was curious. What had the delegates been doing behind closed doors all this time? "Doctor," she called out to Franklin, "what have we got, a Republic or a Monarchy?"[1] For the first time all summer, Franklin was free to answer the question. His response was simple: "A Republic, if you can keep it."[2]

Unfortunately, the statement is often misquoted. Too many Americans have been told that Franklin responded: "A democracy, if you can keep it."[3] The mistake reflects Americans' declining understanding of their own heritage.

The Founders would not have made such a mistake so easily. They were well aware of the important differences between a republic and a democracy, and they knew better than to create a *simple* democracy.[4] The Founders wanted to be self-governing, of course. They had just fought a revolution in part because they had no representation in Parliament. They weren't likely to abandon the principle of self-governance so soon. But their desire to be self-governing was tempered by their study of history: They knew that pure democracies have a tendency to implode. The Founders would surely be surprised to find that modern Americans hold simple democracy in such esteem. The Founders' goal had been to create something different—and better. They knew they needed something unique if the citizens of a diverse nation, composed of both large and small states, were to live together peacefully.

THE CONSTITUTIONAL CONVENTION

The Constitutional Convention of 1787 got off to a slow start.[5] Delegates were supposed to meet in Philadelphia on May 14, but travel was tough in those days. Most delegates couldn't make it on time, and only a handful were present on that Monday morning. Indeed, a quorum wasn't achieved for almost two weeks. Finally, on May 25, those who were present decided to proceed, even though some states still had no representatives in attendance.[6]

The delegates had been given the task of revising the Articles of Confederation, the governing charter of the United States since 1781. The Confederation Congress hoped to restrict the Convention to "the sole and express purpose *of revising the articles of Confederation*," but many states had given their delegates much broader authority,[7] and it's likely that at least a few delegates went into the Convention believing that a mere revision of the Articles would not be enough. Certainly delegates such as James Madison and Alexander Hamilton felt that a stronger national government was needed to handle interstate commerce and foreign relations, among other matters.

Only twenty-nine delegates were present when the Convention finally got under way, but fifty-five would eventually attend at least some portion of the Convention. Nineteen delegates never made an appearance, and Rhode Island refused to send any delegates at all. The delegates' average age never exceeded forty-three. Benjamin Franklin was the oldest at eighty-one, while Jonathan Dayton of New Jersey was the youngest at twenty-six.

Despite their youth, the delegates were unusually accomplished. Most had served in Congress or the colonial or state legislatures. They were well versed in the works of such philosophers as John Locke and Baron de Montesquieu. They were students of history, and they could speak knowledgably about the successes and failures of other political systems. Many were lawyers. Notably, their deliberations were relatively free of the partisanship that plagues modern American politics. Remember that political parties hadn't been created yet. Instead, the delegates' strongest allegiances were to their home states. Perhaps most importantly, though, the delegates were realistic about human nature. They knew that people are fallible and that power corrupts.

Thomas Jefferson, then serving as an emissary in Paris and not himself a delegate, was certainly impressed when he read the names of the delegates. "It is really an assembly of demi-gods," he wrote to his friend John Adams.[8] Indeed, the Convention of 1787 was a historically singular assembly. Nothing of its kind had ever occurred before—and nothing of its kind seems likely to occur again.

George Washington was the Convention's president, but he contributed little to the discussions. He considered it inappropriate for the presiding officer to express himself on pending matters.[9] Moreover, the former general was already being called the "Father of the Country,"[10] and he may have worried that his celebrity would give his opinions too much weight. Whatever his motivations may have been, Washington never rose to speak until the last day of the Convention. He voted with the Virginians, however, and he was known to favor a stronger national government.

The delegates worked through the sweltering summer with the windows and blinds in Philadelphia's State Hall closed. They considered it imperative that the discussions be conducted secretly so all delegates would feel free to speak their minds. Throughout the debates, the thirty-six-year-old James Madison took comprehensive notes. He said later that his labor in that hot room throughout the summer nearly killed him. "I was not absent a single day, nor more than a casual fraction of an hour in any day, so that I could not have lost a single speech, unless a very short one," he later confirmed.[11] Others took notes too, but Madison's notes remain the best source on the debates in the Constitutional Convention.

Of all the issues that shaped the summer's deliberations, none was more important than the ever-present tension between the large and the small states.[12] Friction among the states was perhaps unavoidable. Each had operated with nearly sovereign independence for decades, first as a colony, then as a state under the Articles of Confederation. It would be no easy matter to convince the states, especially the smaller ones, to sacrifice their much-valued sovereignty to a new union of states.

The delegates would spend months in a deep, intellectual discussion and debate. Absolutely everything was on the table. Should Americans have one or several presidents? Would the nation rely on "one state, one vote" representation or "one person, one vote"? Should Congress propose constitutional amendments or would the states be better stewards of that responsibility? Should states have a veto over congressional legislation? The delegates discussed the successes and failures of ancient Greece and Rome. What lessons could be learned from history? How could a diverse nation composed of both large and small states govern itself, even as it treated minority groups fairly? How could it protect itself against government officials who would abuse their power?

Surely such philosophical discussions are rarely heard in the halls of today's Congress! This eminently qualified group of men understood how hard it would be to protect freedom in the face of so many challenges. They were determined to make it happen anyway.

THE EVILS OF DEMOCRACY

The authors of the Constitution have been accused of all sorts of dishonorable motives. Conventional wisdom has it that America's Founders were too "aristocratic."[13] They were elitists who "distrusted the people," so they "placed elaborate barriers between them and the actual power to govern."[14] When it came to selecting the president, the Founders certainly "did not trust the people with such an important task."[15]

Such statements betray a gross misunderstanding of the motives that drove the delegates at the Constitutional Convention. True, they were skeptical of simple, unfettered democracy. They knew that people are imperfect. Emotions can grip a mob and propel voters into unreasonable action. History shows that minority groups tend to be tyrannized in such situations. But the Founders were, if anything, equal-opportunity skeptics. While they didn't always trust voters, they didn't trust another group of people, either: those who are elected to hold office. The Constitution they created is therefore full of checks and balances aimed at everyone— voters and officials alike. The Founders knew that unrestrained power is always dangerous. No person or group is immune from mistakes, selfishness, and greed.

The delegates' skepticism was supported by their deep knowledge of history. They knew how and why other governments had failed. Indeed, about two years before the Constitutional Convention, an interesting exchange occurred between Thomas Jefferson and James Madison. Jefferson was then in Paris, where he had easy access to a wide variety of books. Did Madison want some? Yes! Madison certainly did. He quickly took Jefferson up on the offer, asking for "treatises on the antient or modern fœderal republics, on the law of Nations, and the history natural and political of the New World; to which I will add such of the Greek and Roman authors where they can be got very cheap, as are worth having and are not on the common list of School classics."[16]

Madison studied these works, developing strong ideas of what would and would not work in a constitutional government. When the Convention opened, many of his ideas formed the basis for the delegates' discussions.[17] His study had convinced him that Americans would need something better than a simple democracy. Unfettered majorities such as those found in pure democracies tend toward tyranny. In a pure democracy, Madison later explained,

> [a] common passion or interest will, in almost every case, be
> felt by a majority of the whole; a communication and concert
> results from the form of government itself; and there is nothing

to check the inducements to sacrifice the weaker party or an obnoxious individual. Hence it is that such democracies have ever been spectacles of turbulence and contention; have ever been found incompatible with personal security or the rights of property; and have in general been as short in their lives as they have been violent in their deaths.[18]

Others agreed with him, and the rhetoric became quite strong during the Constitutional Convention. Early in the debates, Elbridge Gerry, a delegate from Massachusetts, forcefully asserted that "[t]he evils we experience flow from the excess of democracy."[19] Edmund Randolph of Virginia concurred that "the general object was to provide a cure for the evils under which the [United States] laboured; that in tracing these evils to their origin every man had found it in the turbulence and follies of democracy."[20] Later in the Convention, Randolph reaffirmed his words, noting that the "democratic licentiousness of the State Legislatures proved the necessity of a firm Senate. . . . to controul the democratic branch of the [National] Legislature."[21]

Other delegates also sought controls on the impulsiveness and emotion that they believed would sometimes characterize public opinion. As Gouverneur Morris of Pennsylvania remarked, "Every man of observation had seen in the democratic branches of the State Legislatures, precipitation—in Congress changeableness, in every department excesses [against] personal liberty private property & personal safety."[22]

The arguments against pure democracy continued after the Constitutional Convention had concluded. Madison spoke to Jefferson of the danger that could arise when the government becomes "the mere instrument of the major number of the constituents."[23] Alexander Hamilton continued these arguments against democracies in a speech before the New York ratifying convention on June 21, 1788:

It has been observed, by an honorable gentleman, that a pure democracy, if it were practicable, would be the most perfect government. Experience has proved that no position in politics is more false than this. The ancient democracies, in which the people themselves deliberated, never possessed one feature of good government. Their very character was tyranny; their figure, deformity.[24]

Others in the founding generation concurred. John Adams, who signed the Declaration of Independence and later became president, declared, "[D]emocracy never lasts long. It soon wastes, exhausts, and murders itself. There never was a democracy yet that did not commit suicide."[25] Another signatory to the Declaration of Independence, Benjamin Rush, warned, "A simple democracy . . . is one of the greatest of evils."[26] A third signer, John Witherspoon, agreed: "Pure democracy cannot subsist long, nor be carried far into the department of state—it is very subject to caprice and the madness of popular rage."[27] And Fisher Ames cautioned the delegates to the Massachusetts convention that ratified the Constitution, "A democracy is a volcano, which conceals the fiery materials of its own destruction. These will produce an eruption, and carry desolation in their way."[28]

Why would the Founders fear simple democracy so much? Simple. They recognized a danger that is too often shrugged off today: in a pure democracy, 51 percent of the people can rule the other 49 percent—*all the time, without question.* (In some situations, even a plurality might suffice.) Imagine how simple democracy might play out today. What dangers might a mob mentality lead to in the wake of an event such as 9/11? In fear, anger, or immediate emotion, a bare majority could enact any law it wanted to, regardless of its effect on the other 49 percent. Even very sizable minorities can be tyrannized in such a system. Religious freedoms and civil liberties can easily be infringed.

The Founders knew these dangers all too well. They'd fought a revolution partly because they had no representation in Parliament, but they also remembered something else: representation alone would not have been enough to protect the American colonies. After all, Americans would still have been a minority in that governmental body. Without some other protection, Americans' needs and opinions could easily be forgotten by the majority of citizens at home in England.[29] They would simply be outvoted time and time again.

The Founders' distrust of emotional mobs wasn't the end of the discussion, of course. These men who spoke so forcefully in 1787 against the vices of a pure democracy were the same men who had declared in 1776 that governments "deriv[e] their just powers from the consent of the governed."[30] Their distrust of democracy implied no opposition to self-government. To the contrary, the Founders knew and often spoke of the need to allow the will of the people to operate in the new government that they were crafting.

"Notwithstanding the oppressions & injustice experienced among us from democracy," argued George Mason of Virginia, "the genius of the people is in favor of it, and the genius of the people must be consulted."[31] One legislative branch, he argued, should be directly elected by the people, serving as the "grand depository of the democratic principle of the [Government]."[32] It would "know & sympathise with every part of the community."[33] He admitted that the state governments "had been too democratic"[34] in the past but cautioned his fellow delegates not to use these past failures as an excuse to "incautiously run into the opposite extreme."[35]

He need not have worried. Other delegates also realized that the government would not be legitimate or sustainable if it didn't reflect the voice of the people. James Wilson of Pennsylvania argued that the "most numerous branch of the Legislature [should come] immediately from the people," because "[n]o government could long subsist without the confidence of the people."[36] Madison also "considered the popular election of one branch of the National Legislature as essential to every plan of free Government."[37]

The delegates, then, faced a dilemma. Their opposition to simple democracy ran headlong into their determination to allow the people to govern themselves. How could they let the people rule themselves while protecting the country from momentary passions or irrational majorities? How could minority political interests, especially the small states, be protected from the tyranny of the majority? What constitutional provisions would allow majorities to rule but also require them to take the needs of the minority into account?

They solved the problem by writing a Constitution that combines democracy (self-governance) with federalism (states' rights) and republicanism (deliberation and compromise). The national government is divided into three co-equal branches: executive, legislative, and judicial. Each serves as a check on the others. The Constitution includes many other checks on power: supermajority requirements to amend the Constitution, presidential vetoes, and, of course, a presidential election system that operates state by state instead of nationally.

When the checks and balances in the Constitution are respected, they enable Americans to accomplish the near-impossible: to be self-governing, even as mob rule and majority tyranny are avoided.

DISCUSSIONS ABOUT PRESIDENTIAL SELECTION

The mode of electing the executive was discussed early and often that summer in Philadelphia. The delegates considered it one of the hardest questions that they would be asked to address. Indeed, they tackled the question almost immediately after the Convention opened and established its standing rules.

In many of those early discussions, the delegates compared the merits of legislative selection of the president with those of other modes of appointment, such as a national, direct popular election. Imagine if Congress were to select the president every four years. The idea was discussed. The possibility of presidential electors was also raised a few times, but these early proposals were usually variations of the legislative and direct election proposals already under consideration. They weren't the focus of discussion.

The small states were concerned about the prospect of direct popular elections, in which they would always be outnumbered. Roger Sherman of Connecticut felt that the people "will generally vote for some man in their own State, and the largest State will have the best chance for the appointment."[38] Charles Pinckney of South Carolina concurred: "An Election by the people [is] liable to the most obvious & striking objections. They will be led by a few active & designing men. The most populous States by combining in favor of the same individual will be able to carry their points."[39]

One delegate was much more direct. Gunning Bedford of Delaware voiced the fear felt by the delegates of every small state: "*I do not, gentlemen, trust you,*" he blasted. "If you possess the power, the abuse of it could not be checked; and what then would prevent you from exercising it to our destruction?"[40] Imagine the tension that such a scolding must have injected into the room, despite Bedford's obvious struggle to maintain at least a modicum of politeness and civility!

The small states would not accept a national popular vote, but the alternative, legislative selection, could not gain steam either. Many delegates worried that such a method of appointment would rob the president of his independence from the legislature. Gouverneur Morris declared that such an executive would be the "mere creature of the [Legislature]: if appointed & impeachable by that body."[41] The president, he thought, "ought to be elected by the people at large, by the freeholders of the Country. . . . If the Legislature elect, it will be the work of intrigue, of cabal, and of faction."[42]

Morris's fellow delegate from Pennsylvania, James Wilson, had related concerns. How can the president "stand the mediator between the intrigues & sinister views of the Representatives and the general liberties & interests of the people" if he is dependent on Congress for his election?[43] James Madison generally concurred with all these sentiments:

> If it be a fundamental principle of free [Government] that the Legislative, Executive & Judiciary powers should be *separately* exercised, it is equally so that they be *independently* exercised. There is the same & perhaps greater reason why the Executive [should] be independent of the Legislature, than why the Judiciary should: A coalition of the two former powers would be more immediately & certainly

dangerous to public liberty. It is essential then that the appointment of the Executive should either be drawn from some source, or held by some tenure, that will give him a free agency with regard to the Legislature.[44]

The proposal for legislative selection of the president was bogged down by yet another problem: the concern over the composition of the legislature. After all, if the small states were not equally represented in the legislature, then they would not have equal representation in selecting the executive, either. The large and small states simply could not agree on a solution, and their disagreement nearly tore the Convention apart. Luther Martin of Maryland later recalled that the Convention at this juncture was "on the verge of dissolution, scarce held together by the strength of a hair."[45] The division was finally resolved when the delegates agreed to give small states equal representation in one of the two legislative houses. Afterwards, the discussions surrounding the election of the president changed. The question was no longer *whether* to incorporate the principle of equal state representation into the election process but *how* to implement it.

The Electoral College, when it was eventually proposed, included concessions to both the large and the small states. States with larger populations would get more electoral votes in the college, but the small states were guaranteed at least three votes, regardless of population.[46] One further concession was made to the small states: in the event of a contingent election in the House, each state delegation would have one vote, regardless of its size.[47] The compromise was quite an important gesture by the large states, as many delegates believed that most elections would be resolved in the House.

Both sides, then, sacrificed interests at different stages in the election process.[48] The result, wrote James Madison, was "a compromise between the larger & smaller States, giving to the latter the advantage in selecting a president from the Candidates, in consideration of the advantage possessed by the former in selecting the Candidates from the people."[49]

BUT ISN'T THE ELECTORAL COLLEGE RACIST?

The framers of the Constitution might have been focused on negotiating compromises between the large and small states, but commentators today sometimes assume more nefarious motives. The Electoral College, these critics say, was established because some Founders wanted to protect slavery. Any institution with such racist roots, they conclude, should be eliminated.[50]

This view threatens to become conventional wisdom, but nothing could be further from the truth.

Obviously, some of the Founders owned slaves. Compromises were made in America's early years because North and South couldn't agree on whether to continue the institution.[51] Just as obviously, virtually all Americans today wish that slavery had never existed. It's a part of America's heritage that is clearly at odds with America's founding principles. That does not mean, however, that the Constitution and its presidential election process are simply a "relic of slavery." The discussions at the Convention were shaped more by the delegates' study of history and political philosophy, as well as their own experiences with Parliament and the state legislatures. They wanted to avoid the mistakes that had been made in other governments. They sought to establish a better constitution that would stand the test of time.

George Washington expressed this conviction, felt so strongly by the founding generation: "[T]he preservation of the sacred fire of liberty, and the destiny of the Republican model of Government," he concluded, "are justly considered as *deeply*, perhaps as *finally* staked, on the experiment entrusted to the hands of the American people."[52] His words echoed an argument that James Madison had made about a year and a half earlier. Only a republic, Madison had written, "would be reconcilable with the genius of the people of America; with the fundamental principles of the Revolution; or with that honorable determination which animates every votary of freedom to rest all our political experiments on the capacity of mankind for self-government."[53] He thought the experiment worthwhile. The Constitution met these criteria.

Nevertheless, some modern commentators brush this history aside and insist that the compromises at the Convention were nothing more than attempts to preserve slavery. Americans, they say, have been fooled into thinking that their heritage is more admirable than it is. The specific charges about the Electoral College in this context are inaccurate, but they need to be addressed since they are raised so often.

First, critics sometimes cite the Constitution's "three-fifths" compromise, which determined how slaves would be counted in apportioning congressional representation.[54] The South wanted to count each slave as a whole person. The North did not want to count slaves *at all*—a larger population would give the South more voting power.[55] In the end, Convention delegates agreed to count each slave as three-fifths of a person. But did that compromise really do more for the South or for the North? If slaves had been counted as whole persons (as the South wanted), then the South would have had even *more* representatives in Congress. In other words, while the three-fifths compromise is often cited as an advantage for the slave-holding South, it can also be interpreted as a win for the North.[56]

One additional nuance complicates an assessment of the three-fifths compromise—the Convention applied the same formula for apportioning direct taxes. The North effectively offered the South a compromise: in return for having fewer representatives in Congress, the South would be assessed less in federal taxes.[57]

A more honest assessment of the three-fifths compromise shows what it really concerned—congressional representation and taxation, *not* the Electoral College. Indeed, the discussions about the compromise and the discussions about the presidential election system were largely separate. The main reason the compromise is cited today is because, late in the Convention, it was decided that each state's electoral vote allocation would match its congressional allocation.

Overriding all these discussions is a much bigger compromise that was brokered between the large and small states: the large states agreed that representation in the Senate would be based on the principle of "one state, one vote." The small states agreed that representation in the House of Representatives would be based on population. This blend between the two types of representation was later reflected in the Electoral College, which gives every state three electors, regardless of its size. The rest of the electors are allocated according to population.

Critics of the Electoral College ignore the larger context of the three-fifths compromise, focusing instead on one statement made by James Madison. Taken in isolation, it certainly sounds damning. "The right of suffrage," he told the Convention in July, "was much more diffusive in the Northern than the Southern States; and the latter could have no influence in the election on the score of the Negroes."[58] Since Madison mentioned presidential electors in his very next sentence,[59] Electoral College opponents contend that he was proposing such a system in order to increase Southern political power and to protect slavery. But Madison wasn't the first to suggest the use of electors that day. Rufus King of Massachusetts had already mentioned them.[60] King was not in favor of slavery. To the contrary, he worked against it during his lifetime. William Paterson of New Jersey, another slavery opponent, also endorsed the concept of electors that day.[61]

The reality is that the discussion that day wasn't about slavery or the three-fifths compromise. Madison's statement was a tangent to the main discussion, which revolved around the president's eligibility for a second term of office. If the president were chosen by the legislature and also eligible for reelection, some delegates feared that he would end up working too hard to satisfy legislators. After all, he'd be worried about winning their support so he could be reelected. Executive independence would ultimately suffer. Indeed, Madison made exactly this point just before his now-controversial comment about the "right of suffrage" in the South: "[T]he appointment of the Executive should either be drawn from some source," he told the delegates, "or held by some tenure, that will give him a free agency with regard to the Legislature."[62]

The delegates were discussing separation of powers. Slavery was not their focus. Indeed, the debates about the presidential election process never focused on slavery. Instead, the delegates discussed whether legislative selection or a national popular vote was preferable. The division was between large and small states, not between slave and free states. Some of the larger states had slaves, some did not. Some of the smaller states had slaves, some did not. *All* of the small states, however—slave and free—were worried about the dangers of a simple national popular vote. As slavery opponent Gunning Bedford of Delaware had said so eloquently, the small states simply feared that they would be outvoted by the large states time and time again.[63]

***

The Framers deliberately avoided the creation of a simple democracy. They wanted something even better. They came up with a government that combines self-governance with the checks and balances necessary to protect freedom.

Power in America is divided among three co-equal branches of government. It is also divided between the national and state governments. Each arm of government has the opportunity and the responsibility to act as a check on the others. Such safeguards protect Americans against abusive governmental officials and the whims and passions of the majority. The state-by-state nature of the Constitution's presidential election process reflects these same principles.

The Founders were proud of their work—especially their new presidential election system. "The mode of appointment of the Chief Magistrate of the United States," Alexander Hamilton wrote, "is almost the only part of the system, of any consequence, which has escaped without severe censure . . . . I venture somewhat further, and hesitate not to affirm that if the manner of it be not perfect, it is at least excellent."[64]

The Constitution—and its Electoral College—was considered by the Founders to have struck the perfect balance between minority protection and majority rule.

CHAPTER TWO

WHAT ACTUALLY HAPPENS ON ELECTION DAY?

The 2016 election highlighted nuances of America's presidential election system that generally go unnoticed. Many Americans discovered that they do not vote for the presidential candidates themselves. How surprising! The candidates' names are on the ballot. By all appearances, voters are directly casting their ballots for the Republican or Democratic nominee—but they aren't. They are actually voting for a slate of electors pledged to a particular candidate. The winning slate of electors in each state will represent that state in the *real* presidential election. This election occurs about a month after the day that most Americans think of as Election Day.

The Founders established the framework for these procedures in Article II of the United States Constitution. The tumultuous presidential election of 1800, however, soon prompted a single amendment to that Article II process. The Twelfth Amendment corrected one logistical problem that had arisen because of the unanticipated emergence of political parties, but it otherwise left the Founders' original design intact.

Today, American presidential elections are governed by the Twelfth Amendment and two still-effective clauses in Article II.

The process of electing American presidents is admittedly not as straightforward as a national popular vote, and many find it confusing. It is perhaps easiest to think of the election in two phases: first, the Electoral College vote, and second, the contingent election procedure, which is used only if no candidate wins a majority of electoral votes.[1]

UNINTENDED CONSEQUENCES IN 1800

The country's first two elections were relatively uneventful. Nearly everyone expected that the revered General George Washington would be the nation's first president. The bigger question was who would serve as his vice president. John Adams was elected to the post.

American politics had become more complicated by the time Washington announced his retirement in 1796.[2] Political parties were coalescing, and they were identifying specific nominees for president and vice president. Today, voters expect each party to nominate one person for president and one person for vice president. In 1796, however, this practice was just taking shape, and it caused an unanticipated conflict with the original Article II election process. The Constitution did not then allow electors to cast votes specifically for vice president. Instead, each elector was to cast two ballots for president. When these electoral votes were tallied, the candidate receiving the most votes became president, and the runner-up became vice president.

When the new political parties began nominating candidates for vice president, they were nominating candidates for an office for which there was, in a sense, no election. The elections of 1796 and 1800 revealed that American presidential politics had, in this single respect, outgrown its constitutional framework.

Two major-party candidates competed for the presidency in the country's third presidential election in 1796. The Federalist Party nominated Vice President Adams for president and Thomas Pinckney for vice president. The Democratic-Republican Party nominated

Thomas Jefferson for president, but it could not agree on a nominee for vice president. When the electors cast their votes, Adams placed first with seventy-one electoral votes, and he became the country's second president. The Federalist Party's vice presidential nominee, Pinckney, did not place second in the electoral voting. That honor went to Jefferson, who had received sixty-eight electoral votes. His second-place finish made him vice president, even though he and Adams were from different political parties. Pinckney placed third with fifty-nine electoral votes. The remainder of the electoral vote was divided among ten other men.[3]

The Federalist Party, recognizing the possibility of an unintended tie if all Federalist electors voted both for Adams and Pinckney, had instructed some of its electors to cast one ballot for Adams but to leave their second ballot blank instead of voting for Pinckney. The strategy backfired, however. Too many Pinckney votes were held back, and Jefferson squeaked in between Adams and Pinckney to place second in the balloting.[4]

The fourth presidential election was more eventful,[5] and it brought the flaw in the Article II process more sharply into focus. In 1800, the Democratic-Republican Party nominated Jefferson for president and Aaron Burr for vice president. They defeated the Federalist nominees, Adams and Charles Pinckney (Thomas's brother), by eight and nine electoral votes, respectively. The presidential election should have ended there—but it didn't. The Democratic-Republican Party had unfortunately failed to ensure that one elector would abstain from casting his vote for Burr, the strategy that the Federalist Party had bungled in 1796. The result was an electoral tie, triggering for the first time the Constitution's secondary election procedure, in which the House of Representatives selects the president.

More trouble brewed in the House, which was still controlled by the outgoing Federalist Party. Many Federalists searched for a way to thwart Jefferson's election. Eventually, these congressmen decided to throw their support to Burr. Other Federalists, relegated to the minority for the first time, sought concessions from Jefferson in return for their vote.

A stalemate continued for the better part of a week.[6] The votes of nine states' delegations were needed to win the election in the House, but neither candidate could obtain this majority. Over five days of voting, thirty-four ballots were taken, but the vote remained unchanged: eight states for Jefferson, six for Burr, and two states divided. The sixth day of voting opened with yet another unchanged ballot, but after this thirty-fifth ballot, one congressman yielded. James Bayard, the only representative from Delaware, indicated his decision to switch his vote to Jefferson, placing the critical ninth state in Jefferson's column. His announcement broke the deadlock, which in turn made his vote for Jefferson unnecessary. In the end, Bayard abstained from voting on the thirty-sixth ballot, as did congressmen from Maryland, Vermont, and South Carolina. Jefferson ultimately won, ten states to Burr's four.

RESULTS: ELECTION OF 1800

	Party	Nominee For	Electoral Votes	House Votes
Thomas Jefferson	Democratic-Republican	President	73	10
Aaron Burr	Democratic-Republican	Vice President	73	4
John Adams	Federalist	President	65	—
Charles C. Pinckney	Federalist	Vice President	64	—

Allegations later surfaced that the impasse had been broken because Jefferson cut a deal with Bayard through an intermediary, General Samuel Smith of Maryland. Jefferson, however, denied these claims. In a letter to Dr. Benjamin Rush, he later described his reaction to Adams at the time of the House deliberations: "I will not come into the government by capitulation. I will not enter on it, but in perfect freedom to follow the dictates of my own judgment."[7]

In all likelihood, Jefferson did not cut a deal, but Smith may have taken it upon himself to ascertain Jefferson's views regarding certain matters of concern to Bayard. Armed with this new information, Smith was able to reassure the wavering congressman, and Bayard decided to change his vote.[8] Jefferson's election may also owe much to the intercession of Alexander Hamilton, who had no great fondness for Burr. Hamilton wrote many letters to congressmen, urging them to obtain concessions from Jefferson and then to vote for him. In a letter to Bayard he scathingly wrote of Burr, "[G]reat Ambition unchecked by principle, or the love of Glory, is an unruly Tyrant."[9] The new vice president had no great fondness for Hamilton, either. Just a few years later, he would kill Hamilton in a duel.

Amending the Constitution to separate the voting for president and vice president might seem like an obvious solution to these electoral problems, but many congressional representatives in the early 1800s did not see it that way. Indeed, a fair amount of argument over the subject ensued.[10] The minority party, the Federalists, opposed such an amendment, arguing that the election process as it then stood made it possible for the minority party to have a representative in the executive branch. In all likelihood, they feared that the Democratic-Republicans were taking advantage of the situation to deprive them of such an advantage in a future presidential administration. Some Democratic-Republicans, for their part, could see the possibility that they would be in the minority again someday. They hesitated to change the election procedure as well. After all, the Article II process had helped them to gain the vice presidency in 1796, when Jefferson defeated the Federalist vice presidential candidate, Thomas Pinckney.

An amendment to the election procedure failed to pass the Senate when it was first proposed in 1801. In 1803, however, with a presidential election looming, the Twelfth Amendment finally gained enough support to pass both the Senate and the House. North Carolina became the first state to ratify the amendment on December 21, 1803. The amendment became effective when New Hampshire ratified it on June 15, 1804.[11]

The Twelfth Amendment still provides the framework for American presidential elections today.[12] Its procedures are virtually identical to those originally established in 1787 except that the amendment established separate elections for president and vice president. It also made minor changes to the contingent election procedures, used when no candidate wins a majority of the electoral votes.[13]

THE ELECTORAL COLLEGE VOTE

The Constitution does not provide for a national, direct popular vote for president. Instead, it provides for an election in which each state is granted a certain number of representatives, called electors, to cast votes on its behalf.[14] These electoral votes determine the outcome of the presidential election. The national popular vote tally might be of interest to some people, but the number has no legal significance.

This state-by-state electoral process is colloquially referred to as the Electoral College, although that term does not appear in the Constitution.

Who decides how many electors each state gets? The numbers change with each census, which by constitutional mandate is conducted every ten years. States are allocated one elector for each of their representatives in Congress—both senators and representatives.[15] Each state therefore receives a minimum of three votes, because it is entitled to at least two senators and one representative, regardless of population.[16] Puerto Rico and the Island Areas have no electors, because they are not states. The District of Columbia is not a state, either, so it originally didn't have electors. This situation changed with the adoption of the Twenty-Third Amendment in 1961, which provides the national capital with at least three electoral votes, as if it were a state.[17] At this time, there are 538 total electors.

The state legislatures have a great deal of discretion in deciding who their electors will be. The Constitution simply provides that "[e]ach State shall appoint, in such Manner as the Legislature thereof may direct, a Number of Electors . . . ."[18] The general rule is that the legislatures may appoint their electors in any manner that they choose, assuming that they do not violate another constitutional provision in the process.

Few Americans realize that they don't have a constitutional right to vote for president. State legislatures retain the right to appoint their electors directly, although they have generally relied on statewide popular votes for nearly two centuries.[19] Most states follow a "winner-take-all" system, whereby the presidential candidate winning the state's popular vote is awarded the state's slate of electors in its entirety. Maine and Nebraska have been the only recent exceptions to this general rule, despite occasional rumblings from other states that they too might abandon winner-take-all.[20] Maine and Nebraska follow a congressional district system of allocating electors. They give two electoral votes to the statewide winner and allocate the remaining electors according to which candidate carried each congressional district.[21]

While the state's authority to determine a method for appointing electors is not in doubt, one issue is still sometimes disputed: How far does congressional authority extend if there is controversy regarding which slate of electors rightfully represents a state?[22] The 1876 election was contentious because of this very issue. Three states had submitted multiple sets of election returns,[23] and Congress had to decide which of the conflicting returns to accept. No one seemed to know what to do, but Congress eventually established an electoral commission to tackle the problem.[24] After that election, Congress approved the Electoral Count Act of 1887,[25] hoping to forestall similar problems in future elections. In that statute, Congress claimed authority to supervise the Electoral College process, although the boundaries of this power have never been tested.[26] The law limits state discretion as to certain issues of timing and grants Congress final authority in counting electoral votes. This federal law, as updated and expanded through the years, provides a timeline for the various procedures described in the Constitution.

Election Day is the Tuesday following the first Monday in November of a presidential election year.[27] On that day, each state holds its own internal election; there is no such thing as a single, nationwide election in America. Think about that for a minute. Fifty-one completely separate presidential elections are held in this country each and every presidential election year—one in each state and the District of Columbia. The purpose of these purely democratic, state-level elections is to determine which individuals—electors—will represent each state at the meetings of the Electoral College.

In other words, American voters never cast ballots directly for a presidential candidate, even though the candidates' names are on the ballot. Instead, voters in the states are actually casting their ballots for a slate of electors (Republican, Democrat, or third-party). Each state relies on the outcome of its own statewide popular vote to determine who won its own election. If a Republican candidate wins the state, then the Republican slate of electors is elected to represent that state. Likewise, if a Democratic or third-party candidate wins, then a slate of electors committed to that candidate is elected instead. (In Maine and Nebraska, as discussed above, the procedure is slightly different.) Once an elector is elected, everyone expects him to vote for his party's nominee in the Electoral College vote among the states.

It's worth emphasizing that each presidential candidate has his own slate of electors prepared to vote for him. No one is asking a slate of Democratic electors to vote for a Republican candidate or vice versa. The third-party candidates also have their own slates of electors. The electors affiliated with each party were appointed prior to the election, usually at the state party convention during the election year.[28]

During the 2016 campaign, amid speculation that one of the candidates might drop out in the wake of certain scandals, headlines warned that "it's too late" because ballots had already been printed. This was a fake problem. It didn't matter whose name was on the ballot: voters weren't voting for the candidates anyway. They were voting for slates of electors. If an emergency had prompted one candidate to drop out, the political party or state legislatures would have directed electors to vote for an alternative candidate.[29] The bigger concern would have been educating voters that, for example, a vote for Hillary Clinton was really a vote for electors committed to Tim Kaine, or that a vote for Donald Trump was really a vote for electors committed to Mike Pence.

Naturally, early voters might have wished for a redo, but it's unclear what remedy would have been available. These voters were always voting for the electors (unchanged) not the candidate (changed). Such possibilities are an argument against early voting for those people who see contingencies that could change their minds, but they do not prevent political parties from replacing their nominees at the last minute.

Once state officials have tallied the votes cast on Election Day, each state certifies a slate of electors to represent it at the meetings of the Electoral College. A "Certificate of Ascertainment" naming these electors is forwarded to Washington, DC.[30]

These electors assemble in their state on the first Monday after the second Wednesday in December and cast the votes that officially determine who will be the next president of the United States.[31] These votes are recorded on "Certificates of Vote," one of which goes to the president of the Senate.[32] These votes are due in the Senate by the fourth Wednesday in December,[33] and they are counted on January 6 in a joint session of Congress, with the president of the Senate presiding.[34] This ceremony is occasionally heavy with historical irony, as on January 6, 2001, when Vice President Al Gore announced the victory of his opponent, Governor George W. Bush, in the hotly disputed election of 2000.

To be elected president, a candidate needs a majority of the electoral votes, which are cast in December. He does not need a majority of the direct popular vote on Election Day. At this time, 270 electoral votes constitute a majority of the Electoral College and will win the presidency for a candidate.

THE CONTINGENT ELECTION

If no candidate wins a majority of the Electoral College vote, the election is decided according to the Constitution's contingent election procedure, in which the election of the president is sent to the House of Representatives, and the election of the vice president is sent to the Senate.[35] The House must choose from the top three recipients of electoral votes for president, and the Senate must choose from the top two recipients of electoral votes for vice president.[36]

In the House vote for president, each state delegation is granted one vote. California, which had fifty-three congressmen in 2016, would cast one vote, as would South Dakota, with its single congressman. If a state's delegation is evenly divided, that state cannot vote unless the tie is broken. For instance, if one of Maine's two congressmen votes Republican while the other votes Democrat, one of them will have to abstain or switch his vote before the state's vote can be cast for a candidate. Otherwise, the state of Maine must abstain from the election.

A president is elected when one candidate wins a majority of the votes of the state delegations (currently twenty-six). Voting is repeated until a majority is achieved. A similar procedure is employed for the election of the vice president, except that each senator is granted one vote.[37]

The Constitution provides this procedural outline for a contingent election, but it leaves many other logistical details unaddressed. If a contingent election were ever needed in the future, numerous questions about the procedures to be followed would arise, especially in the House presidential election.[38]

First, is a state's vote determined by majority or plurality within its House delegation? A closely related question is whether a quorum is required within each state delegation before the delegation may take its vote. The Constitution does not provide an answer,[39] so the House would likely turn to the rules that it passed during the contingent election of 1825. Under these rules, a state could not cast a vote except by "majority of the votes given."[40] As an example, consider a hypothetical vote in the Massachusetts delegation (nine representatives) in 2016. If four representatives voted for Hillary Clinton, three for Donald Trump, and two for Bernie Sanders, the state's vote would be deemed "divided" and would not be counted, because Clinton had only a plurality of the votes within the delegation. The state could vote if, for instance, one representative switched to Clinton. Alternatively, if the two Sanders representatives abstained, then Massachusetts's vote would go to Clinton because four votes constituted a "majority of the votes given."[41]

Second, is the election conducted by secret ballot? The Constitution requires that "the House of Representatives shall choose immediately, by ballot, the President,"[42] but it does not otherwise address whether balloting must be done publicly.[43] In 1801 and 1825, many congressmen felt that votes should be cast by secret ballot, but the rules they passed do not necessarily require the ballots to be secret. In fact, many newspapers in 1801 and 1825 reported the votes of congressmen.[44]

Last, is the contingent election conducted in the incoming or outgoing House of Representatives? The Constitution provides that the new House is sworn in on January 3,[45] and federal law provides that the electoral votes are counted on January 6.[46] Accordingly, many scholars believe that the newly elected House is responsible for conducting the contingent election. A few others, however, observe that the counting of the votes on January 6 is a mere formality. The outcome of the Electoral College vote is generally known much sooner. Under the right set of circumstances, some might urge that the contingent election be held earlier, in the lame-duck House.

When Ross Perot entered the 1992 presidential race, the House did some investigation into the logistical aspects of a contingent election. Unfortunately, it dropped the issue when Perot dropped out of the race (temporarily, as it turned out).[47] The issue was never raised in any serious manner again. The lack of consideration regarding this issue is unfortunate. During the 2016 election, a contingent election again seemed like a possibility, at least for a while. The House was nearly caught unprepared, yet again.

Obviously, fair contingent election procedures can most easily be identified before the outcome of any one election hangs in the balance. Once a contingent election is triggered, partisan considerations are certain to taint any discussion of logistical procedures that remain unresolved. The House of Representatives should adopt procedures for a contingent election, even though no immediate need for them appears on the horizon.[48]

**

America's method of electing its president remains largely as it was first conceived by the Founders in the summer of 1787. The procedure seems unnecessarily complicated to many Americans today, yet the Founders believed the Electoral College to be an ingenious solution to the problems facing the new country.

Would they still think so today? Life has changed since that long Philadelphia summer in 1787, and presidential elections obviously operate differently than anticipated in many ways. For instance, the Founders did not anticipate the emergence of political parties or the states' nearly universal adoption of a winner-take-all allocation of electors. Some Founders might be surprised to discover that Americans haven't used the House contingent election more often. And surely no Founder could have predicted the ways in which technology would improve communications and enable voters to learn about their presidential candidates. Yes, the presidential election system has evolved in unexpected ways. Nevertheless, the system still serves the important goals of the Framers: it still encourages presidential candidates to remember just how big and diverse the nation is, and it still protects small states and other political minorities from being trampled by bare or emotional majorities.

Further examination of the system, as it operates in modern presidential elections, will show how useful the system remains today.

CHAPTER THREE

MODERN BENEFITS OF AN OLD INSTITUTION

The Electoral College may be one of America's most misunderstood institutions. Media outlets gratuitously bash the system as "outdated" or "archaic." School textbooks dismiss the Electoral College as a reflection of the Founders' fear that "ordinary citizens, most of whom could neither read [n]or write, were too poorly informed to choose wisely."[1] The presidential election system is said to be a relic of the horse-and-buggy era—a process devised by slaveholding Founders who didn't trust the people to govern themselves.

Aren't Americans more enlightened now? Shouldn't such a broken process be eliminated, once and for all?

The media never seem to consider an alternative perspective: what if it's the narrative about the Electoral College that is broken, not the institution itself? After all, spotty teaching in schools, combined with skeptical media, has left the general electorate remarkably ill-informed about its presidential election process. A little education reveals that the

Electoral College still serves many important purposes today. Americans hurt only themselves when they dismiss these benefits too quickly.

As a matter of history, the Electoral College encourages coalition building and prevents America's political process from degenerating into a fractured, European-style, multi-party system. It raises hurdles to fraud and prevents elections from being "rigged." It ensures certain and stable election outcomes. Any of these benefits could be lost if the Electoral College were eliminated.[2]

Then-Senator John F. Kennedy once defended the Electoral College on the floor of the U.S. Senate. He worried that eliminating the Electoral College would have a domino effect, with many unanticipated consequences. "[I]t is not only the unit vote for the Presidency we are talking about," he noted, "but a whole solar system of governmental power. If it is proposed to change the balance of power of one of the elements of the solar system, it is necessary to consider all the others."[3]

The Founders' Constitution employs an elaborate system of checks, balances, and separated powers, each safeguard working hand-in-hand with the others to protect American liberty. Eliminating any one of them is certain to have unintended and potentially devastating consequences.[4] To elaborate on Kennedy's metaphor, changing the gravitational pull of the sun would affect more than only the sun. Indeed, even such a simple change would begin a ripple effect. The orbit of each planet would be affected. The changed orbits would, in turn, change weather patterns. Ultimately, Earth's atmosphere could become uninhabitable for human beings.

No one knows what would happen if the Electoral College were removed from America's political system, but some benefits would surely be lost. Perhaps the most helpful solution to any perceived problem is to clear up misunderstandings about the system. The Electoral College serves Americans in many ways that tend to go unnoticed and unappreciated today.

COALITION BUILDING IN A DIVERSE NATION

Many members of the founding generation worried about the prospect of extending a republic across a country as large and diverse as the

United States. "[A] free elective government," one member of the founding generation concluded, "cannot be extended over large territories."[5]
He was an "anti-Federalist," working against ratification of the Constitution. Another anti-Federalist concurred with these sentiments. He was
convinced that nothing "short of despotism" could "bind so great a
country under one government."[6] A third anti-Federalist spoke of the
importance of representatives knowing the "minds of their constituents"
in a free republic.[7] The United States, he believed, was simply too big.
The legislature would either be too small to adequately represent everyone or it would become so numerous as to be unwieldy and unproduc-
tive.[8] These issues could, of course, become even more complicated when
the election of a single, national executive was taken into account.

Remember, these men were discussing the prospect of a "large"
nation composed of only thirteen states. Modern America is far bigger:
fifty states, plus several territories. Whatever problem these Founders
feared has only grown over time. Now more than ever, Americans need
the protection of devices such as the Electoral College, which encourage
presidents and political parties to consider a wide variety of voters.

Anti–Electoral College activists tend to be dismissive of this history.
They bemoan the fact that the president is the only American official
who is not chosen in a straightforward popular vote. Yet they have
forgotten something far more important: the president is also the only
elected official who must represent every voter in the entire nation.
Senators, by contrast, represent only the citizens of a single state and
can speak to the concerns of that state. Similarly, members of the House
represent only the citizens of a single congressional district. The president must represent fishermen in Maine, environmentalists in California, and the oil industry in Texas—simultaneously! A special election
process for the nation's chief executive is not only appropriate but also
necessary.

The Electoral College enables this nation of states to elect a president
who is truly representative of the diverse interests of the various states. The
federalist (state-by-state) nature of the presidential election requires candidates to broaden their base of appeal. The alternative, a direct national

election, would most likely produce a president who represented narrower special-interest groups, such as those based on region, state, or ideology.

Perhaps the best method of demonstrating the benefits of a federalist presidential election process is to compare today's world, with the Electoral College, to a world in which the Electoral College does not exist.

As it stands today, presidential candidates have no incentive to run up a large margin of victory in any one state. Except in Maine and Nebraska, winning 50.1 percent of the votes in a state is as effective as winning 100 percent of the votes. Either way, the winner is awarded the entire slate of electors for that state. Candidates therefore tour the nation, campaigning in all states and seeking to build a coalition of voters that will enable them to win in the most states.[9] They can't simply camp out in one part of the country that is already friendly to them. A Democratic candidate can't get all of his votes from San Francisco or New York. He can't get all of his votes from pro-choice or pro-gun control activists. Similarly, Republicans can't rely only on big, Southern urban centers. They can't focus only on the concerns of the pro-life lobby or the National Rifle Association.

The result? Both parties are encouraged to reach out to as many people as they can. No one can win the White House unless he wins the votes of many different states, in many different regions, simultaneously.[10] The best way to accomplish this goal, of course, is to focus on the similarities among voters. What shared values transcend other interests? How can a cross-regional coalition be built on this common ground?

Those candidates who do the best job of building such coalitions win in massive landslides, as Ronald Reagan did in 1984 and Franklin D. Roosevelt did in 1936.[11]

Now imagine an America in which the president is elected by a direct popular vote. In this new world, winning 100 percent of the votes in a state would be infinitely preferable to winning 50.1 percent of the votes. In fact, it may be easier to rack up votes in a friendly state than to gain 50.1 percent of votes in each of two states of similar size, although the pay-off would be essentially the same. Obviously, campaign strategies would soon change in response to these new rules. Why would a candidate bother to build diverse coalitions with such incentives in place? It's much harder to build that kind of support, and candidates' time and resources are limited. Without some kind of pressure to broaden their campaigns, candidates would simply hunt for individual votes wherever they're most easily obtained. It's a matter of efficiency. Political parties would have no reason to care if their base of support is lopsided, too heavily concentrated in one region, or too reliant on a handful of big urban areas. Any president elected under such a system would have difficulty claiming that he truly represents a large, diverse nation.

Perhaps unsurprisingly, Electoral College opponents dispute this description of America's presidential election system. An election has nothing to do with coalition building, they argue. It's *really* just about the so-called swing states. But even a cursory review of American history shows one major flaw in their argument: the list of "swing states" changes all the time. No state is permanently "safe" or "swing."

During the 2008 election cycle, Americans heard a fair amount of commentary about "new" swing states such as Virginia and North Carolina.[12] Eight years later, the normally predictable state of Utah became competitive for a time, with third-party candidates showing surprising strength in the traditionally Republican state.[13] Final results in 2016 showed that Republicans had flipped three states that had been voting blue for decades: Wisconsin, Pennsylvania, and Michigan. The results mimicked a similar result in 2000 when George W. Bush flipped then-safely blue West Virginia. Indeed, Bush would have lost the election that year if he hadn't flipped West Virginia.

The examples are seemingly endless. Texas used to be as reliably Democratic as it is Republican today. Georgia, Kentucky, and Louisiana all voted for Bill Clinton in the 1990s, but they were considered safe Republican states in 2016. California is often viewed as irreversibly Democratic, but it used to be just as stubbornly Republican. Indeed, the state even sent two Republican presidents to the White House in 1968 and 1980. The experience of California shows that both demographics and voting behaviors can (and do) change.[14]

Electoral College opponents pretend that only swing states are relevant in presidential elections, but that's simply not true. Safe states are vitally important. Democrats do not want to go into an election without California's electors in their back pocket, just as Republicans do not want to lose Texas. Hillary Clinton (2016) and Al Gore (2000) both lost their elections because they could not hang on to blue states. They surely realize, in retrospect, that they should have paid more attention to those states. Safe states must never be taken for granted. They are bound to exact a price for such dismissiveness.

Anyone who calls safe states "unimportant" badly misunderstands presidential politics. Generally speaking, safe states are simply states that made up their minds earlier in the process. After all, presidential elections are not only about the TV commercials and campaign visits in the months and weeks before Election Day. They're also about the four years of governance before the election. How did some voters react when President Barack Obama blocked construction of the Keystone pipeline? How did others react when President George W. Bush prohibited federal funding for certain types of embryonic stem cell research? How many people refused to vote for Hillary Clinton because of Benghazi? Such decisions and their ramifications are part of governing, but they're also part of campaigning. They influence voting decisions as much as TV ads do—maybe more—as candidates and incumbents certainly know.

At the end of the day, political parties and presidential candidates can't ignore any state for very long.[15] Instead, they must build coalitions that include both swing and safe states. Without the Electoral College, candidates and their parties could easily forget the importance of working to unify the citizens of a nation as large and diverse as America.

A STABLE TWO-PARTY SYSTEM

The Electoral College, in combination with the winner-take-all allocation of electoral votes, reinforces the two-party system. This fact was perhaps driven home with particular force during the 2016 election. In a year when polls showed that most people did not want to vote for either of the two major-party nominees, only 6 percent of voters ultimately cast their ballots for any of the third-party candidates.[16]

In the wake of such events, many Americans doubtless view the two-party system as a liability. Why would any nation keep a system that limits the choices of voters so drastically? Why should voters feel stuck with two nominees they dislike? These voters might have a hard time believing that the Electoral College's tendency to uphold the two-party system is actually a *benefit* of the system. At first glance, it seems like the complete opposite.

Arguments against the two-party system usually focus on the frustrations of individual voters who wish they had more choices. Such arguments are understandable, but it's not enough to have complaints about the status quo. It's equally important to consider what the proposed changes will accomplish. What would replace the two-party system? Would it be an improvement? Or would the cure be worse than the disease?

To adapt something that Winston Churchill once said: the two-party system is the absolute worst type of political system—except for all those others that have been tried![17]

Perhaps the most important benefit of the two-party system is that it prevents American politics from degenerating into the fractured, multi-party state of affairs that is sometimes found in Europe. These multi-party systems can reward divisiveness and do not do enough to discourage extremist candidates. The Republican primaries of 2016 ended in such anger because that process acted too much like one of these divisive, multi-party systems. As a matter of history, the Electoral College stands in sharp contrast to all these problems: it rewards coalition building, and it tends to squash the influence of extremist candidates.

Third-party candidates have a tough row to hoe in America. Defeating two major-party nominees in a single national election pool would be difficult enough. But in America's federalist presidential election process, the task is even more daunting. A third-party candidate must overcome both of the major parties, not just one time in one national pool of voters, but many times in many state pools. And he must accomplish these against-the-odds victories simultaneously. The third-party candidate who came closest to accomplishing this feat was George Wallace, in 1968.[18]

Support for the segregationist candidate was concentrated in only one region of the country—the South. Wallace hoped this support would be enough to force a contingent election in the House, where he expected to have some bargaining power.[19] When vote totals came in, however, Wallace's presence in the race made barely a blip on the screen. The final results were 301 electoral votes for Richard Nixon, 191 for Hubert Humphrey, and forty-six for Wallace. A segregationist candidate had won five states, but it didn't stop him from losing the election in a landslide. The Electoral College helped Americans in this instance by limiting the influence of an extremist.

Wallace hasn't been the only regional candidate to face difficulties in America's state-by-state election system. In 1836, one of the then-existing major parties, the Whigs, could not agree on a nominee.[20] Rather than settling on one candidate with national appeal, the party decided to deliberately fracture its vote among several regional candidates. Whigs hoped to divide the vote so badly that the Democratic nominee, Martin Van Buren, would be unable to obtain a majority of electoral votes. One of the Whig candidates could then win in the resulting House contingent election.

RESULTS: ELECTION OF 1836

	Party	Electoral Vote	Popular Vote
Martin Van Buren	Democrat	170	764,176
William H. Harrison	Whig	73	550,816
Hugh L. White	Whig	26	146,107
Daniel Webster	Whig	14	41,201
W. P. Magnum	Independent Democrat	11	-0-

It didn't work. Instead, Van Buren benefited from the Whig strategy and won a resounding victory in the Electoral College. He defeated his nearest opponent by ninety-seven votes.

With the Electoral College, America's presidential election system minimizes the influence of candidates who have only isolated support, even as it rewards those who strive for national appeal. Yet the experience of other countries shows how vulnerable American politics would be without its constitutional defenses against extremist or regional candidates.

Consider the French presidential election of 2002, in which sixteen candidates competed for the presidency.[21] The incumbent, Jacques Chirac, finished in first place, with 19.88 percent of the vote. A radical right-wing candidate, Jean-Marie Le Pen, was just a few points behind Chirac at 16.86 percent. The Socialist candidate, Lionel Jospin, came in third with 16.18 percent. More recently, in 2012, ten candidates fractured the electorate in a similar manner.[22] The top vote-getter, Socialist François Hollande, obtained 28.6 percent of the vote, with 27.2 percent going to the incumbent, Nicolas Sarkozy. The third-place candidate, the National Front's Marine Le Pen, was close behind at 17.9 percent, while the Communist-backed Left Front candidate, Jean-Luc Mélenchon, placed fourth with 11.1 percent.[23]

In both elections, a run-off was held between the top two contenders, and a president was elected. But did the average French voter *really* feel like he had much choice at that point? Ironically, the multi-party system left French voters in the same spot that Americans sometimes complain about—an election in which they are forced to choose between two people they don't like. But the American system at least includes important coalition-building benefits that are harder to find in the French system.

In a country as big and diverse as America, incentives for coalition building seem especially important. Americans are an independent-minded people with a wide variety of opinions on many subjects. "Most" people will never agree on a single candidate. Instead, given the opportunity, voters would divide their support among a dozen or more candidates, as

Republican primary voters did in 2016. The two-party system has its frustrating moments, but it generally serves Americans better than a multi-party system would.

Having said all of this, are the Electoral College and the two-party system completely inflexible? Do they put a straitjacket on voters? Must voters always cast their ballots for one of the two major-party candidates? Of course not. The Electoral College strikes a healthier balance than that. Large, reasonable third parties have influenced the process in the past and could do so again. Major parties have weakened and imploded. Consider that Abraham Lincoln was elected soon after the collapse of the Whig Party, while the Republican Party was still in its infancy. The victory of a relatively new party is unusual, of course. Typically, third parties don't win, but they can influence the process in other ways.

A case in point is the election of 1992, a three-way race among Ross Perot of the Reform Party, Republican George H. W. Bush, and Democrat Bill Clinton. Conventional wisdom then held that a vote for Perot was a vote for Clinton, so those planning to vote for Perot were under pressure to switch their support to Bush.[24] Indeed, the main reason many people didn't vote for Perot was their fear that their vote would be "wasted." Such incentives are usually sufficient to push voters toward one of the two major parties, as the 2016 election results prove. In 1992, however, Perot pulled off a feat that has been accomplished only a handful of times in American history: as a third-party candidate, he received a whopping 18.9 percent of the popular vote. Bush received 37.4 percent of the vote, and Clinton received 43.0 percent.[25]

Perot's Reform Party ticket didn't win a single electoral vote, but his campaign was large and healthy with much mainstream appeal. It captured the attention of both the major parties. In the years that followed, both Democrats and Republicans worked to address the financial concerns of Perot voters. It is no coincidence that both parties made a push for fiscal responsibility before and during the 1994 mid-term elections. Democrats supported a 1993 budget reconciliation bill that raised taxes,[26] arguing that increased taxes were necessary to bring the budget back into balance. As the election neared, Republicans countered with their "Contract with America," which promised an "audit of Congress for waste, fraud or abuse" and other budgetary cuts.[27]

In short, Perot's campaign achieved something, even if that something wasn't the White House.

A similar dynamic existed in 1912, when the Republican vote was split between the sitting president, William Howard Taft, and former President Teddy Roosevelt.[28] In a weird twist, the incumbent president's campaign was effectively the third-party ticket that year. Taft was contending against a popular ex-president who'd decided to re-enter the political arena when he became discontented with how things were going without him. Actually, Roosevelt was more than just mildly discontent—he was irate! Roosevelt thought that Taft was doing a terrible job, and he planned to take back the Republican Party nomination for himself—but then he didn't quite succeed.

Roosevelt still enjoyed a lot of support among the Republican base, and he won more Republican primaries than Taft did. Nevertheless, party leaders chose Taft as their nominee at the party convention. When the announcement was made, Roosevelt's supporters were furious, and they promptly marched out. The Bull Moose Party was born!

Members of the Bull Moose Party felt that they were standing up to the establishment.[29] Their voices needed to be heard, and Roosevelt had promised to stand up to "political crookedness."[30] Taft's supporters viewed the issue differently. Taft believed that Roosevelt was "the greatest menace to our institutions that we have had in a long time."[31] Roosevelt favored more government regulation than Taft did, and the populist Roosevelt was ready to ditch certain constitutional principles to make the government more purely democratic.

Taft ultimately earned only eight electoral votes to Roosevelt's eighty-eight. Democrat Woodrow Wilson had won in a landslide with 435 electoral votes. Nevertheless, Taft's supporters felt that they'd achieved their goal: to preserve a constitutionalist arm of the Republican Party.[32] Many historians have since agreed with that assessment, and the election stands as an example of a large, reasonable third-party effort influencing American politics, despite an electoral loss.

By contrast, the other third-party candidate in that election cycle, Socialist Eugene V. Debs, could not garner a mainstream following. When election results came in, Debs was unable to obtain any electoral votes, although roughly 900,000 people had voted for him.

RESULTS: ELECTION OF 1912

	Political Party	Electoral Votes		Popular Votes	
		Actual	*Percent*	*Actual*	*Percent*
Woodrow Wilson	Democrat	435	81.9%	6,294,326	41.8%
Theodore Roosevelt	Bull Moose	88	16.6%	4,120,207	27.4%
William H. Taft	Republican	8	1.5%	3,486,343	23.2%
Eugene V. Debs	Socialist	0	—	900,370	6.0%

Does the Electoral College rob voters of choices? No, it does not. But it does make the decision to vote for a third-party more difficult. When are things so bad that a voter is willing to deviate from one of the two major parties? Will that third-party vote have the intended effect? Is the voter willing to cast that ballot only if he is guaranteed an outcome like that of 1860? Or is a statement like those of 1912 and 1992 sufficient?

With the Electoral College in place, a third-party vote is best cast thoughtfully, not emotionally. But voters are not "stuck" with only two choices unless they believe they are. Americans ultimately benefit from the difficulty of this choice. After all, the alternative is a fractured electorate and empowered extremists. The Electoral College provides a better way. It encourages Americans to come together, build coalitions, and focus on their shared values and goals.

DISCOURAGING FRAUD, LITIGATION, AND RECOUNTS

"Our new Constitution is now established," Benjamin Franklin wrote to a French physicist in 1789, "and has an appearance that promises permanency; but in this world nothing can be said to be certain, except death and taxes."[33]

Perhaps Franklin should have added one more item to his list of certainties: dishonest people will always exist—and they will always cheat. It's part of the human condition. Unfortunately, no election system can turn dishonest people into honest ones. Where people are vying for power, there will always be motivation for fraud. The best that an election system can do is to throw up as many hurdles as possible to dishonesty and to minimize its effects. The Electoral College accomplishes both of these goals far better than a direct national election can.[34]

With the Electoral College in place, an election cannot be stolen unless a few factors come together simultaneously. First, at the national level, the election needs to be close enough that altering the results in only one or two states would change the outcome. Second, the margins in those contested states must also be very close. Such elections are fairly rare. The election of 2000 was one such election: Florida could have changed the outcome, and the margin in that state was vanishingly small. The election of 1960 was another: both Texas and Illinois had narrow margins; they could have flipped the election to Nixon. Most elections are won by wider margins.

A third criterion may be the hardest to meet. Assuming the election is close, dishonest actors must be able to predict which state (or states) will be close enough to influence the final results. This is harder than it sounds. In 2000, no one could have known in advance that a few hundred stolen votes in Florida could change the election outcome. In fact, if the media had not called the state for Gore too early—before polls closed in the Republican-leaning panhandle—the result might not have been so narrow. But imagine that someone is able to make such a prediction. If one person can do it, then probably many people from both parties have made the same prediction. Poll watchers will descend upon the potentially problematic state.

In 2004, it was widely expected that the election in Ohio would be extremely close and that the state might tip the election one way or the other. Unsurprisingly, then, the election was closely monitored. Poll watchers and lawyers from all over the country swarmed the state. Voting fraud has probably never been more difficult to pull off than it was in Ohio in 2004.

With the Electoral College, stealing votes is easiest where they do not matter to the national outcome (e.g., safe states dominated by one political party), and it's hardest where they do matter (e.g., swing states, which are usually closely watched). It is probably naïve to believe that fraud can ever be completely eliminated, but the Electoral College at least makes it as difficult as possible.

Now consider a world without the Electoral College. Suddenly, the situation is reversed. Any vote stolen in any part of the country can change the outcome of an election. Even votes that are easy to steal suddenly become critical to the national outcome. Imagine how easy it must be to steal votes in the bluest California precinct or the reddest Texas one. These easily stolen votes are now able to change the national results. There is no need to predict which swing state could change the outcome of the election. This is a dangerous situation and the opposite of what Americans experience today.

The Electoral College provides one final benefit in this context. If problems do occur during the election, either because of fraud or because of human error, those problems can be limited to one or a handful of states. The elections of 1876, 1960, and 2000 demonstrated this remarkable ability of the Electoral College to provide certain and stable outcomes, even when matters are otherwise threatening to fall apart.

In 1876, Republican Rutherford B. Hayes faced off against Democrat Samuel J. Tilden. Final election results were thrown into doubt when Florida, Louisiana, and South Carolina each submitted votes from multiple slates of electors. State officials couldn't agree—had the Republican electors won their states or had the Democratic electors? Adding to these problems, one electoral vote in Oregon was disputed because that elector was not qualified to hold his office. Hayes needed all twenty of these contested electoral votes to obtain a majority of 185 and the presidency; Tilden needed only one.[35]

The Republican-controlled Senate and the Democrat-controlled House had difficulty determining which slates of electors to accept. They eventually agreed to appoint an electoral commission to resolve the challenges. Unsurprisingly, the Republican-controlled commission awarded all twenty disputed electoral votes to Hayes, throwing the election to him. Many aspects of the commission's decision can be disputed, of course, but the Electoral College nevertheless provided an important benefit that year. It limited election problems to only four states, preventing the election from spinning out of control.

The Electoral College performed an almost identical function in the 2000 election. That election was also close at the national level. Republican George W. Bush had won, but barely. If the outcome in Florida were reversed, then Democrat Al Gore would win the presidency instead. Making matters worse, Bush was ahead in Florida by only a few hundred votes. The nation waited in suspense for weeks as lawsuits were filed and recounts were conducted. The Supreme Court eventually ended the recounts in Florida, bringing the contest to an end. But the situation could have been much worse. With the Electoral College, the focus was on only a handful of counties in Florida. Under a direct-election scheme, the recounts (and accompanying lawsuits) could easily have spread across the country, leaving the United States without an elected president for months.

Today, some might question whether Bush "really" won Florida's vote, but the votes in other states are not questioned. The broad national coalition that Bush pieced together outside Florida is undeniable. Without the Electoral College, even this certainty would be absent. Instead, given the close popular vote in 2000, many today could be questioning whether Bush or Gore "really" won the national popular vote.[36] There would have been no certain point at which the country could have stopped the legal wrangling over recounts.

The 1960 election provides one last illustration of the ability of the Electoral College to control a situation that could otherwise degenerate into chaos and uncertainty. Republican Richard Nixon had ample reason to demand recounts in Illinois and Texas, as there appeared to be a fair number of problems in those closely contested states. For example, journalist Richard Reeves reports that 6,138 votes appear to have been cast by 4,895 voters in Fannin County, Texas, while in Chicago's sixth ward, forty-three voters apparently cast 121 votes in one hour.[37] Nixon ultimately decided not to pursue recounts, but he could have done so.

In his memoirs, Nixon explains why he conceded the election rather than demand a recount in Texas and Illinois. "A presidential recount would require up to half a year," he wrote, "during which time the legitimacy of Kennedy's election would be in question. The effect could be devastating to America's foreign relations."[38] He was right, and his decision spared the country a fair amount of disorder and confusion. But recounts without the Electoral College would have caused even more chaos than the situation Nixon was trying to avoid.

The national results in 1960 revealed a difference of only 118,574 votes between the two men.[39] Under a direct election system, Nixon easily could have demanded a recount of such a close vote. The Electoral College system, however, made the closeness of the national popular vote irrelevant. Instead, had Nixon demanded recounts, these disputes would have been limited to Illinois and Texas. Moreover, the allegations of fraud have focused on these two states for a reason. Even if votes were stolen somewhere else in the country on that Election Day in 1960, they would not have affected the final outcome one way or another.

The Electoral College successfully limits the effects of fraud and error to one or a handful of states. The remaining electoral votes can remain above the fray, as they are undisputed. The country is given a clear set of problems to resolve before moving on to a definitive election outcome.

DIFFICULTY IN RIGGING ELECTIONS

The 2016 election highlighted a growing concern about "rigged" elections. Republican candidate Donald Trump tweeted before the election that the process "is absolutely being rigged. . . ."[40] Such perceptions are real among the general public, but any animosity toward the Electoral College in this context is misguided. To the contrary, the decentralized structure of the Electoral College works against such a systematic rigging of election results.[41] Indeed, a direct election system would make it far easier for an incumbent class of federal officials to work behind the scenes, paving the way for their favorites.

The prior section discussed the difficulty of stealing elections through fraud and stolen votes, but there are other ways to "rig" elections. Who makes the laws that govern elections? After all, those in control of the government have the power to tilt laws and regulations to the advantage of one party or another. As a small example, consider the ease with which incumbent candidates and political parties get on the ballot compared with the obstacle course that independent candidates sometimes have to negotiate.

As the Electoral College operates today, election laws are primarily made at the local level, not at the national level. Americans hold fifty-one completely separate elections each and every presidential election year—one in each state, plus one in the District of Columbia. Each election is conducted in accordance with state and local laws. The relevance of federal laws is limited to a handful of items, such as the date by which electoral votes should be submitted to Congress.

In other words, at least fifty-one legislative bodies write the laws that govern presidential elections. Such a decentralized process makes it harder to systematically rig an election in favor of one party or the other. A direct election system, by contrast, would be much more centralized. Consider the changes that would soon follow: a new federal election code would be written. And a new federal agency would be created; it would be needed to handle the multiple election responsibilities now managed by local election judges. Someone would be needed to run this new bureaucracy, of course. The president would appoint someone.

In other words, if Americans replace their Electoral College with a direct election system, they will also replace a state-driven, decentralized process with a process that gives most power to the incumbent president and his administration. Incumbents would become responsible for their own re-election processes. Obviously, this single national process would be much easier to rig than fifty-one separate state-level processes.

A centralized federal election bureaucracy seems at odds with the Founders' thinking in yet another way. The Constitution explicitly separates federal officials from much of the presidential election process. Article II, Section 1, prohibits any "Senator or Representative, or Person holding an Office of Trust or Profit under the United States" from being appointed an elector.[42] The Founders wanted an independent body of representatives, completely separate from Congress. They had at least two good reasons for their decision: first, they wanted to ensure that the voice of the people drove the process. Congress should be separated from the electoral vote, unable to elect their political cronies to office and unable to protect an incumbent. The Constitution, Alexander Hamilton explained in *Federalist No. 68*, "exclude[s] from eligibility to this trust all those who from situation might be suspected of too great devotion to the President in office."[43]

Second, they hoped that a temporary body of electors would be less corruptible than other legislative bodies. The selection of the president, Hamilton explained, does not "depend on any preexisting bodies of men who might be tampered with beforehand to prostitute their votes."[44]

In modern-day parlance, the Founders thought decisions reached by this body of electors would be more difficult to "rig."

The Founders did not want federal officials to be electors, at least in part to protect the process from being politicized and corrupted. If congressmen can't be trusted to be electors, then why should they be trusted to enact a federal election code governing presidential elections? The danger of politicization and corruption is the same.

Some aspects of presidential elections have already been centralized by default, and Americans are not always happy with the results. For instance, they grumble about the bias of the mainstream media and twenty-four-hour cable news stations. They dislike decisions made by the Commission on Presidential Debates. If too much power has already been put in the hands of a few for media and debate purposes, why would anyone expect it to go better in other contexts?

The freedom of American presidential elections is protected, in part, by the fact that they are so decentralized. What if centralizing them into one national effort throws the physics of the entire political system, as JFK would say, out of balance? The risk isn't worth taking.

***

The Founders were proud of the Constitution that they had written and deemed the Electoral College to be among its best features. They would likely consider it a great pity that most Americans now believe the Electoral College to be an anachronism serving no real purpose in a global economy transformed by technological advances.

Obviously, the world has changed since that summer in Philadelphia when the Founders drafted a new form of government. But the Founders didn't create a system of checks and balances in the Constitution because the Internet hadn't been invented yet. They created constitutional protections because they knew that freedom needs to be protected from the flawed nature of human beings. That concern is as valid today as it was in 1787.

Human beings are still imperfect. Power still corrupts. Ambition, power, and greed are still dangerous to self-government. Minorities still need to be protected. Some states are still smaller than their neighbors, with unique interests that should be represented in the federal government. Moderation and compromise are still beneficial in a large, diverse nation. Americans still need a president who represents the variety of subcultures, regions, and industries that span this great country.

Perhaps American historian Max Farrand said it best. In his classic work *The Framing of the Constitution of the United States*, he summarized the attitude of the Founders toward the new presidential election process that they had devised: "[F]or of all things done in the convention the members seemed to have been prouder of that than of any other, and they seemed to regard it as having solved the problem for any country of how to choose a chief magistrate."[45]

"*Any* country." They surely believed the phrase would include twenty-first-century America.

PART TWO

PRESIDENTS WHO LOST THE POPULAR VOTE

CHAPTER FOUR

POPULAR VOTE LOSERS: LEGITIMATE WINNERS

I n the wake of the 2016 election, a *Washington Post* poll found that one-third of Hillary Clinton supporters believed Donald Trump's win was illegitimate.[1] Clinton had just become the second Democratic candidate in sixteen years to win the popular vote but lose the electoral vote. Indeed, Trump himself seemed a bit uncomfortable with the situation at first.

"In addition to winning the Electoral College in a landslide," he tweeted on November 27, "I won the popular vote if you deduct the millions of people who voted illegally."[2] Trump never proved the allegation, but at least one poll soon showed that 52 percent of Republicans believed that Trump had won both the electoral and the popular vote.[3] Were they perhaps trying to resolve a bit of cognitive dissonance? Are modern Americans so democratic-minded that they can't accept a president elected according to republican and federalist principles?

Others seemed to have trouble swallowing the legitimacy of Trump's win. "The presidency is the only office in America where the candidate who wins the most votes can still lose the election," outgoing Democratic Senator Barbara Boxer fumed in late 2016 as she filed legislation to eliminate the Electoral College.[4] "[T]he winner doesn't win, maybe. The winner doesn't win! It's crazy."[5] Her complaints echoed those heard in 2000 when Al Gore won the popular vote but lost the election to George W. Bush.[6] Curiously, one of those complaints came from then-Senator Hillary Clinton. "[W]e should respect the will of the people," she said at the time, "and, to me, that means it's time to do away with the Electoral College and move to the popular election of our president."[7]

But is a victory illegitimate because the candidate did not reach a goal that he was not trying to attain?[8] Neither Bush nor Trump was working to get the most individual popular votes nationwide. Why should either man be judged for his failure to get them? If the candidates had been striving for a popular vote win, they would have used their time and resources differently. President Bill Clinton's solicitor general, Walter Dellinger, made this point in 2000, while the Bush-Gore contest was being decided. "There's no real legitimacy argument," he observed. "If the presidency was decided by the popular vote, the two candidates would have run different races. We simply don't know who would have won."[9] Moreover, in a different system, it's entirely possible that a third-party candidate could have had a larger effect.

"The winner should win" might make an easy sound bite, but a national popular vote victory is not the only route to legitimacy, as the Founders well knew.

PLAYING BY THE RULES OF THE GAME

"At 3:36.30 p.m. yesterday," the *Pittsburgh Post-Gazette* reported on October 14, 1960, "all hell broke loose in Pittsburgh. At that precise moment Pirate second baseman Bill Mazeroski's game winning home run cleared the left field wall touching off one of the wildest, noisiest, happiest, and most raucous celebrations in Pittsburgh's history. The bedlam—and there is no other way to describe the scene Downtown after the game—continued on and on and on into the night."[10]

The Pittsburgh Pirates had defeated the New York Yankees to win the World Series! It was the team's first championship in thirty-five years. Needless to say, people across town were ecstatic. Before Mazeroski had even finished his lap around the bases, joyous fans were already throwing scrap paper out windows in downtown Pittsburgh. The makeshift confetti rained down on the city, stopping traffic and adding to the pandemonium.[11]

The Pirates had barely pulled off their surprising win in the closing moments of Game Seven. Indeed, they'd spent much of the World Series being soundly defeated by the Yankees. Game One had started well with a 6-4 victory for the Pirates, but they'd lost in blowouts in Games Two and Three. The Yankees routed them 16-3 and 10-0! The Pirates were back in contention only because they'd won with bare victories in Games Four and Five. Game Six had been yet another embarrassing 12-0 rout by the Yankees.

In the end, the championship came down to Game Seven. At the seventh-inning stretch, the Pirates were losing again, 5-4. They came back during the eighth inning, but the Yankees were scoring too. When Bill Mazeroski stepped to the plate at the bottom of the ninth inning, the two teams were tied 9-9. Mazeroski watched the first pitch go by, then smashed the second pitch over the left field wall. The home run brought the game to a stunning 10-9 conclusion.

Against all odds, the Pirates were the champions that year. They'd barely scraped by, of course, but they'd done it. As Pirates fans celebrated in downtown Pittsburgh late on October 13, no one cared that the Pirates had scored only twenty-seven total runs to the Yankees' fifty-five during the course of the seven World Series games. No one seriously questioned the legitimacy of their title. The rules of the game are clear: winning four of seven games is sufficient to earn the championship. The total number of runs scored across the seven games is irrelevant.

The criteria are consistent with the priorities of Major League Baseball throughout the baseball season. The rules emphasize games won instead of total runs scored. Any baseball fan knows that teams do not get to the World Series by scoring the most runs throughout the course of the season. Instead, teams earn their spot in the playoffs by winning the most games in their division. Major League Baseball could revise these rules, of course. It could send the two teams that score the most runs throughout the season to the World Series. It could also look to total runs scored during the course of that seven-game series. Baseball commissioners could even shorten the series to a single game like the Super Bowl. They don't make any of these changes, however, because such revisions would not accomplish their objective. They are not trying to reward teams who can run up the score in a single game or in a single circumstance. Instead, they strive to reward the team that can win consistently over the course of a full season or an entire set of games.[12]

Revising the rules might allow a team, for instance, to earn a spot in the World Series by having one great month and several poor months. A team that was great at taking advantage of weak opponents, even if it did poorly against good opponents, could win a berth in the World Series. Perhaps a team could excel by relying too heavily on one fantastic pitcher. Excellent performances throughout the baseball season would not be required to earn the championship. Occasional, stellar performances could be sufficient.

The rules for the presidential election contest have a similar purpose. The system seeks to identify the best overall candidate, favoring those whose strengths play out evenly over those who perform brilliantly in one part of the country but terribly in other regions. The Pirates were the legitimate champs in 1960 because they won by the rules that governed their sport. The same holds true for presidential candidates.[13] No president who has been elected according to the rules of the game is "illegitimate."

FAIR RULES, LEGITIMATE RESULTS

All that can be expected of a presidential election system is that the rules are fair and that they accomplish their stated objectives. Similarly, all that can be expected of a presidential candidate is that he plays by the rules of the game then in effect. If he wins under the existing set of rules, then he is the legitimate winner.

Some academics cannot accept this reasoning simply because they cannot accept the legitimacy of any election procedure that allows a candidate to win despite losing the nationwide popular vote. Other commentators accept the reasoning to some extent, but they are afraid to accept it fully. They may agree that the Electoral College is beneficial to the degree that it produces winners of "federal pluralit[ies]," but they argue that if a candidate won a "large majority of the popular vote" while losing the electoral vote, reform would be necessary.[14] After all, a president should have the "support of the people."[15]

Either stance betrays a lack of understanding of the Electoral College. The system was devised to ensure that a president will have the "support of the people," but this support must be broad-based. Candidates almost never win the electoral vote when they've lost the popular vote by a wide margin, as Donald Trump did in 2016. In fact, Hillary Clinton was the first (and so far only) losing candidate to run up such a high national popular vote total without also achieving an electoral victory. Her loss occurred because she relied too heavily on a small handful of like-minded states—precisely the type of behavior that the Electoral College is designed to prevent. The Clinton campaign deserved to lose. She might have had the support of the majority of individuals, but it was the kind of majority that threatens to be a tyrannical or regional majority. The Constitution looks for a different type of majority: a *federal* majority.

Electoral College critics who deny the legitimacy of a presidency not won with a majority of popular votes have assumed the need for the very matter in question.[16] Is a majority of individual votes necessary for legitimacy? Or could some other kind of majority—perhaps a majority of states, counties, or families—confer legitimacy? Many today dismiss such questions, but the Framers evaluated them at length. They concluded that freedom would be protected best if presidential candidates were required to win a majority of states' electoral votes.

To the degree that voters perceive an election as illegitimate because the victor didn't win a majority of the popular vote, this problem can be cured through simple education. The Founders had important reasons for establishing the Electoral College. Lack of understanding is an insufficient reason for abolishing it.

Americans accept the winner of the World Series even when the winner does not score the most runs during the baseball season. They accept the winner because they understand and accept the validity of the rules. Similarly, voters will accept the legitimacy of the Electoral College winner, even when he loses the popular vote, if they understand the rules of the game. Education is the key to any legitimacy problem that may exist.

***

The rules of American presidential elections are certainly unique, but that doesn't detract from their validity. Far from it. The Founders established the rules of their presidential election contest with certain purposes in mind. The system works as intended.

The task facing the Founders was difficult. How could a large, diverse country be self-governing, even as the dangers of majority tyranny and emotional mob rule are avoided? Achieving these two objectives simultaneously would seem to be impossible. No wonder the rules of the Founders' presidential election game turned out to be a little unusual. They found a way to let the people rule themselves, even as voters and states maintained their individuality.

Professor Russell Muirhead of Dartmouth once offered a thoughtful defense of the Electoral College as "part of the most fundamental idea in the Constitution."[17] The system reflects the answer to the question of "who should rule" in America:

> The Constitution's answer is this, the Constitutional majority should rule. . . . What's the Constitutional majority? The Constitution says it's not just a bare majority of the citizens, as Gallup might register in a poll tomorrow or next week, it's a more enduring, temporally enduring and geographically dispersed

majority . . . . The Constitutional majority is larger in space and more enduring in time than any ordinary majority would be. The idea there, the idea of the founders was that a larger more enduring majority would more likely be thoughtful, reflective, right, design policies that are actually effective, and just, design policies that are really fair, even to minorities.[18]

For more than two hundred years, the system has proved successful in achieving its objectives. It strives to identify those candidates or political parties best suited to represent the large, diverse American republic at a given time. Perhaps the best way to demonstrate the fairness—and, thus, the legitimacy—of the system is to look at the dynamics of five historical elections in which there was a discrepancy between the recorded popular and electoral votes.

CHAPTER FIVE

1824 AND 1876: MUCH ADO ABOUT NOTHING

C onventional wisdom has it that as many as five American presidents have been elected without winning the popular vote: John Quincy Adams (1824), Rutherford B. Hayes (1876), Benjamin Harrison (1888), George W. Bush (2000), and Donald Trump (2016). None of these men garnered either a majority or even a plurality of the recorded individual popular vote before being elected. Some critics contend that these elections are evidence that the presidential election system is "flawed."[1] Worse, they note, six presidential elections since 1948 were allegedly "problematic" in that a "shift of a relatively small number of votes in one or two states would have elected . . . a presidential candidate who lost the popular vote nationwide."[2]

Such claims certainly make the situation sound dire. To listen to these critics, it would seem that the presidential election system is constantly on the brink of disaster, and Americans are tempting fate to leave the system standing for so long. The country's luck is sure to run out soon.

The reality, of course, is nothing like these ominous claims. To the contrary, more than two hundred years of stability suggests that America's presidential election system is far more reliable than Electoral College opponents are ready to acknowledge.

First, at least two of the presidents commonly included on critics' lists of popular-vote loser presidents may not belong there, because the "real" national popular vote tallies for 1824 and 1876 remain in doubt.[3] Second, switching a "relatively small number of votes in one or two states" is much harder than it sounds. Finally, even if *every* election showed a discrepancy between the popular and electoral votes, the Electoral College would still be serving its underlying purpose: rewarding coalition building and discouraging candidates with isolated or only regional appeal.

THE ELECTIONS OF 1824 AND 1876

People had been pouring into Washington, DC, for days.[4] As many as twenty thousand people descended upon a city that simply didn't have room for them all. Hotel rooms were expensive—and packed. Some people shared beds with strangers; others slept on the floor in taverns. Travelers could be found sleeping under doorways or under staircases. Some even slept in fields around the city. They had come from all parts of the country to witness Andrew Jackson's historic presidential inauguration on March 4, 1829.[5] The oath of office was to be administered in front of the Capitol on the east side. Every aspect of this presidential inauguration would be fully public, which was a departure from usual practice. Voters were excited.

When the big day finally came, thousands of people stood outside the Capitol, waiting for the grand event. One Washington socialite, Margaret Bayard Smith, described the scene: "Thousands and thousands of people, without distinction of rank, collected in an immense mass round the Capitol, silent, orderly and tranquil, with their eyes fixed on the front of that edifice, waiting the appearance of the President in the portico."[6]

Except the "silent, orderly and tranquil" crowd didn't stay that way for long. After Jackson's inaugural address, a barrier separating the public from the Capitol steps came down, and the crowd was unrestrained. Smith described the mass of people that broke through: "[T]hey rushed up the steps all eager to shake hands with [Jackson]. It was with difficulty he made his way through the Capitol and down the hill to the gateway that opens on the avenue. Here for a moment he was stopped. The living mass was impenetrable."[7]

Jackson rode his horse back to the White House with the crowd close behind. By tradition, the executive mansion was open to the public on Inauguration Day. In the past, relatively small receptions had been held, but this time the White House was completely overrun. People flooded the mansion, knocking over furniture, spilling beverages, and breaking china. At one point, Jackson was reportedly backed up against a wall, completely surrounded by well-wishers.

Smith's description continues: "Ladies fainted, men were seen with bloody noses and such a scene of confusion took place as is impossible to describe,—those who got in could not get out by the door again, but had to scramble out of windows."[8] Jackson himself was finally forced to escape, either climbing out a window or fleeing through a back door and retreating to a local hotel. In the meantime, the White House staff moved washtubs of whiskey and orange juice to the front lawn, hoping to lure the revelers outside.

Some of Jackson's supporters later insisted that the tales of drunkenness and damage at the inaugural party had been exaggerated by his political enemies, but neither side disputed that an enormous crowd descended upon the White House that day, forcing the new president to make an escape.

Voters had much to celebrate! The raucous inaugural came soon after an election that had disappointed many people. Four years earlier, Andrew Jackson had lost a bitterly contested election to John Quincy Adams—but just barely.[9] Jackson had won a plurality of both the electoral and the recorded popular vote, but he had fallen short of a majority of either. Without a majority of electoral votes, the election was sent to the House of Representatives. Congressmen were to choose from the top three contenders in the electoral vote—Jackson, Adams, and William H. Crawford. Henry Clay, who had come in fourth, was excluded from consideration because the Constitution limits the field to the top three vote-getters.

Perhaps Jackson ended up wishing that Clay had somehow squeaked into third place ahead of Crawford? Once Clay was out of the running, he threw his support behind Adams. Clay didn't really like either man— he called it a "choice of evils"—but he thought Adams was slightly better.[10] Clay was then still Speaker of the House of Representatives, and his influence made a difference in many of the state delegations. Ultimately, Clay's support was enough. Adams defeated Jackson in the House vote and became president, even though he'd placed second in the Electoral College vote.

RESULTS: ELECTION OF 1824

	Electoral Votes		Popular Votes		House Votes
	Actual	*Percent*	*Actual*	*Percent*	
John Quincy Adams	84	32.2%	113,122	30.9%	13
Andrew Jackson	99	37.9%	151,271	41.3%	7
William H. Crawford	41	15.7%	40,856	11.2%	4
Henry Clay	37	14.2%	47,531	13.0%	—

Jackson's supporters, already unhappy, became even more upset when Adams made Clay his secretary of state. Had a "corrupt bargain" been struck between the two men?[11] Reports emerged that Clay had initially tried to strike a deal with Jackson, but Jackson refused to "go to that chair" except "with clean hands."[12] Historian Paul Johnson concludes, "We shall probably never know whether there *was* a 'corrupt bargain.' Most likely not. But most Americans thought so. And the phrase made a superb slogan."[13]

The allegations were enough to provoke a fair amount of dissatisfaction with the election results, particularly when combined with the fact that Jackson had won the popular vote. There was just one problem hiding among these claims: true, Jackson had indeed won a plurality of the *recorded* popular vote in 1824, but many individual votes had never been recorded in the first place.[14] At the time, many state legislatures were still directly selecting presidential electors to represent their states in the Electoral College.[15] Many of those states also happened to be ones in which the citizens generally preferred Adams.[16]

In short, there is no way to know what the popular vote would have been in 1824 if all states had then relied upon a statewide popular vote as their method of elector selection. Adams may or may not have been a so-called "runner-up" president. Either way, the election of 1824 is not representative of today's electoral system, which relies upon popular votes in all the states and a winner-take-all system of appointing electors.

The next election that allegedly produced a president who lost the popular vote was that of 1876, an election that makes the 2000 dispute over Florida look like child's play.[17] The popular vote tallies showed that Rutherford B. Hayes had received about 250,000 fewer votes than his opponent, Samuel J. Tilden. But that wasn't the worst part. Twenty electoral votes in Florida, Louisiana, Oregon, and South Carolina were disputed.[18] Three of those states submitted votes from multiple slates of electors, and one electoral vote in Oregon was also challenged. Hayes needed all twenty of these contested electoral votes to obtain a majority of 185 electoral votes and the presidency; Tilden needed only one.

The country waited for weeks to see which candidate would be declared the victor. The Senate was then controlled by Republicans, while the House was controlled by Democrats. Unsurprisingly, no one knew what to do about the conflicting sets of election returns. Finally, the divided Congress established an electoral commission composed of fifteen senators, congressmen, and Supreme Court justices.

The commission was supposed to be divided evenly, with seven Republicans, seven Democrats, and one independent. Except it didn't quite work out that way. Independent Justice David Davis declined to serve on the commission when he was unexpectedly elected to the Senate by the Illinois state legislature. He was replaced by Justice Joseph Bradley, a Republican appointee. Perhaps predictably, the Republican-controlled commission soon awarded all twenty disputed electoral votes, and thus the presidency, to Hayes. A Democratic filibuster nearly scuttled congressional acceptance of the commission's findings, but eventually Congress brokered a compromise. Republicans indicated that they would be willing to bring Reconstruction to an end. In return, Southern congressmen began withdrawing their objections.[19]

Hayes was finally declared the winner of the presidential election at about four o'clock in the morning on March 2, 1877, only two days before President Ulysses S. Grant's term expired.[20]

Samuel Tilden led Hayes by about a quarter-million popular votes as they were officially recorded, but those figures are potentially incomplete. In those post–Civil War years, elections in the South were not always free, and blacks often were not allowed to vote. Fraud pervaded the election as the Northern and Southern portions of the country struggled to reunite. At least one study has concluded that a "fair and free election" would have resulted in a popular vote victory for Hayes.[21] Under such circumstances, many more ballots would likely have been cast for Hayes in states such as Mississippi, Alabama, and North Carolina. Adding to the confusion, the election shares at least one similarity with the 1824 election: the appointment of electors was not always based on a statewide popular vote. One state legislature—Colorado's—directly selected electors for Hayes that year. It's impossible to know what a full national popular vote total would have been if Colorado had conducted a statewide popular vote instead.

Either way, with so much doubt about the results, it seems unfair to use the 1876 election as a case in point against the Electoral College. If anything, the state-by-state nature of the election saved the country that year. Instead of sparring endlessly over the fairness of a national popular vote tally, election problems were isolated in four states. The country was given a finite set of problems to resolve before moving on to a definitive election outcome.

WORRIES ABOUT NEAR-CALAMITIES

The state-by-state nature of the presidential election system is less comforting to Electoral College opponents. They worry about some presidential elections in which a "shift of a relatively small number of votes in one or two states" could have resulted in the election of yet another president who lost the popular vote.[22] These critics are able to cite quite a few examples.[23] In fact, given the frequency of these supposed near-crises, one would think that the country should be perpetually living with a "popular-vote loser" as president.

In reality, of course, such crises remain purely theoretical most of the time. Practically speaking, the mathematical scenarios dreamed up by Electoral College opponents remain possible but not very probable. The reason? Real life gets in the way.[24] If something causes people in one part of the country to change their minds, then it can just as easily cause people in other parts of the country to change their minds in the opposite direction.

Professor Judith Best, an expert on the Electoral College, has cited the election of 1844 in this context.[25] A shift of a mere 2,555 votes in New York would have given the election to Henry Clay instead of James Polk, despite Polk's decisive victory in the national popular vote. However interesting it might be to imagine that scenario, obtaining those votes in the real election was not quite so easy. To win New York, Clay probably would have had to change his position on the annexation of Texas. But modifying his position on annexation to win New York probably would have cost him Tennessee. That state approved of his position on annexation, yet he carried it by a mere 113 votes. Had he gained New York but lost Tennessee, Clay still would have lost the election.

In a similar vein, Electoral College opponents sometimes worry that a presidential candidate could win with the support of "only" eleven states, if they were the eleven biggest states. Once again, the contention is mathematically true but practically infeasible. In real life, any presidential candidate who could get the support of both Texas and California—simultaneously—would easily win the support of other states as well. Indeed, the last president to win both of those states was George H. W. Bush, in 1988. Bush had built a good cross-regional coalition, and he won the electoral votes of forty states.

In sum, the scenarios dreamed up by opponents of the Electoral College are possible as a purely abstract matter, but in reality they are highly unlikely. Their math is correct, but their grasp of the practicalities of American presidential politics is tenuous.

The historical record confirms just how much Americans need the Electoral College. The system encourages presidential candidates to seek national support and to build cross-regional coalitions. The loser of the popular vote is not elected often, but when he is, the reasons for such an outcome are always the same: the candidate who won the popular vote failed to build support across state boundaries. He spent too much time focused on a particular region or interest group.[26] Such a candidate does not deserve to win the presidency. The president should be an *American* president, not a regional one.

THE ELECTION OF 1960

"Any election night is an emotional roller coaster ride," Richard Nixon once wrote, "but election night in 1960 was the most tantalizing and frustrating I have ever experienced."[27] For hours, it was impossible to tell whether John F. Kennedy or Nixon would carry the day. The election is often commented on because of the close outcomes in Texas and Illinois, but some academics take matters a step further: they argue that Richard Nixon "really" won the national popular vote that year and that the Nixon-Kennedy race is yet another example of a popular-vote loser gaining the presidency. This argument falls apart upon further inspection, but it's made often enough that it is worth addressing.

The crux of the issue has to do with how Alabama's vote is tabulated. If Alabama is omitted from the national total, Kennedy has a slight lead in the popular vote—33,902,681 votes compared to Nixon's 33,870,176.[28] Kennedy's lead was clear, although the race was tight.

Adding Alabama to the mix complicates any attempt to come up with a precise national popular vote total. The problem stems from a ballot that would leave a voter today scratching his head. Alabama voters in 1960 did not cast a single vote for president. Instead, they cast eleven ballots for eleven electors of their choice. They could vote for Republican electors, Democratic electors, independent electors—or even some of each. Making matters still more confusing, some of the Democratic electors were committed to Kennedy, but others were not. Six of Alabama's Democratic electors would ultimately vote for Harry F. Byrd.

How should political scientists tally the popular votes of Alabamians? Each elector received a different number of votes, indicating that not everyone voted a straight ticket. At least some voters divided their ballots among Republican, Democratic, and independent electors. If someone voted for five Kennedy electors, five Nixon electors, and one independent elector, then how is his vote to be counted? Is that a vote for Kennedy or a vote for Nixon? Or perhaps it was actually a vote for his friend, the independent elector, to be a free agent.

The votes in Alabama can't be tabulated in any kind of coherent way, yet some have still tried to twist the confusing situation into a claim that Nixon "really" won the national popular vote. How odd. Nixon lost the popular vote in all states, excluding Alabama. Within the state of Alabama, his top elector received fewer votes than the top elector pledged to Kennedy—237,981 votes for the Nixon elector versus 318,303 votes for the top Kennedy elector.[29] If Nixon's top Alabama elector received fewer votes than the top Kennedy elector, then how does Nixon suddenly leap ahead in the national popular vote total? Mathematicians might come up with ways to twist the statistics, but it doesn't seem like an accurate reflection of what was happening on the ground in Alabama that year.

Despite critics' claims to the contrary, the fairest assessment of the 1960 election is an acknowledgment that there is no good way to count Alabama's votes accurately toward a national total. The independent State of Alabama constructed its ballot with other purposes in mind.

***

Five elections won by the popular-vote loser—with at least six more close calls—sounds like a lot. But a closer look shows that many of these concerns are simply much ado about nothing. The system has been operating as intended for more than two hundred years.

There have been only three elections in which the Electoral College denied the White House to the clear winner of the popular vote. Each of these can be explained by a failure of one party to build coalitions—a fatal mistake in a diverse republic such as America.

CHAPTER SIX

1888, 2000, AND 2016: WHEN STATES OUTVOTE INDIVIDUALS

Three men have become president despite losing the nationwide individual popular vote: Benjamin Harrison, George W. Bush, and Donald Trump. The elections of the latter two, in particular, have been criticized as cases in which the electoral process has failed the American people. Yet they are the precise opposite.

A closer examination of these elections reveals that, in each instance, the Electoral College rewarded the party that had built the strongest cross-regional coalition—or perhaps simply punished a party that had failed in that regard.

1888: CLEVELAND'S OVEREMPHASIS ON THE SOUTH

Adjutant-General Richard Drum surely had no idea what a ruckus he would raise with his well-intentioned letter of April 30, 1887.[1] He'd discovered that the War Department had quite a few old flags that had been captured or recovered during the Civil War. Some were Union flags, but others were "Confederate flags which the fortunes of war placed in our hands . . . ."[2] Drum thought it might be a "graceful act" to return all these war standards, including the Confederate flags, to their home states.[3] "While in all the civilized nations of the world," he wrote to the secretary of war, "trophies taken in the war against foreign enemies have been carefully preserved and exhibited as proud mementoes of the nation's military glories, wise and obvious reasons have always excepted from the rule evidences of past [internal] troubles . . . ."[4]

In other words, given that the country intends to continue as a united front, wouldn't it be better to treat the South like friends instead of enemies?

The secretary of war spoke to President Grover Cleveland and returned the memo to Drum with a handwritten notation: "Approved by the President."[5]

The outrage was immediate. Several governors protested, including the governor of Ohio. He wrote Cleveland that the people of his state were "shocked and indignant beyond anything I can express."[6] He instituted legal proceedings to prevent the return of any Confederate flag captured by Ohio troops.[7] He was joined in his outrage by Lucius Fairchild, commander of the Grand Army of the Republic (GAR), an enormously influential organization of Union veterans. Fairchild took to the stage at a rally and stormed, "May God palsy the hand that wrote that order. May God palsy the brain that conceived it; and may God palsy the tongue that dictated it."[8]

Needless to say, Cleveland soon retracted his order, writing that he'd taken time to consider the matter "with more care than when the subject was orally presented me."[9] Upon further reflection, he'd decided that "[a]ny direction as to final disposition of [the flags] should originate with Congress."[10]

Unfortunately, Cleveland's political enemies wouldn't let the matter drop.[11] Those years were hard anyway, of course, as the country struggled to reunite following the Civil War. Now Republicans shoved the flag issue upon Cleveland, too. It became one of several issues convincing voters that Cleveland cared more about the South than about the rest of the country.

The flag controversy was made worse by another touchy subject that had been plaguing Cleveland for years: abuse of the pension system following the Civil War. Congress tended to be highly sympathetic to any claim put forth by Union veterans, whereas Cleveland repeatedly vetoed claims that he viewed as weak or fraudulent. He would eventually veto a record 414 bills during his first term in office.[12] Some voters respected his attempts to curb the fraud and waste, but others weren't quite so enthusiastic. They thought Cleveland was being disrespectful to their veterans and the "bloody shirt."[13]

Needless to say, Cleveland became increasingly unpopular with Union veterans. His poor relationship with that group soon led to another political debacle, just as he was trying to regroup from the Confederate flag controversy. The president had accepted an invitation to the national encampment of the GAR in St. Louis. Cleveland was excited about the opportunity. He thought it would be helpful to meet and shake hands with voters, so he suggested that his reception there be public. The veterans, however, were offended by what they perceived as Cleveland's political opportunism. The *National Tribune* scolded, "Does anyone want the National Encampment running in conjunction with a grand political mass meeting?"[14] Protests were threatened, and some feared for the president's safety. Reluctantly, Cleveland canceled his plans to attend the meeting.

As if souring relations with Union veterans weren't enough, tariff reform also became a contentious issue.[15] Cleveland himself pressed Congress to lower tariffs, but the bill that emerged from the Democratic House was a watered-down bill that favored the South at the expense of the North. Congress never passed a meaningful reform, and the perception that Cleveland was currying favor with the South dogged his re-election campaign in 1888. Perhaps making matters worse, his Republican opponent, Benjamin Harrison, brought up the tariff issue repeatedly, creating a picture of Cleveland as a president who cared mostly about the South.[16] For his part, Cleveland never did a good job of responding to the Republican allegations.[17]

When election results came in, they revealed a discrepancy between the electoral and popular votes. Harrison easily won the electoral vote (233 to 168), but Cleveland led the national popular vote tally by nearly ninety thousand votes. His lead was based on landslide victories in just six southern states. Those states had backed their president wholeheartedly, giving him 72.2 percent of the votes cast for both men.[18] Cleveland's support elsewhere was lackluster, and he'd lost the independents who had supported him in 1884. Meanwhile, Harrison's support was less intense than Cleveland's, but it was spread across the North and West. He'd also picked up many of the independents who had abandoned Cleveland.

Cleveland's proposals may have been sound from the standpoint of economics and constitutional law, but he did not present them in a manner that enabled him to obtain strong cross-country support. Instead, he ran the type of campaign that ought to lose under the system devised by the Founders. If Cleveland had won in 1888, it would have been because an extremely high margin in a bloc of six Southern states had overcome the votes of the North and West combined. A candidate would have prevailed not with a message of national appeal, but by amassing landslide victories in a few key states.

The Electoral College sent a message in 1888 to future presidential candidates: do not ignore the interests of the many by catering to the few. Interestingly, Cleveland himself learned this lesson and returned to win a second presidential term in 1892.

2000: RURAL VS. URBAN VOTERS

"Are you saying what I think you're saying?" one presidential candidate asked the other. "Let me make sure that I understand. You're calling back to retract [your] concession?"[19]

"You don't have to be snippy about it," his opponent responded.[20]

It was 2:30 a.m. local time on November 8, 2000. Vice President Al Gore had been on his way to Nashville's War Memorial Plaza, where he'd planned to offer his concession speech. A crowd waited for him there, refusing to leave despite the cold, drizzly weather. It had been quite a night. Early election returns had made Gore's victory seem all but certain. The important swing state of Florida had been called in the Democrat's favor at 7:49 p.m. Eastern time. States such as Michigan and Minnesota were soon also placed in the Gore column, causing the candidate's aides to feel hopeful. Their hope ripened into glee when the networks called New Mexico for Gore at 9:44 p.m. The Democratic candidate now seemed certain to win.[21]

Gore's campaign spokesman would later call those few minutes of jubilant celebration "our seven-minute presidency."[22]

The final outcome would prove to be much messier than those few moments of joy. Minutes later, the early call for Florida was retracted. Instead, the networks began calling Florida—and the presidential race—for George W. Bush at 2:16 a.m. Eastern time. Al Gore called Bush to concede, but an hour later, he retracted his concession when it became apparent that the networks had made another premature call.

The results of the 2000 election would remain in doubt for weeks. The outcome hinged on the count in Florida, which then had twenty-five electoral votes.[23] Bush was ahead in the state tally, but his lead was razor-thin. Lawsuits were filed and recounts were requested. Weeks of doubt followed as state officials and judges attempted to determine whether Bush or Gore had won Florida's electoral votes. The legal wrangling endured for more than a month until a Supreme Court ruling finally put an end to the turmoil.[24] Bush had won Florida by only 537 votes. The victory gave him a bare majority of 271 votes in the Electoral College, even though Gore had won the national popular vote by 537,179 votes.[25]

The 2000 election made George W. Bush the first president in more than one hundred years to win the presidency without also winning the national popular vote. The election year had been odd in other ways, too. The issues that motivated the electorate were harder to pinpoint than the regional, post-war issues that drove Benjamin Harrison's victory in the 1888 election.[26]

As the presidential election year began, the country was doing well economically. This peace and prosperity should have weighed in favor of Vice President Al Gore, the heir-apparent to incumbent President Bill Clinton.[27] In fact, if Gore had taken advantage of the situation, then perhaps he would have won after all.[28] As it was, Gore never effectively capitalized on the nation's economic health.[29] Instead, the notoriously hard-to-define concept of "values" would drive the outcome of the 2000 election.[30]

Many people felt that Clinton had performed well in office, but they did not like him personally. His presidency had been scandal-ridden, and the president had even been impeached. The moral decline affected the mood of voters, making Clinton a political liability for Gore. Rural voters in the South and the Midwest seemed especially disillusioned and ready for the country to steer back toward a healthier moral track.[31] Bush capitalized on this discontent, even as he acknowledged one of his opponent's strengths: the country's economic prosperity. Bush's nomination acceptance speech at the Republican National Convention in Philadelphia opened, "Prosperity can be a tool in our hands used to build and better our country, or it can be a drug in our system dulling our sense of urgency, of empathy, of duty. . . . Our generation has a chance to reclaim some essential values."[32]

Bush's campaign worked to link Gore with the dishonest and unprincipled behavior that voters perceived had intensified during the Clinton administration. Vice presidential candidate Dick Cheney declared, "Mr. Gore will try to separate himself from his leader's shadow. But somehow we will never see one without thinking of the other."[33] Gore further contributed to his own downfall, binding himself to Clinton's failings in the minds of many voters. Many remained upset that he'd failed to strongly condemn Clinton's actions during the 1998 impeachment proceedings. Diane Wright, a homemaker in Gore's home state of Tennessee, expressed this sentiment. She would likely vote for Bush, she said, "[p]robably because of Clinton. Gore should have been stronger. He could have distanced himself. A lot of people in Tennessee feel that way."[34]

Gore came to be perceived as experienced but insincere and too ambitious. This perception, accurate or not, contributed to his inability to distance himself sufficiently from Clinton's moral failings. Gore made the mistake of thinking that peace and prosperity would carry the day with most of the country. He was right in thinking that it would carry the day with most *individuals*; however, most of these voters resided in the more liberal East and West coasts. Voters in the majority of states, particularly in the more conservative Midwest and South, voted on a different range of issues. Honesty and other virtues were important to them, and they believed that Bush was the better man.[35] "[W]e didn't do enough," one Gore adviser later wrote, "to reassure voters about what is true: Al Gore is a man of strong values and bedrock integrity."[36]

Bush was ultimately able to build a solid cross-regional coalition of voters, whereas Gore could not. Bush also made significant inroads into the Democratic vote, earning the votes of 11.3 million people who had not voted for the Republican ticket in 1996.[37] New Hispanic voters alone grew by 1.5 million.[38] Further, Bush won a number of traditionally Democratic states, such as West Virginia.[39] Gore also increased the number of votes cast for his party since the 1996 election, but these additional votes were from constituencies that consistently vote Democratic anyway. For instance, he gained new votes among labor unions and black voters.[40]

An examination of the vote totals by state or county reflects a nation that leaned heavily toward Bush. Sixty percent of the states favored Bush. He carried 2,434 counties, while Gore carried only 677.[41] The population in the counties won by Bush was 143 million people, compared with the 127 million people who resided in the counties won by Gore.[42] Bush carried the election in about 2,427,000 square miles of the country, compared with the roughly 580,000 square miles carried by Gore.[43] Bush earned the votes of at least one state in every region of the country. Most of Gore's support was concentrated in several heavily populated regions in the Northeast and on the western seaboard.

The election of 2000 demonstrated, once again, why the Electoral College exists. If America operated under a direct election system, Gore would have won despite losing the election in 60 percent of states and more than three-quarters of the counties in America. He would have won with virtually no support in two large regions of the country and the bulk of his support isolated on the East and West coasts. The rural and less populous states would have been trampled by the will of a few heavily populated regions.

The Electoral College appropriately awarded the better coalition-builder that year.

2016: REBELLION AGAINST THE ELITES

If the Electoral College is about coalition building, then what happened in 2016? At various points in the campaign, the winning candidate seemed pretty unconcerned about unity and coalition building. If anything, he seemed intent on the opposite.

"I have to be honest—I think I'll win without the unity," candidate Donald Trump told a crowd in Raleigh, North Carolina, in July 2016.[44] For weeks, he'd been calling some of his fellow Republicans names: they were "liars," "losers," or "overrated."[45] When his rallies were protested, he called the protestors "thugs" or "criminals."[46] He urged attendees to "knock the crap out of" a protestor if they saw one.[47] He praised one audience when it "hit back," noting "that's what we need a little bit more of."[48] Months earlier, he'd already been accused of mocking a disabled reporter, although Trump later said that he'd only intended to imitate a "flustered reporter."[49] At a rally in New Hampshire, he declared that American businesses that were moving operations out of the country could "go [expletive] themselves because they let you down, and they left."[50]

Not exactly the type of language that one would expect from a candidate who is striving to build a national coalition. But the Democrats were doing even worse: they'd nominated Hillary Clinton, a candidate whose problems should have been obvious. She'd admitted to mistakes with her handling of classified information during her time as secretary of state, and she was under FBI investigation for much of the campaign. Whether wrongly or rightly, broad swaths of the voting public believed that she had done more than just make a few mistakes: they believed that she was guilty of crimes and had endangered the lives of American agents overseas. Perhaps the Democratic Party shouldn't have chosen the campaign trail as the moment in which to try and prove her innocence.

Many voters distrusted Clinton because of events surrounding the murder of an American ambassador in Benghazi during her tenure as secretary of state. But Clinton's final problem may have been the worst of all: she was viewed as a member of the wealthy "elite" and a long-standing member of the liberal establishment in Washington. She represented everything that mainstream America was coming to distrust: the liberal, elitist class in the media, Hollywood, academia, and the government.[51] Voters were tired of being told what to think, how to think it, and when to think it!

At some point, perhaps even with the best of intentions, Democrats and liberals had quit respecting the diversity of thought and opinion in America. They'd been trying to fit everyone into a one-size-fits-all mold and denouncing them as "racists" and "bigots" when they didn't go into the mold quietly. Perhaps Democrats shouldn't have been so surprised when things went badly.

One journalist nicely summarized the reasons that Hillary Clinton—and the Democratic Party in general—could not build a coalition that would propel them on to election in 2016. "It happened because you banned super-size sodas. And smoking in parks," he wrote, "And offensive ideas on campus. . . . Because you treated owning a gun and never having eaten quinoa as signifiers of fascism. Because you thought correcting people's attitudes was more important than finding them jobs. . . . Because you treated people like trash. And people don't like being treated like trash."[52]

Given the level of frustration in some parts of the country, Trump's encouragement to "hit back" undoubtedly struck a chord with some voters. What might have offended them in any other election year delighted them in 2016. They took it as a sign that someone was finally willing to stand up and fight the establishment for them. Mike Rowe, who stars in the surprise hit television show *Dirty Jobs*, put it simply: "The people did not want a politician. The people wanted to be seen. Donald Trump convinced those people that he could see them. Hillary Clinton did not."[53] Actually, Clinton more or less did the opposite. In September 2016, she infamously commented that "you can put half of Trump supporters into what I call the basket of deplorables."[54]

Rowe's comments reflect discoveries made by Diane Hessan, an entrepreneur working for Clinton's campaign during the final months of the election cycle. "[Voters] didn't like either candidate," she concluded. "They just wanted to be understood. At the end of the day, they cared less about Trump's temperament and more about whether he 'got' them. They were smart, they knew the cheers, Trump gave them a voice, and he certainly didn't think they were deplorable."[55]

Michael Reeb, an Air Force combat veteran and a lifelong Democrat, explained why he'd pulled the lever for Trump in Pennsylvania: "Butler is my hometown, and Butler is in trouble. My hometown friends and I understand this plain as day, but the nation hasn't been listening to the decades-old problem of hometown humiliation."[56] He was surprised to discover a champion in Trump: "Somehow, up in a multimillion-dollar New York tower overlooking what seemed like the whole world, Trump heard that our jobs had been fabricated—and he sounded like the only one who had heard."[57] Clinton, on the other hand, didn't seem to care about the problems confronting many voters. Reeb noted dryly, "Clinton could be found ducking reporters."[58]

The longtime Democratic strategist David "Mudcat" Saunders announced that he would be voting Republican for similar reasons. "Hillary Clinton's record . . . she's not been a friend of rural America and rural America knows that," Saunders told a reporter, "and it's shining in the primaries and caucuses. It's a huge ABC feeling out here, Anybody But Clinton."[59]

Against all odds and amid some pretty unusual rhetoric, a coalition was formed in America during the 2016 election: it was a coalition *against* much of what had been going on under the Barack Obama administration—and even under prior administrations. The coalition included some people who genuinely trusted Trump, the man who had finally "seen" them after years of being taken for granted by the political establishment. And it included others who felt less comfortable with his crass approach but who shared the desire to shake things up in Washington. They distrusted Clinton and felt that Trump was more likely to disrupt the status quo. They were tired of watching elites focus on a liberal social agenda, even as health insurance premiums skyrocketed and lower and middle-income brackets took an economic hit.[60] Most of all, voters were simply tired of Washington insiders, who live by a different set of rules than everyone else does. They voted for change.

In fact, when later asked what had most influenced their vote, 39 percent of those polled replied that they voted for the candidate who "can bring change." Trump won a whopping 82 percent of these voters.[61] The election, one Stanford professor later said, had come down to "the ultimate establishment candidate" versus "someone who vowed to break things."[62] A coalition of Americans came together with a common purpose—destroying the status quo. They hoped to "drain the swamp" in Washington, DC.[63]

When election results came in, Clinton led Trump by nearly three million votes in the national tally—she'd obtained 65.8 million votes to Trump's 62.9 million. Her huge popular vote lead in the face of an electoral loss was unprecedented. At first glance, the results would seem to confirm the worst fears of Electoral College opponents. But a more thorough analysis of the numbers shows that the election actually confirmed the best hopes of Electoral College supporters. The system prevented one or two states from dictating an outcome to the rest of the nation. It enabled voters in less populated parts of the country to make themselves heard.

Clinton repeated the mistake that Grover Cleveland had already made a century earlier. In 1888, Cleveland's support was concentrated in six southern states. Similarly, Clinton's support was concentrated in only two states, New York and California. More than 20 percent of

Clinton's 65.8 million votes came from only those two states. Indeed, if those states are removed from the national total, then the results are reversed: *Trump* leads the national popular vote by more than three million votes. His electoral victory was less heavily reliant on one particular part of the country. He won thirty states across the country, compared to Clinton's twenty (plus the District of Columbia). Trump carried more than 2,600 counties, but Clinton carried fewer than five hundred.[64]

Oddly, the Clinton campaign had made a decision in the closing days of the campaign that likely contributed to the huge discrepancy. Fearing that Clinton would win the Electoral College but lose the national popular vote, the campaign switched its focus to driving up the popular vote in "safe" areas where it already felt sure of winning.[65] The strategy, of course, is the opposite of that required by the Electoral College. Clinton would have spent her time more wisely shoring up support in less safe parts of the country.

Democrats didn't seem to understand their mistakes at first. After the election, former President Bill Clinton fumed that Trump "doesn't know much. One thing he does know is how to get angry white men to vote for him."[66] Yet the coalition that voted for Trump was less white and less male than Clinton's words would suggest. In fact, Trump improved on Republican Mitt Romney's 2012 performance in several areas. Among blacks, a traditionally difficult group for Republicans, Trump obtained 2 percent more of the vote than Romney did. He did not improve among married women, but he stayed within two points of Hillary in that voting group, and he improved over Romney's performance among unmarried women. Similarly, Trump improved on Romney's performance among Asian-Americans, and he also earned the votes of one in three Hispanic males. Overall, 28 percent of Hispanics voted for him. Given the concern about Trump's positions on immigration, those numbers suggest that something more was at play when people were considering how to vote.[67]

Shortly after the election, Trump tweeted that he'd won "the Electoral College in a landslide."[68] It was an interesting statement to make.

At the time, it appeared that Trump would win by seventy-four electoral votes, compared with Barack Obama's 126-point margin in 2012 and 192-point margin in 2008. Indeed, since 1804, most elections have been won by at least one hundred electoral votes, if not considerably more. Of the thirty elections held between 1900 and 2016, seventeen presidents were elected after winning the electoral vote by a margin of two hundred votes or more. As a historical matter, Trump's win wasn't a landslide; it was a rather modest victory.

MARGIN OF VICTORY IN THE ELECTORAL COLLEGE: 1804 TO PRESENT

	1804 – 1896 elections	1900 – 1996 elections	2000 – 2016 elections	Total
N/A—Decided in contingent election	1	0	0	1
1-50 electoral votes	4	1	2	7
51-100 electoral votes	8	2	1	11
101-200 electoral votes	8	5	2	15
200 or more electoral votes	3	17	0	20
TOTAL	24	25	5	54

Perhaps the most astounding thing about the 2016 election is that Trump did not defeat Clinton by more than he did, given the amount of baggage that she carried into the election. The divisive commentary, it would seem, was not without consequence after all.

On Election Day, Clinton's "highly unfavorable" rating sat at a stunningly high 39 percent.[69] By contrast, when Barry Goldwater was defeated in a massive landslide in 1964, his "highly unfavorable" rating was a much smaller 26 percent.[70] By contrast, his opponent, incumbent President Lyndon B. Johnson, then had an unfavorable rating of only 13 percent. Johnson easily defeated Goldwater, 486–52. Similarly, George McGovern's "highly unfavorable" rating was 20 percent in 1972, but he was going up against an incumbent Richard Nixon who then had a highly unfavorable rating of only 11 percent. Nixon decimated McGovern in the Electoral College, 520–17.

Obviously, other factors come into play besides only disapproval ratings, but these simple examples demonstrate what might have been expected. When one party nominates someone controversial or out of the mainstream, the other party should be able to win, in a landslide, simply by nominating the opposite: someone uncontroversial and more mainstream. A strong coalition against an extremist or untrusted candidate is easy to build.

Prior to the 2016 election, no major-party candidate had ever matched the high disapproval ratings that both Trump and Clinton obtained. Clinton's were bad, but Trump's were even worse: 42 percent of voters held a highly unfavorable view of him in a poll taken mere days before the election.[71] These simultaneously high unfavorable ratings made the election close when it never had to be. They also ensured that a few third-party candidates received unusually high vote totals.

The independent candidate Evan McMullin started his campaign late in the election cycle. The former CIA agent was a virtual unknown when he threw his hat into the ring, yet he still managed to achieve 21.3 percent of the vote in his home state of Utah. He achieved more votes in a single state (on a percentage basis) than any third-party candidate since Ross Perot in 1992. The discontent with the two major-party choices was felt in other parts of the country as well. Roughly 6 percent of voters cast their ballots for a third-party candidate in 2016, and almost 1 percent of voters chose to write in the name of an alternative candidate. Writing in a name—during a presidential election, no less—is a pretty serious expression of discontent.[72] Topping it all off, Libertarian Gary Johnson received 3 percent of the vote nationally, the best overall showing by a third-party candidate since Ross Perot's campaign in 1996.

In the weeks before the election, many Republican loyalists blasted those voters who planned to cast their ballots for McMullin, Johnson, or another third-party candidate. They seem to have missed the point. The divisive nature of the Republican primaries and the general election campaign had exacted a price, as reflected by the third-party votes and the close election outcome. It was a price that would have cost Republicans the White House in any other election year.

The Electoral College rewarded a coalition of voters that was built outside California and New York in 2016, but it was a coalition built on ideas more than people or party. Indeed, the challenge facing *both* political parties in the wake of the 2016 election is the same—quit focusing on the failures of the other party. Instead, take an honest look inward, address internal failures, and move on to better coalition building in the future.

***

In the late 1800s, America suffered through a series of close elections. It must have been painful. At least one, if not two, elections showed a discrepancy between the popular and electoral votes. The country was in turmoil, and both parties were struggling to right themselves after a heated Civil War. The Electoral College provided stability during those years by forcing candidates to reach out to voters beyond their home base.

Democrats could never win without obtaining votes outside the South—as the 1888 election convincingly demonstrated. Republicans couldn't get too comfortable, either. They *could* win without Southern voters, but only by a dangerously narrow margin. The presidential election system rewards coalition building. Over time, the parties responded to these incentives, and agonizingly close elections became a thing of the past—for a while.

More than one hundred years later, Americans find themselves in a similar situation. Within a period of only sixteen years, two elections have shown a discrepancy between the electoral and the popular votes. Perhaps the close elections and the contentious atmosphere are unsurprising. Both parties are broken; neither is as focused on coalition building as it should be.

The Democratic Party received a stinging rebuke in 2016, but Democrats were also blessed with an opportunity to assess what they have been doing wrong and to chart a new direction for themselves. Republicans, despite the latest victory, ought to engage in the same sort of introspection. They won in 2016, but only because they were being graded on a curve. The emergence of third-party candidates, the #NeverTrump crowd, and other forms of protest reveal the huge gaps in Trump's appeal.

The first party to correct its course will benefit at election time. As a matter of history, the Electoral College always rewards any political party that excels at building coalitions and that recognizes the diverse, federalist nature of the American republic.

PART THREE

WHO'S IN CHARGE HERE?

CHAPTER SEVEN

THE STATES VS. THE RNC, THE DNC, AND THE FEDS

A mere five days into his presidency, Donald Trump threw down the gauntlet with a pair of tweets: "I will be asking for a major investigation into VOTER FRAUD," he wrote, "including those registered to vote in two states, those who are illegal and even, those registered to vote who are dead (and many for a long time). Depending on results, we will strengthen up voting procedures!!"[1]

His words came on the heels of a startling decision by the outgoing Barack Obama administration. Only a few weeks earlier, Secretary of Homeland Security Jeh Johnson had designated American election systems as "critical infrastructure" that deserved special federal assistance.[2] "[E]lection infrastructure will, on a more formal and enduring basis," Johnson announced, "be a priority for cybersecurity assistance and protections that the Department of Homeland Security provides . . . ."[3]

The designation was a striking grab of authority by the federal government. One election official immediately blasted out a protest. "This action politicizes elections," Christy McCormick of the U.S. Election

Assistance Commission wrote. "There is a reason that the Founding Fathers gave the authority of conducting elections to the States. . . . Our nation['s] elections should not be handled or governed by a partisan branch of the Federal Government."[4] Sharing her concern were other EAC commissioners as well as numerous state election officials. Georgia's secretary of state, Brian P. Kemp, for example, decried the "federal overreach into a sphere constitutionally reserved for the states."[5]

Nevertheless, Johnson's announcement went mostly unnoticed in the flurry of news surrounding Donald Trump's inauguration. Later, the new president's tweets inadvertently piled on to this idea that the federal government should intervene in presidential elections to prevent fraud. Unfortunately, Trump's tweets were met with praise from his supporters. After all, who doesn't want to stop hacking or fraud?[6] The decision seems like a no-brainer. Yet the decisions of both the Obama and the Trump administrations share one fatal flaw: they depart from America's constitutional structure of decentralized, state-driven elections.

The system has operated in the background for so long that many Americans may not have focused on the important differences between a centralized and a decentralized approach to presidential elections. A *centralized* approach would establish all power in the hands of a single federal authority. By contrast, America's *decentralized* approach separates power among fifty-one different authorities—fifty states and Congress.

The Constitution ensures that *states* are the driving force behind presidential elections. The *states*, not the federal government, bear primary responsibility for anything that is happening. The Constitution does not envision federal involvement in presidential elections beyond the counting of electoral votes and the congressional duty to "determine the Time of chusing the Electors, and the Day on which they shall give their Votes . . . ."[7] When it comes to congressional elections, the Constitution grants Congress slightly more authority to intervene, but the states still bear most of the responsibility.[8]

The decentralized system that the Founders designed protects presidential elections from being politicized and controlled by an incumbent class of federal officials, as explained in chapter three.[9] But it also gives the states great flexibility to act on behalf of their citizens in other ways. Not only can states handle fraud within their own borders, but they can also take other actions to ensure that their citizens' voices are heard. In the past, states have sometimes used their power when they disagree with the direction of the national political parties. They have spent time experimenting with different methods of awarding electors. Or they have even used their power to protect themselves financially.[10] As a general matter, states have great latitude to act so that they may best serve their own citizens.

Nevertheless, most Americans today are unaware of the great discretion that their states have in this area. The Electoral College may have been designed partly to give the states a voice, but Americans have been abandoning that idea in recent years. As states have abandoned their power, entities such as the Republican National Committee, the Democratic National Committee, the Commission on Presidential Debates, and even the mainstream media have stepped into the void.

The Founders would surely be surprised that the states have been giving up their power so easily in recent years—and equally *un*surprised that the longer this trend continues, the more dissatisfied Americans seem to be with their presidential nominees.

"SIGNALS OF GENERAL ALARM"

The first presidential election would have seemed strange to modern Americans. The states took the constitutional directive to appoint electors "in such Manner as the Legislature thereof may direct" quite literally. They had a lot of freedom to act, and they came up with all sorts of crazy ideas.[11]

Five legislatures decided not to hold a presidential election at all. Instead, state legislators simply appointed men whom they trusted to act as electors.[12] Imagine if the legislature in Connecticut were to cancel its 2020 presidential election and pick seven men and women to represent it in the Electoral College. Even today, Connecticut retains the right to do exactly that, and it would merely be repeating a decision that was already made for the state during the 1789 presidential election.

Other states had different ideas about the best way to select a president. For instance, one state created special districts for the election of electors.[13] Today, Americans often live in areas that have been assigned to multiple districts for election purposes: one for their congressman, a different district for a state representative, and a third district for a state senator. Such a system would introduce a fourth district for a presidential elector into the mix. On Election Day, voters would cast ballots for the elector they trust the most.

Another state came up with a different scheme, in which voters effectively narrowed down a list of potential electors when they cast their ballots on Election Day. Then the state legislature selected electors from the short list of pre-approved men.[14] Other states had still other ideas— one state even lost its vote altogether because the legislators couldn't agree on how to proceed.

No one swooped in from the federal government to save New York's votes that year. It was a matter for New York voters to resolve. The state took care of itself, and that was the last time that New York ever lost its vote.

The Founders would have expected nothing less. Ultimately, states are in charge of themselves—a fact that holds especially true in presidential elections. The federal government doesn't get to decide whom states will select as their own representatives. This division of responsibility was a natural outgrowth of the conversations at the Constitutional Convention. The delegates had spent a fair amount of time considering the comparative advantages of a national popular vote and the legislative selection of a president. But underlying every discussion at the Convention was a more important question: who is in charge here, the federal government or the states?

The question was a difficult one, and the delegates struggled with it quite a bit. Remember that the original purpose of the Convention was to address the problem of a national government that was too weak to handle many necessary tasks. George Washington and his army had struggled throughout the American Revolution because the Continental Congress had been unable to raise sufficient funds to support them. Congress couldn't force the states to cooperate. Even after the war, the weaknesses of Congress continued to surface. By then, the country had adopted its first national charter, the Articles of Confederation, but that system was failing too. The problems raised by interstate commerce had become increasingly difficult. Moreover, states weren't working together as they brokered treaties with foreign nations, and the country was in debt because the Confederation Congress still couldn't raise funds.

Washington summarized the situation pretty succinctly: "Thirteen Sovereignties pulling against each other, and all tugging at the fœderal head, will soon bring ruin on the whole."[15] Many delegates were keenly aware that the Convention needed to strengthen the national government; otherwise, the United States was bound to fail. As the Convention opened, some delegates spoke of their desire to reduce the states' grip on the national government. In one extreme statement, Rufus King of Massachusetts even lamented the impossibility of "annihilating the States," but he at least thought that "much of their power ought to be taken from them."[16]

On the other hand, most delegates still felt great loyalty to their states, and they believed in the principle of local governance. They knew that strong states were needed, too. John Dickinson of Delaware summarized this position early in the Convention. "One source of stability is the double branch of the Legislature," he concluded. "The division of the Country into distinct States formed the other principal source of stability. This division ought therefore to be maintained, and considerable powers to be left with the States."[17] Later, a delegate from Pennsylvania echoed this sentiment when he noted that the states "were absolutely necessary for certain purposes which the [national government] could not reach."[18]

As with so many other issues at the Convention, the debate over the balance of power between the states and the federal government would end in compromise.[19] The Constitution establishes a national government that can act with strength in the areas in which it has been delegated

power—but that can't act at all otherwise. The state and national governments are intended to act as checks upon each other. After all, neither
state nor federal officials, acting on their own, would be reliable guard-
ians of liberty. Human beings are too imperfect. Rather than expecting
perfection where none exists, the Founders structured their government
to make the imperfections of human nature work in their favor.

The Father of the Constitution, James Madison, described this
dynamic, noting that "[a]mbition must be made to counteract ambition."[20] In other words, the harmful self-interest of one set of officials
should be set against the harmful self-interest of other sets of officials.
If properly counterbalanced, "opposite and rival interests" can make up
for bad motives.[21] Every man's "private interest" can be a "sentinel over
the public rights."[22]

Every school child is taught a little bit about the separation of powers among the three branches of the national government: executive,
legislative, and judicial each have its own area of responsibility. But the
balance between national and state governments provides another layer
of protection for American freedom. "In the compound republic of
America," Madison wrote in *Federalist No. 51*,

> the power surrendered by the people is first divided between
> two distinct governments, and then the portion allotted to
> each subdivided among distinct and separate departments.
> Hence a double security arises to the rights of the people. The
> different governments will control each other, at the same
> time that each will be controlled by itself.[23]

Madison viewed this balance as a great benefit. The states wouldn't
long tolerate a federal government that became tyrannical or intruded
on the states' prerogatives. To the contrary, Madison foresaw a situation
in which

> ambitious encroachments of the federal government on the
> authority of the State governments would not excite the

opposition of a single State, or of a few States only. They
would be signals of general alarm. Every government would
espouse the common cause. A correspondence would be
opened. Plans of resistance would be concerted. One spirit
would animate and conduct the whole.[24]

In other words, Madison was certain that the states could be trusted
to keep the national government in line.

When it comes to the election of federal officials, this balance
between the national and state governments is very much in evidence.
State legislatures are given primary authority over the process, but
the national government is also given a few tools with which it may
protect itself. State legislatures are to prescribe the "Times, Places
and Manner of holding Elections for Senators and Representatives,"
although Congress may "make or alter such Regulations, except as
to the Places of chusing Senators."[25] Alexander Hamilton defended
the system as one that would leave the states in charge most of the
time, but that would also give the federal government authority to act
in "extraordinary circumstances."[26] His primary concern was that
the federal government have the power to protect its own existence.
After all, if the states' power over elections were left completely
unchecked, then the states could "annihilate" the federal government
simply by refusing to hold an election and refusing to send congressmen to Washington.[27]

Despite these concerns about self-preservation, the federal government was given even less power over the selection of presidential electors.
Instead, the Constitution provides that each "State shall appoint, in such
Manner as the Legislature thereof may direct" its electors.[28] Congress is
given limited responsibility: it "may determine the Time of chusing the
Electors, and the Day on which they shall give their Votes; which Day
shall be the same throughout the United States."[29] Later, of course, the
electoral votes are to be counted in a joint session of Congress.[30]

Notably, the executive branch is not given any authority over the
election of federal officials, especially the president's own election. Any

responsibility delegated to the national government is specifically given to Congress.[31]

For the most part, however, the states are left to their own devices. Over the years, they've expressed their opinions in many ways—and they've done it in many different contexts. The states are independent authorities charged with protecting their own citizens. Importantly, they are no more beholden to the national political parties than they are to the federal government.

IN SUCH MANNER AS THE LEGISLATURE MAY DIRECT

Katharine Lee Bates was overwhelmed by the beauty of the American countryside. She was on a train traveling West, headed toward a summer teaching position in Colorado.[32] It was a long ride. She was leaving Massachusetts and her job at Wellesley College for the summer position. Her trip had taken her past Niagara Falls and through Chicago. The view outside her window was breathtaking. Cities gave way to countryside. Rivers merged into plains or grassy pastures. Plains gave way to mountains. The land was beautiful—and diverse.

Finally, Bates arrived in Colorado. As she settled into her summer teaching job, she was given the opportunity to visit Pike's Peak, a prominent summit on the front range of the Rocky Mountains. A horse-drawn carriage took her and a few other teachers halfway up the mountain, but it could go no farther. Mules helped the group to complete their trek. As Bates finally stood atop the peak, she was overcome by all that she saw. She later wrote, "It was then and there, as I was looking out over the sea-like expanse of fertile country spreading away so far under those ample skies, that the opening lines of the hymn floated into my mind."[33]

The "hymn" she referenced was the song that Americans have come to know as "America the Beautiful." The lyrics were inspired by an English professor's encounter with the vastness and beauty of America, and they were written in a state that was then relatively new. Interestingly, one of the very first things that Colorado did when it joined the Union was to express its individuality. It used its discretion in the presidential election system to serve the interests of its citizens, even though its action was then outside the mainstream.

The new State of Colorado was looking at a tight timeline. Colorado had been admitted into the Union on August 1, 1876, only three months before a presidential election. It would have been logistically difficult and fairly expensive to hold a statewide popular vote that year. So the state simply didn't do it. The legislature appointed electors instead.[34] Every other state in the Union was then conducting popular elections for this purpose, but Colorado did what it had to do to be represented with minimal trouble and expense. The state later switched to a popular vote system like everyone else.

A winner-take-all, statewide popular vote has been the norm in virtually every state since about 1836.[35] Such an arrangement seems appropriate, reflecting as it does the desire of citizens to participate directly in the process. On a few occasions, however, legislators have reacted to other events in their state, and they have modified their election processes. This is also appropriate. A state legislator's job is to reflect the concern of his constituents, not to stick with a system just because it is preferred by others in the nation.

If Colorado wanted to save money and avoid logistical difficulties in 1876, then that was exactly what needed to happen. State legislators owed a duty to their own citizens, first and foremost. The Florida legislature has also recognized this reality on at least two separate occasions. In 1868, the state would have had trouble conducting a full-fledged election because it was just emerging from Reconstruction. The state legislature appointed electors directly that year, rather than lose its votes.[36] More than one hundred years later, Florida again found itself in a difficult situation. During the contentious 2000 election, many state legislators feared what would happen if court battles over the state's popular vote total continued past statutory deadlines for submitting slates of electors. State legislators met in special session, determined to directly appoint electors. They did not want ongoing legal challenges to prevent their state from being represented in the Electoral College. Fortunately, those challenges were resolved before such intervention became necessary.[37]

On other occasions, Massachusetts, Michigan, Maine, and Nebraska have deviated from the winner-take-all rule, each for its own reasons. Massachusetts once had a system in which the state legislature would select electors if no one received a majority of the state's popular vote. That happened in 1848 when the Whig slate of electors fell 5 percent short of an outright majority. Legislators selected electors that year, but they also honored the Whigs' 45 percent plurality by selecting the Whig electors to represent Massachusetts.[38]

Another deviation from winner-take-all occurred in Michigan, although this change admittedly occurred mostly for political reasons. Democrats won control of the Michigan legislature in 1890, enabling them to implement a district plan of allocating electors. The party won five of nine electoral votes in 1892, but the change was short-lived. Republicans soon regained control of the state government and reversed the change.[39] By contrast, Maine and Nebraska have used the district plan for decades with relatively little political upset.

States have wide discretion in determining how to best reflect the interests of their citizens in presidential elections. They may cast their electoral votes as a bloc, divide them among multiple candidates, or even introduce a new candidate into the mix if the major-party nominees are unacceptable from the state's perspective. Some states allow felons to vote. Others do not. The brand new state of Wyoming allowed women to vote in 1892, long before the Nineteenth Amendment ensured that women could not be denied the opportunity to vote because of their gender.[40] The first state to make this decision, Wyoming didn't wait around for other states to agree; it simply did what it thought was best.

Each state legislature has "plenary" power when choosing a manner of allocating its state's electoral votes[41]—and it does not have to agree with neighboring state legislatures on the best method. Each state legislature determines how the state and its citizens can best be served in the electoral vote and adopts a method accordingly. If citizens disagree with the chosen method, they simply need to appeal to their state legislators to change the rules.

Other provisions of the Constitution do, nevertheless, impose a few limits on the states' discretion.[42] For instance, a state may not conduct a popular vote in which men are allowed to vote, but women are turned away from the polls. Such an election would violate the Nineteenth Amendment.[43] States also do not have the authority singlehandedly to centralize the state-driven, decentralized system discussed in this chapter, despite the pretense of one anti–Electoral College group. The so-called "National Popular Vote" effort has been lobbying states to change the manner in which they allocate their presidential electors: NPV wants states to join an interstate compact (a contract among states) in which they promise to award their electors to the winner of the national popular vote. The compact would go into effect only when states representing a majority in the Electoral College had signed on, but that threshold could be reached with as few as eleven states.[44] The NPV initiative is constitutionally dubious, to say the least. It flies in the face of Article V, which requires approval from three-quarters of the states (currently thirty-eight) before such a drastic change can be made to the presidential election system.[45]

The Supreme Court has repeatedly recognized the states' discretion, assuming they stay within these constitutional parameters. As early as 1892, the Court held that the Constitution "recognizes that the people act through their representatives in the legislature, and leaves it to the legislature exclusively to define the method of effecting the object. . . . In short, the appointment and mode of appointment of electors belong exclusively to the States under the Constitution of the United States."[46]

Indeed, many Americans might be shocked to hear that their state has such broad discretion that individuals don't really have a "right" to vote for president (or even presidential electors). "The individual citizen has no federal constitutional right to vote for electors for the President of the United States," the Supreme Court reaffirmed in 2000, "unless and until the state legislature chooses a statewide election as the means to implement its power to appoint members of the Electoral College."[47]

A presidential election truly is a state-driven process. "[T]he electoral college system as embodied in the Constitution," Justice Thurgood Marshall once affirmed, "contemplates the election of the President and Vice President not by the Nation as such, but rather by the individual States."[48]

OTHER STATE ACTIONS, OUTSIDE THE ELECTORAL COLLEGE

Franklin Delano Roosevelt's unexpected death shocked the nation. He'd been president for twelve long years, carrying the country through the Great Depression and much of World War II. "It was all so sudden," one White House staff member would say, "I had completely forgotten about Mr. Truman. Stunned, I realized that I simply couldn't comprehend the Presidency as something separate from Roosevelt. The Presidency, the White House, the war, our lives—they were all Roosevelt."[49]

For quite a while afterwards, many White House aides found themselves unable to call Harry Truman "Mr. President."[50] Others worried that Roosevelt's death would cause the war to drag on much longer than it would have otherwise. General Omar Bradley wrote that "Truman did not appear at all qualified to fill Roosevelt's large shoes."[51] The new president was overwhelmed as well, candidly telling a group of reporters that he "felt like the moon, the stars, and all the planets had fallen on me."[52]

Under the circumstances, perhaps no one was surprised when Truman's reelection bid in 1948 turned contentious. The party nomination processes, in particular, were a bit of a circus.[53] These processes are independent of the Electoral College and the general election in November, but the states and their political parties have historically taken a cue from the decentralized, state-driven process found in the Constitution. They have remembered their ability to act independently when needed, although they typically (and appropriately) strive for coalition-building and a nominee who can unify the party. After all, coalition building is the best way to win the Electoral College and the White House.

None of this is to say that the states are perfect or have always acted from noble motives. They aren't, and they haven't. "If men were angels," James Madison famously wrote, "no government would be necessary."[54]

The 1948 election was a case in point. It simultaneously illustrated the ability of the states and their political parties to act independently, expressing their own point of view, even as it wrestled with the kinds of ignoble motives that prompted the Founders to build checks and balances into the Constitution in the first place. Fittingly, the 1948 election story concludes with the most reasonable coalition winning the White House. States expressed their differing opinions, and yet the Electoral College managed to sort out reasonable motives from less admirable ones.

In the wake of FDR's death, the Democratic Party had difficulty finding someone who could hold the party together. By the time of its convention in July 1948, some Southern Democrats had had enough. They were irate about changes to the party platform, and they weren't terribly happy with the nomination of Harry S. Truman for president, either.

The cause of the split wasn't too pretty, of course. At the core of the conflict was a disagreement about segregation and civil rights. Northern Democrats, impatient with the bland generalizations about equality in the party platform, wanted more specific commitments. Southern Democrats preferred the language as it was. Unfortunately, Hubert Humphrey, the mayor of Minneapolis and a candidate for the Senate, delivered an emotional speech to the convention, defending the new language. If only he'd stuck to a defense of civil rights! Instead, he took the opportunity to blast states' rights as well.[55] It was the exact wrong thing to do as far as some Southern delegates were concerned.

The party adopted the new civil rights plank soon afterwards, and, as *Life* magazine put it, "the convention blew up."[56] The vice chairman of the Alabama delegation announced that he and others were "compelled to walk out."[57] All of the Mississippi delegates marched out, along with half of the Alabama delegation.[58] Not all Southerners left the Democratic Party, but those who did formed a new party, the States' Rights ("Dixiecrat") Democratic Party. Governor Strom Thurmond of South Carolina was their nominee and appeared on many ballots in the South. In some states, he was the official Democratic nominee instead of Truman.[59] In other states, he was listed under a States' Rights label.

The State of Alabama went further and refused to list Truman on the ballot at all.[60]

Southerners were unfortunately driven partly by a dishonorable motive—protecting segregation—but they had another, better justification for their actions, too. They remembered the importance of protecting the compound nature of the American republic, a structure that protects freedom even when one arm of the government is failing. In fact, it succeeds *precisely because* occasional corruption and base motives have already been factored into the equation. The system of checks and balances is the remedy, administered in advance for predictably imperfect human institutions.

Perhaps it's ironic, then, that Southerners, motivated partly by a desire to protect segregation, were then stymied by the state-by-state process that they were also protecting.

Normally, a third-party candidate would have been a drag on the Democratic Party, ensuring victory for the Republicans. In this instance, however, the Dixiecrats' exit freed Truman from a racist taint that threatened to drag down his campaign. Once the Dixiecrats were gone, Truman was able to present himself as a reasonable, mainstream candidate, appealing to a greater variety of voters. He was able to obtain the votes of many Northerners who had felt unsure about him.[61] Ultimately, he carried twenty-eight states (303 electors) to Thomas E. Dewey's sixteen states (189 electors) and Thurmond's four states (thirty-nine electors), easily winning the presidency.[62]

States and their political parties have made independent decisions about which nominees to accept in other presidential elections. In 1836, for example, Virginians flatly refused to accept the Democratic nominee for vice president.[63]

The race that year was among multiple candidates, including the Democratic nominee Martin Van Buren and several Whigs. Van Buren himself would go on to win the election fairly easily, but his running mate wouldn't enjoy that luxury. Richard M. Johnson of Kentucky was controversial in some circles, having lived with a slave of mixed lineage until her death in 1833. The couple even had children, whom Johnson freely acknowledged.[64]

All in all, it was more than many Virginians could bear. When the national Democratic Party nominated Johnson at an early political convention in 1835, the Old Dominion's delegates "hissed most ungraciously."[65] Their chairman got to his feet and announced that Virginia could not support Johnson for vice president as they had "no confidence in his principles nor his character—they had come there to support *principles*, not *men*, and they had already gone as far as possible in supporting Mr. Van Buren."[66] Virginia was done. The state would not support Johnson, too.

The Virginians were true to their word. Several months later, the state chose electors pledged to William Smith of Alabama, not to Richard M. Johnson. Later, at the state's Electoral College meeting, the Virginia electors voted for Van Buren for president (as the party wanted), but they also kept their promise to vote for Smith for vice president.[67] Those twenty-three votes prevented Johnson from receiving an electoral majority, which forced a contingent election in the Senate.[68]

The presidential election of 1860 brought more displays of independence by states and their political parties. An unusually high number of people were running for president that year: four men vied for the White House. Nevertheless, many states chose not to list all four of these candidates (or their electors) on ballots.[69] Most Southern states, for instance, refused to place Lincoln on their ballots at all.[70] In the meantime, a state like New Jersey took a completely different approach.[71] Republican voters could cast ballots for seven electors who would vote for Abraham Lincoln, but on the other side of the political aisle, an effort was made to coalesce the various Democratic and former Whig factions behind a "fusion" slate of electors. This latter slate consisted of three electors for Stephen A. Douglas (Democrat), two for John C. Breckinridge (Southern Democrat), and two for John Bell (Constitutional Union).

RESULTS: NEW JERSEY, ELECTION OF 1860[72]

Republican Electors		"Fusion" Electors	
Name	Vote Total	Name	Vote Total
*J.C. Hornblower	58,345	*William Cook	62,801
*Edward W. Ivins	58,341	*Joel Parker	62,387
*George H. Brown	58,335	*Theo. Runyon	62,309
*Chas. E. Elmer	58,334	Peter D. Vroom	58,210
Isaac W. Scudder	58,323	Alexander Wurts	56,182
David Thompson	58,322	Edmund Brewer	57,801
Andrew K. Hay	58,315	Silas Condit	57,553

* Elected

Democrats hoped to combine their strength and defeat Lincoln on Election Day. It might have worked, too, except some Douglas supporters did not cast ballots for the Breckinridge and Bell electors like they were supposed to. In the end, Lincoln obtained four of New Jersey's seven electors even though the Democrats arguably had more overall support.[73] Ultimately, of course, Lincoln went on to victory during that unusual election year.[74]

States have exercised control over their own ballots in other years, too. In 1892, some states did not include the Democratic candidate, Grover Cleveland, on their ballots. In Wyoming, for instance, state Democrats agreed to a fusion ticket.[75] Local Populists would support the Democratic gubernatorial and congressional candidates. In return, Democrats would support the Populist presidential candidate, James Weaver. The Populist candidate ultimately lost in Wyoming, but he won in several other states that had rejected Cleveland.[76] Despite Cleveland's troubles, the Republican incumbent, Benjamin Harrison, was too unpopular to win. Cleveland won his second, non-consecutive term as president.[77]

States and their political parties are independent in many other areas. Some states hold caucuses, while others hold primaries. Some states allocate their delegates to political conventions on winner-take-all terms.

Some do not. States and their political parties may also have differing rules regarding how long their delegates are bound at a national convention.[78] They have differing ballot-access rules and differing provisions for write-in candidates. Some states include the names of presidential electors on their ballots, but most do not. Each of these decisions is an opportunity for state lawmakers to reflect the needs and priorities of their own voters. Agreement with the rest of the nation is not required.

When they are operating at their best, states and their political parties are working together to find a candidate who can appeal to a broad coalition in November. They are responding to the incentives for unity that are baked into the Constitution's presidential election process. But if they see national forces going astray, they retain the power to act independently and to make their voices heard.

Should more power be given to national forces just because states have occasionally used their power for dishonorable reasons, such as defending Jim Crow laws? Of course not. Such a solution misses the point: the Founders designed a constitutional system of checks and balances because they expected that *every* arm of government would occasionally act for inappropriate reasons. The political parties and their nomination processes operate best when they respect these principles and include checks and balances in their nomination processes as well. After all, if the states or state political parties can make mistakes, then so can the national government or the national political parties.

Any system of checks and balances is built upon the expectation that poor decisions will be made. It is the structure itself—"ambition against ambition"—that protects Americans at election time. No human institution is without flaws.

THE PLENARY POWER OF THE STATES

Late in 2016, a New York state senator introduced the T.R.U.M.P. (Tax Returns Uniformly Made Public) Act in his state legislature. The filing was a direct response to Republican presidential candidate Donald

Trump's refusal to release his federal income tax information during the 2016 presidential election cycle.

"For over four decades," Senator Brad Hoylman, a Democrat, wrote, "tax returns have given voters an important window into the financial holdings and potential conflicts-of-interest of presidential candidates. Voters deserve to know that personal priorities will never take precedence over the national interest."[79]

The bill he proposed would require candidates for president and vice president to file their federal income tax returns with New York's Board of Elections. A failure to do so would prevent that candidate from being listed on New York's presidential ballot. New York's electors would also be prohibited from independently voting for that candidate.

Similar bills were introduced in California, Maine, Maryland, and Massachusetts,[80] although all were met with ridicule. "To me, it just looks like sour grapes over the election," Maryland Senate Minority Leader J. B. Jennings, a Republican, concluded.[81] Legal scholars soon jumped into the fray, with one side invoking the broad plenary power of states and the other arguing for the "uniquely important national interest" of having consistent ballots across the country.[82]

Of course, any argument based on "national interest" is a funny one to make, given the deliberately decentralized nature of the presidential election system and the states' history of including or excluding candidates according to their own priorities. In 1892, some states excluded a major-party candidate from their ballots in part because of a disagreement about monetary policy.[83] Why couldn't New York reject any candidate who refused to disclose his or her income tax returns? New York is within its rights to take such action as long as it does not violate some other constitutional provision in the process. For instance, it could not impose a religious test for office, as prohibited by Article VI.[84]

A state's ability to act on its own behalf hasn't changed. What *has* changed is the average American's knowledge about what is possible. Any state can reject a national party's nominee at any time. What is more important is that states use this power wisely. After all, a decision can be constitutional but still be a bad idea.

Imagine a scenario in which the Watergate scandal blows up several months earlier than it did in real life. The scandal hits headlines mere weeks after Republicans select Richard Nixon as their nominee. Many Republicans are concerned because their party refuses to abandon its ethically challenged nominee even though he is being investigated by the FBI. In such a scenario, a governor would be well within his rights to call his state legislature into special session, asking legislators to reconsider the manner in which that state will allocate its electors that year. (In our democratic-minded society, hopefully the governor would also make a point of providing a website, planning town halls, or creating some venue by which constituents may easily contact their legislators and express their opinions.) Together, legislators and voters could consider their options. The state could leave Richard Nixon on its ballot. After all, he is the national nominee. Maybe the state doesn't want to buck the system or disregard its primary results. Alternatively, the state could put a different Republican on the ballot, either with Nixon or in his stead. If time were running short, the state might choose to cancel its presidential election and appoint electors directly, introducing a replacement candidate with fewer ethical concerns into the pool of candidates.[85]

The states have many options. Legislators' main duty would be to listen to the voters in their state and to do their best to accurately reflect the state's priorities. In America's system of checks and balances, there is a safety valve on the legislators' power in this realm, of course: most of them are running for reelection during a presidential election year and are thus extra motivated to keep constituents happy.

Does all this mean that every presidential election can or should devolve into a chaotic mess in which states refuse to work together? Should nominating conventions routinely turn into contentious affairs from which state delegations march out, intent on starting their own political parties? Should states obstinately refuse to work with their neighbors?

Of course not. Historically, the American presidential election system has been characterized by coalition building and a quest for nominees who can unify the electorate. Such practices are not only healthy for the nation, but they remain the best way to win the Electoral College and the White House. States have the power to dissent, but they serve their voters best if they use that power carefully. They will shoot themselves in the foot otherwise. Perhaps it's worth remembering that, while some states dissented from Grover Cleveland's nomination in 1892, a Democratic candidate was back on their ballots by 1896.

***

Americans do not have a right to vote for president or for presidential electors, but they have increasingly run their presidential election system as if they do. They have forgotten the role that states are entitled to play. Strangely enough, the more that Americans focus on their individual "right" to cast a ballot on Election Day, the more dissatisfied they seem to be with their nominees. They have deprived themselves of choices without realizing it. As it turns out, the states were not only protecting voters from centralized power in the national government, but they were also acting as a check on the RNC and the DNC.

The Constitution leaves the bulk of power with the states, and the states can intervene when they see things going awry. They do not have to blindly follow the RNC, DNC, or the mainstream media. In 2016, polls showed that a majority of Americans were unhappy with their choices, yet the states bypassed several opportunities to intervene. There are reasons for and against these different types of interventions—and there are certainly solid reasons to avoid using them often. Nevertheless, voters in a healthy republic will know their options. Knowledge is power, as Founders such as James Madison knew all too well. America's fourth president wrote that a "people who mean to be their own Governors, must arm themselves with the power which knowledge gives."[86]

Sometimes there are no easy answers, just difficult choices. Yet an informed citizenry will know its options, then freely discuss them within state borders, even if some ideas are ultimately rejected. "Knowledge," as George Washington said, "is in every Country the surest basis of public happiness."[87]

CHAPTER EIGHT

FAITHLESS ELECTORS: A PROBLEM OR A VOICE FOR THE STATES?

"The election of the next president is not yet a done deal," a Texas elector, Christopher Suprun, wrote in December 2016.[1] "Electors of conscience can still do the right thing for the good of the country. Presidential electors have the legal right and a constitutional duty to vote their conscience."[2]

The backlash against Suprun's editorial in the *New York Times* was immediate—and harsh. Yet he wasn't the only Texas elector to express discomfort with the idea of casting a ballot for Donald Trump. A few days earlier, Art Sisneros had announced that he would resign rather than cast a ballot for the Republican candidate. Sisneros felt torn between the oath he'd taken to the Texas Republican Party and his inability to vote for someone whom he saw as unqualified. "Since I can't in good conscience vote for Donald Trump," he concluded, "and yet have sinfully made a pledge that I would, the best option I see at this time is to resign my position as an Elector."[3] Nevertheless, Sisneros felt that he should have been free to make an independent judgment. "The Electoral College was corrupted from its original intent once states started dictating the votes of the Electors," he concluded.[4]

Both Sisneros and Suprun received threats—even death threats. "There were several nasty ones," Sisneros told a *Texas Monthly* reporter, "to vote for Trump, or else."[5] Yet the nastiness directed at Suprun was, if anything, even worse. "There is not enough room below to catalog all the things Christopher Suprun has been called since Monday," a columnist for the *Dallas Morning News* wrote, "when the Republican presidential elector said in the virtual pages of *The New York Times* that he would not be voting for Donald Trump on Dec. 19. Pretty sure the bosses here wouldn't even let me list most of the epithets."[6]

In the meantime, another group of electors launched an effort to change how electors planned to vote at the meetings of the Electoral College. "The Founding Fathers intended the Electoral College to stop an unfit man from becoming President," the self-described "Hamilton Electors" asserted on their website. "The Constitution they crafted gives us this tool. Conscience demands that we use it."[7]

Set aside the specific question about whether "conscience demands" that an extraordinary tool should have been used in the 2016 election. Does the tool exist in the first place? Did the Founders expect electors to deliberate freely? Alternatively, could the ability of electors to deviate from the popular vote outcome provide yet another option for state legislatures when they see the need for a last-minute course correction?

Historians and legal scholars disagree on the matter. Some contend that electors were meant to be "distinguished citizens" who would act as representatives of the people.[8] Others believe that the role of elector evolved primarily because the framers of the Constitution did not want to decide for the states how they should cast their electoral votes. Some scholars even argue that the entire thing was slapped together at the last minute and the independence of electors may not have been carefully considered.[9]

As with so many other issues at the Constitutional Convention, it can be difficult to say precisely what the framers intended because many in the founding generation simply disagreed about the best procedure for electing the president.

THE FOUNDERS' EXPECTATIONS

"This process of election affords a moral certainty," Alexander Hamilton wrote in *Federalist No. 68*, "that the office of President will seldom fall to the lot of any man who is not in an eminent degree endowed with the requisite qualifications."[10] Electors, he thought, would be selected because of their ability to act as wise elder statesmen. They would assess the fitness of candidates and prevent demagogues from taking office. Hamilton says it best:

> It was desirable that the sense of the people should operate in the choice of the person to whom so important a trust was to be confided. This end will be answered by committing the right of making it, not to any pre-established body, but to men chosen by the people for the special purpose, and at the particular conjuncture.
>
> It was equally desirable that the immediate election should be made by men most capable of analyzing the qualities adapted to the station and acting under circumstances favorable to deliberation, and to a judicious combination of all the reasons and inducements which were proper to govern their choice. A small number of persons, selected by their fellow-citizens from the general mass, will be most likely to possess the information and discernment requisite to so complicated an investigation.[11]

With such a process in place, Hamilton concluded, "[i]t will not be too strong to say that there will be a constant probability of seeing the [presidency] filled by characters pre-eminent for ability and virtue."[12]

Hamilton wrote these words in an effort to sell the Constitution to his home state of New York. Six states had already ratified that document. Three more were then needed to put the Constitution into effect.[13] The delegates at each of these state ratification conventions would have understood that they were contemplating a new government structure based partly on democratic principles, but also based partly on republican and federalist principles. Whether they agreed or disagreed with making electors independent, they would not have been surprised to hear Hamilton describe the office of elector as just another republican safeguard in the new Constitution. Deliberation, compromise, and state-by-state action were understood to be essential features of the new constitutional scheme.

Did the delegates to the state ratifying conventions agree with Hamilton? Did they believe that electors should be trusted to make independent decisions? Or did they simply assume that each state would soon make its own rules? It is hard to know exactly what they thought because they rarely discussed the presidential election plan in their conventions. The delegates largely seemed to find the plan unobjectionable, so they spent little time debating it. One exception to this general rule occurred in Pennsylvania, when James Wilson took to the floor. Wilson was a well-respected lawyer in his state. He'd served as a delegate to the Constitutional Convention, and he spoke from that perspective.

"The manner of appointing the President of the United States I find is not objected to," he began, "therefore I shall say little on that point."[14] Overall, he thought the compromise struck at the Convention was a good one. He had personally preferred a national popular vote system,[15] but he also recognized that the presidential election system, as proposed, would avoid some practical problems. For instance, he knew that some voters were then already struggling with *state* election districts that were too big—much as rural voters in New York or California might complain today. Wilson believed the problem would only get worse in a nationwide direct election.[16] The proposed system ensured that "the people may elect with only one remove."[17] Better yet, it would "not be easy to corrupt the Electors."[18] The electors would never meet as a single group. Instead, they would be scattered across the nation when they cast their votes—

each state's electors were to meet on their own. How could such widely scattered men be improperly influenced in such a short time?

The difficulty of corrupting electors would be a benefit of the Constitution's electoral system, of course, but Wilson's statement also reflects his assumption that the electors could act with some degree of independence. After all, if they could not act independently, then the possibility of corrupting their votes would not be an issue.

The near-silence at the state ratification conventions followed a similar lack of recorded discussion at the Constitutional Convention itself. The delegates had spent months going back and forth about the benefits of various types of elections, of course, but the final compromises had been made near the end of the Convention in the Committee on Postponed Matters.[19] That committee did not keep records of its proceedings, although one member later wrote that the committee had been about to settle upon legislative selection when an objection was made. "We then all sat down," he reported, "and after some conference, James Maddison took a Pen and Paper, and sketched out a Mode for Electing the President agreeable to the present provision. To this we assented and reported accordingly."[20]

The new plan was proposed to the Convention on September 4. The proposal made that day was fairly similar to the presidential election system that would eventually be incorporated into the Constitution, except that it gave the Senate the task of selecting a president if the Electoral College did not produce a majority. This responsibility would eventually be switched to the House of Representatives.[21]

The Committee's new proposal caused a bit of a flurry in the Convention. Edmund Randolph of Virginia and Charles Pinckney of South Carolina asked for a "particular explanation & discussion of the reasons for changing the mode of electing the Executive."[22] Gouverneur Morris of Pennsylvania undertook the task of answering their question, but in the discussion that followed, the independence of electors was referred to only indirectly. For instance, Morris noted that the new system would allow "the great evil of cabal [to be] avoided. It would be impossible also to corrupt them."[23] At one point, Pinckney expressed his concern that the "Electors will be strangers to the several candidates and of course unable to decide on their comparative merits."[24] Both of these statements reflect an assumption that the electors might be required to deliberate independently,[25] but it is even clearer in a statement James Wilson made toward the end of the day. He predicted that the electors' job would become easier over time: "Continental Characters will multiply as we more & more coalesce, so as to enable the electors in every part of the Union to know & judge of them."[26]

Of course, just because the Founders thought that the electors might occasionally exercise discretion, it doesn't necessarily follow that they thought electors would act entirely independently all of the time. They could just as easily have expected some combination: electors acting partly in reliance on the people's judgment and partly on their own initiative.[27]

Either way, voters themselves didn't always agree with the prospect of elector independence. As early as 1796, electors were being asked to vote in specific ways. When one elector broke with his party to vote for John Adams, some voters were furious. One voter reportedly fumed, "What, do I chuse Samuel Miles to determine for me whether John Adams or Thomas Jefferson shall be President? No! I chuse him to *act*, not to *think*."[28]

Ultimately, of course, the words in the Constitution matter more than the intent of one or two people who happened to express this or that opinion during a debate. Those words grant broad latitude to the states to control the manner in which their electors are appointed: "Each State shall appoint, in such Manner as the Legislature thereof may direct, a Number of Electors . . . ."[29] Is the state's discretion so broad that it can require pledges of its electors before it appoints them? An old Supreme Court decision suggests that the answer is "yes." The Court held in *Ray v. Blair* that Alabama's Democratic Party could require a pledge of loyalty before supporting a candidate for presidential elector.[30] The Court did not directly address the ability of states (as opposed to political parties) to require such a pledge, but states generally have broad authority in this area. It seems likely that they could also demand such a pledge before agreeing to appoint a particular elector.

Naturally, state discretion has its limits. While states and political parties have the ability to demand a pledge before an appointment is made, they don't necessarily have power to punish violations of the pledge afterwards.[31] The *Ray* Court specifically left this possibility open.[32] Once electors are appointed, they are constitutional officers, charged with their own set of responsibilities and duties under the Constitution.[33] By this argument, the state can no more control the elector after his appointment than it can tell a United States senator how to vote on a piece of legislation.

The *Ray* Court refused to address the question, and the issue has never been conclusively decided. One court came close, though. In 1948, the Supreme Court of Alabama was asked to issue an advisory opinion upon the matter. The court concluded:

> It is true that there has grown up a practice under which electors have felt duty bound by virtue of their own consciences to vote for the nominees of the party that nominates them for election and such electors in casting their ballots have felt influenced by the plans and purposes of the party to which they belong. But this course of action has followed their own personal regard for what was their duty and not some statutory mandate. The elector is a constitutional officer and the words used in the original constitution and the amendment thereof show that he is to follow his own judgment and discretion. . . .
>
>   . . . .
>
> When the legislature has provided for the appointment of electors its powers and functions have ended. If and when it attempts to go further and dictate to the electors the choice which they must make for president and vice-president, it has invaded the field set apart to the electors by the Constitution of the United States, and such action cannot stand.[34]

Despite the Alabama court's advisory opinion, disputes remain about whether a state can force an elector to vote in a particular way. Moreover, other questions naturally follow from that open legal question: if an elector violated a pledge, could he be legally punished? Could the state replace the elector with someone who would cast the "correct" vote? Assuming electors can be legally punished, would the faithless vote be retracted and replaced? Or would it stand? How does congressional authority to count votes affect all these issues?[35] In 2016, Minnesota and Colorado each removed electors who had voted the "wrong" way, replacing them with electors who would vote the "right" way. Similarly, in Maine, an elector was told to switch his vote back to Clinton. Congress counted all three of these new votes, apparently ratifying the states' decision to enforce their pledges. As this book goes to press, a court has yet to rule on the underlying constitutional issue, so many questions regarding the enforceability of pledges remain.[36]

As a matter of history, the answers to these questions have been of little importance. Electors rarely cast faithless votes. The way in which they are selected makes them unlikely to waver.

FAITHLESS ELECTORS, THROUGH THE AGES

"The election is over. This should stop," a Republican elector told a newspaper reporter in 2000.[37] She was referring to a lobbying effort spearheaded by a group of Democrats. Those activists hoped to convince electors pledged to George W. Bush to vote for Al Gore, since Gore had won the individual popular vote nationwide.[38] Naturally, the electors were unimpressed. In fact, they were mostly annoyed by the effort.

One elector in Indiana was receiving hundreds of emails, even before the recounts in Florida were resolved. He was the chairman of the Indiana Republican Party and not very likely to change his mind.[39] Another Florida elector was soon feeling similar pressure. "I told a caller last night that 1 a.m. is not a real good time to try and get my vote," she joked.[40] She had no intention of voting for Gore, either. She *wanted* to cast a ballot for Bush. An Arizona elector, Joe Arpaio, agreed: "I am getting aggravated with people calling me and trying to get me to change my vote."[41]

In many ways, the 2000 election was the toughest test that the Electoral College had faced in a long time. As few as two faithless electors could have changed the result, tying the vote and throwing the election into the House of Representatives. Three faithless electors could have handed the election to Gore all on their own.

In the end, not even one Republican elector changed his vote. Only one elector—pledged to Gore—voted differently than expected. Barbara Lett-Simmons abstained to make a political statement about the lack of congressional representation for the District of Columbia.[42] Her abstention was admittedly a bit odd, given the closeness of the election, but it appears that her vote was opportunistic. If Gore had needed the vote to win, she would not have chosen that particular moment to make a political statement. "I would never do anything that would cause George Bush to have the presidency," she told one blogger at the time.[43]

Indeed, presidential electors have historically been remarkably reluctant to break voters' trust. If the Founders expected electors to deliberate independently, few seem to have noticed. No election outcome has ever been changed by a faithless elector. Instead, voters have treated the office of elector as if it were a rubber stamp. They expect electors simply to endorse the outcome of statewide popular elections, and electors have generally complied with this expectation. This situation has endured since the early 1800s, when states and political parties first began choosing electors based on their party loyalty and other similar factors.[44]

The widespread expectation of elector loyalty is reinforced still more by the manner in which electors are chosen. The details vary by state, but electors are often chosen at state party conventions during a presidential election year.[45] They are typically grassroots activists who spent time working for their political party or the party's candidate, and they were probably selected precisely because of this hard work and loyalty. Candidates for elector are hoping their candidate will succeed, and they are looking forward to voting for him, assuming they are given an opportunity to do so. Of course, some electors take an official party pledge, promising to cast their ballots as expected. Others live in states that attempt to bind their electors. The enforceability of these statutes and pledges is uncertain, as discussed above, but this lack of certainty has had little effect on American presidential elections to date. Instead, the "problem" of faithless electors has proved to be mostly theoretical.

The political scientists Lawrence D. Longley and Neal R. Peirce report that no more than seventeen and perhaps as few as nine of the 21,291 electoral votes cast between 1796 and 1996 were "indisputably cast 'against instructions.'"[46] (Keep in mind that Longley and Peirce favor abolishing the Electoral College, so they have no incentive to minimize the number of faithless electors.) The uncertainty of their figures stems from confusion about eight votes cast in the election of 1824. Five North Carolina electors may or may not have been pledged to vote for John Quincy Adams. Either way, they voted for Andrew Jackson. Similarly, in New York, three electors pledged to Henry Clay defected, though they waited until it was clear that Clay could not win.[47]

Only two electors had deviated before the rash of changed votes in 1824. Samuel Miles famously angered a Federalist voter in 1796, as discussed above, but William Plumer soon followed suit in 1820. His unexpected vote kept James Monroe from winning the presidency unanimously.[48] Legend has it that Plumer was trying to protect George Washington's status as the only person who could claim such an undisputed victory, but that's not the case. Plumer genuinely did not want to vote for Monroe.

He later explained his decision. "I was obliged from a sense of duty and a regard to my own reputation to withhold my vote from Monroe and Tompkins," Plumer wrote his son, "from the first because he had discovered a want of foresight and economy, and from the second because he grossly neglected his duty."[49] Plumer remains one of the few electors to have made an independent judgment about whom he could and could not support.

The next electors to defect were in 1948 through 1972. Several of these electors broke their pledges in an effort to make a statement regarding civil rights issues. Three defectors were, oddly, all Nixon electors.

One elector defected in each of his three presidential races. Eleven more electors have broken their pledges since the Nixon races, but seven of these defections occurred in the tumultuous 2016 election. The other four occurred, one each, in 1976, 1988, 2000, and 2004.[50] (The 2004 incident, in which a Democratic elector voted for the vice presidential candidate on a presidential ballot, appears to have been an accident.)[51] None of these faithless votes changed the outcome of an election.

These historical election results provide good anecdotal evidence that the supposed "danger" of faithless electors is not great.[52] The system has been stable and reliable, even when other aspects of the system are more contentious. In fact, the system has been so consistent that even the controversial results in 2000 and 2016 couldn't shake the determination of most electors to vote as they were expected to vote. This is a good situation. By and large, voters do not want (or expect) to cast a vote for one candidate, only to see that vote transformed into a vote for someone else.

Electors who are faithful to the outcome of the popular vote reinforce popular confidence in the electoral system, contributing to its stability. Having said that, are there occasions when Americans might be better served by a different approach? In the wake of the 2016 election, many believe that these questions deserve serious reflection and discussion.

RETHINKING FAITHLESS ELECTORS AFTER 2016

"Several would-be Republican electors are already publicly flirting with the idea of casting their votes for someone other than Mr. Trump," two lawyers wrote for the *Wall Street Journal* in September 2016, "believing that his erratic outbursts have 'disqualified' him from being president. Right or wrong, that is exactly the kind of discernment that the Constitution demands electors exercise."[53]

Others agreed that electors should consider changing their support, although their motivations were surely all over the map. It is one thing to make a calm, rational argument based on the fitness of a candidate and the words of the Founders. It is quite another to throw a temper tantrum because one's preferred candidate lost an election. In the weeks after Election Day 2016, some of each was in evidence.

Within days of the election, a California resident had started a Change.org petition, urging Donald Trump electors to vote for Hillary Clinton instead. His arguments were based partly on Trump's fitness for office, but he also seemed to think that Clinton deserved the victory simply because she'd won the national popular vote.[54] Naturally, the latter argument fell flat with anyone who understood the history and rationale of the Electoral College system. In the meantime, some voters (and even some non-voters) took to the streets in protest. Some of these protests were genuine. Others seemed more opportunistic, and rumors swirled that some of the protests were funded by the liberal donor George Soros.[55]

On the flip side, many of those who voted for Trump were also irate, certain that they were surrounded by a bunch of sore losers. They failed to understand that some Americans were genuinely upset. They weren't simply being sore losers, and they weren't simply being partisan. The long and divisive election year had taken its toll. Many voters remained absolutely convinced that Trump was temperamentally unfit to serve in such an important position. No one was advocating for the electors' independence as a routine matter, but some felt that 2016 was an emergency justifying the extreme measure.

Nevertheless, Trump supporters simply could not see the election through the eyes of these distraught Americans. They were pretty unsympathetic to efforts to sway electors, to say the least. Such an outcome, they thought, would be an insult to the democratic process and a slap in voters' faces.

How ironic. Trump won in an Electoral College vote that deliberately rejects pure democracy and instead tempers the process with doses of federalism and republicanism. Why would pure democracy be bad in one situation, but automatically praiseworthy in the other?

Given all the turmoil, perhaps it is unsurprising that an unusually high number of electors acted independently when the meetings of the Electoral College were finally held on December 19, 2016. One of the deviating electors was a political science professor who cast his ballot for a new candidate despite intense pressure from state and national Republican leaders to stick with Trump.[56] "I take very seriously the oath of office that we had to take," Texas elector Bill Greene later told a journalist at the *Texas Tribune*, "and what the framers of the Constitution, what the founders, wanted electors to do . . . to basically come up with their idea for who would be the best person in the entire United States to be the president."[57] He decided not to vote for Trump but to vote for retired Texas Congressman Ron Paul instead.[58]

Greene was nearly alone among Republican electors. Most of the defectors were Clinton electors.

FAITHLESS ELECTORS: 2016[59]

Name of Elector	State	Pledged To:	Ballot Cast For:
David Mulinix	HI	Hillary Clinton (D)	Bernie Sanders (I)
Chris Suprun Bill Greene	TX	Donald Trump (R)	John Kasich (R) Ron Paul (R)
Bret Chiafalo Esther John Levi Guerra Robert Satiacum	WA	Hillary Clinton (D)	Colin Powell (R) *3 votes* Faith Spotted Eagle (D) *1 vote*
Micheal Baca	CO	Hillary Clinton (D)	*Attempted, but failed:* John Kasich (R)
David Bright	ME	Hillary Clinton (D)	*Attempted, but failed:* Bernie Sanders (I)
Muhammad Abdurrahman	MN	Hillary Clinton (D)	*Attempted, but failed:* Bernie Sanders (I)

Such changed votes could not take the election away from Trump, of course, but these electors and their supporters hoped to offer an olive branch to those who could: the Trump electors.[60] If they voted for a compromise candidate, would enough Republicans follow suit? Some celebrities soon made a video, encouraging Republican electors to "vote their conscience."[61] Thirty-seven deviating Republicans would be needed to force a House contingent election.

To be fair, a few of these Democratic electors had other motivations as well: they acted as they did simply because they were unhappy that Hillary Clinton had been nominated in the first place.[62] Moreover, at least one elector hoped to express his dissatisfaction with the Electoral College system.[63] Final results would show that seven electors had cast ballots contrary to expectations. Three additional electors tried to do so, but their votes were disallowed.

The electors who acted independently in 2016 became folk heroes to some, but were they right to do what they did? Or were the Trump supporters correct that such faithless electors should be scorned?

Perhaps the truth lies somewhere in the middle. Americans value their ability to vote and would certainly lose faith in the process if electors began to cast independent votes on any kind of consistent basis. On the other hand, many Founders considered electors to be one final safeguard in America's system of checks and balances. Perhaps modern Americans should not always be so quick to dismiss the possibility entirely.

Indeed, one can imagine situations in which faithless electors could serve an important purpose. What if a winning presidential candidate were to suffer a debilitating stroke after Election Day but before the meetings of the Electoral College? Should electors really vote in lock step for a candidate whose health was compromised? Perhaps in that situation voters would be relieved that their electors were free to vote for the vice presidential candidate instead.

Alternatively, what if a Wikileaks document dump revealed that a candidate had committed a serious crime? What if the crime were committed hand-in-hand with his vice presidential nominee? Are electors bound to the popular vote winner, or could they vote for an alternative?

Again, voters might be relieved that electors could introduce a new alternative into the mix.

What if a state deliberately gave its electors discretion to choose between two candidates in a race among three? According to at least some reports, this precise situation happened in 1824, when some North Carolina electors were instructed to vote for either Andrew Jackson or John Adams, depending on which one had the better chance of defeating the other two candidates. In 1912, some of Teddy Roosevelt's electors were reportedly in a similar situation. If Roosevelt was undermining William Taft's chances of defeating Woodrow Wilson, then they were supposed to vote for Taft instead of Roosevelt.[64] Such a scenario is not unthinkable, even today. Given the dynamics of the 2016 election, it's not hard to imagine a similar decision from a state like Utah. That state could easily have given its electors freedom to choose between Trump and Evan McMullin, depending on how the electoral map was shaping up.

Nevertheless, some state legislators, moved by the circumstances of 2016, seem bound and determined to run headlong into "fixing" the problem of faithless electors, even though such faithlessness has never been a consistent problem. Almost immediately after the election, many of them introduced legislation attempting to impose stiffer penalties upon faithless electors.[65] But bad facts, as they say, make bad law. Those state legislators run the risk of cutting themselves off at the knees, leaving their states with fewer options in an emergency.

State legislators should instead consider a different approach: they could spend time thinking about *when* and *how* to use electors as a last-minute republican safeguard. Are there *any* circumstances in which electors should deviate from the popular vote? Just how bad does it have to be before elector independence is warranted? Each state will come to its own conclusion. Perhaps some state legislatures would set up a formal process for gathering information and giving electors new directions in emergency situations.

Undoubtedly, many electors would have appreciated such an approach in 2016. In the weeks after the election, stories circulated about possible

Russian interference in the American electoral process. Some electors sought more information from Congress, but they lacked authority to make Congress do much of anything.[66] In the meantime, state legislatures left their electors in the lurch, refusing to intervene in any way. The state legislatures had options, though. They could have sought more information on behalf of their electors. Or they could have passed resolutions expressing either the sense of the legislature that the Russian stories were "fake news" or that the stories warranted concern.

In 2016, the states seemed to forget that they are ultimately in charge of presidential elections. But the states retain the tools they need to exercise their constitutional authority over future elections. Some states might establish guidelines for when they will intervene to obtain further information for their electors and voters. Other states might go in a different direction, trusting their electors more, but also making the selection process for electors more transparent. After all, voters have no reason to trust electors when they don't even know who those electors are. Perhaps candidates for elector could be required to provide more information about themselves so the electorate can judge their character and trustworthiness. Presidential ballots could be changed: perhaps voters would like to see their electors' names on the ballot. Some voters might even want to cast an individual ballot for each elector they approve. In 1960, the State of Alabama did exactly that. Voters could vote for up to eleven electors (because the state then had eleven electoral votes). This meant that they could simultaneously vote for several Republican electors and several Democratic electors, if they really wanted to do so. They could also avoid voting for the Democratic electors who had refused to take a pledge to support John F. Kennedy.[67]

The 2016 election has perhaps taught every American, including this author, an important lesson: most voters have been too nonchalant about the identity of their presidential electors. The country has taken for granted that certain types of emergencies will never occur. Potentially, that has left Americans too quick to dismiss the possibility that electors could serve as one last republican safeguard, although it would be better if electors were chosen with such a possibility in mind. An elector who can act independently can also give the states one final opportunity to make their voices heard when everything else seems to be going haywire.

One final type of emergency has occurred only once in American history, but if it were to occur again, it could leave voters wishing that they were more amenable to the idea of state-directed elector independence. In the case of a presidential candidate who becomes ineligible after Election Day but before Congress counts electoral votes, independent electors could ensure that a losing candidate is not the only option for president in a House contingent election.

INELIGIBILITY OF A CANDIDATE

The 1872 election nearly ended in disaster, yet no one could have anticipated the tragedy that was about to hit. Republican Ulysses S. Grant was then running for re-election against Democratic-Liberal Republican Horace Greeley. Of the campaign season, one author jokingly notes: "With a legendary war hero running against an [allegedly] atheist vegetarian newspaperman, you can probably imagine how things went."[68]

Except no one really could. Greeley's wife unfortunately passed away on October 30, 1872, less than a week before Election Day. Greeley was devastated and wrote of his wish to join her. "My house is desolate, my future dark, my heart a stone," the candidate wrote.[69] A devastating loss on November 5 just made matters worse. The votes cast on Election Day revealed that Greeley had won only sixty-six pledged electors to Grant's 286.[70]

"I was the worst beaten man who ever ran for the high office," the once-renowned newspaper editor declared.[71] The statement was erroneous, but it revealed his mindset. Greeley became so despondent that he was even admitted to a sanitarium.[72] On November 29, he passed away, the first (and only) candidate to die between Election Day and the meetings of the Electoral College.[73]

His electors weren't sure what to do, but each made his own decision. When the Electoral College met, three electors exemplified the great reluctance of electors to break their pledges: they voted for a dead man.[74]

The other Greeley electors felt that they'd been freed from their pledges, and they split their votes among several other Democrats.[75]

When the time came for Congress to count the votes, one representative objected that the votes for Greeley could not be counted because Greeley "was dead at the time said electors assembled to cast their votes and was not 'a person' within the meaning of the Constitution."[76] Both houses of Congress met to vote on the matter. In the end, the votes cast for the deceased candidate weren't counted, but the decision was far from unanimous. Senators had been ready to count the votes, but a bare majority in the House disagreed.[77] Debate was not allowed, so it is hard to know what the senators were thinking. From the few statements on record, however, it appears that some senators simply wanted to complete a "ministerial" task without having to decide a difficult constitutional question.[78] After all, whether the votes were counted or not counted, the result of the election would be the same. They saw no reason to stew over it endlessly when they had other business to conduct.

Is death the only event that can make a person ineligible for office? What if a candidate were impeached after Election Day? Impeachment would make that candidate ineligible for any "Office of honor, Trust or Profit under the United States," including the presidency.[79] Can Congress count votes that have been cast for a candidate who is not eligible to be president?

The question isn't so far-fetched. During the 2016 campaign, some media commentators raised the possibility of impeaching Hillary Clinton.[80] She was a former secretary of state, not a current officeholder, but some lawyers thought that impeachment proceedings against her were still possible. They urged that her handling of sensitive national security information be investigated further. Set aside the question of whether such proceedings would have been appropriate or just a partisan maneuver. If completed, her impeachment would have left her ineligible for the presidency.[81]

If Congress did not count the votes cast for a dead man because he "was not 'a person' within the meaning of the Constitution," would they count the votes cast for a person who was ineligible to be president? What if evidence came to light that a candidate was not a "natural born Citizen" within the meaning of the Constitution?[82]

Needless to say, the death or ineligibility of a presidential candidate before or after Election Day would raise many complications. Before Election Day, each state would handle these complications according to its own laws, the subject matter of which is beyond the scope of this book.[83] For purposes of this discussion, the relevant question is: how might states take advantage of elector independence to avoid the problems posed by the death or ineligibility of a candidate?

As things stand today, there is no other ready cure for this timing hiccup. The Constitution does not provide a contingency plan if a winning presidential candidate dies between the general election and the meetings of the Electoral College or between the meetings of the Electoral College and the counting of the electoral votes by Congress. Federal provisions for presidential succession will eventually take effect, but not until Congress counts the electoral votes in January and officially declares someone president-elect.[84] Once the nation has a president-elect, the Twentieth Amendment and other federal laws kick in, providing that the vice president-elect will succeed the president-elect if the president-elect dies before taking office.[85]

Unfortunately, the Twentieth Amendment is not helpful before this point. If a candidate dies or becomes ineligible between the general election and the meetings of the Electoral College, then the burden falls on the electors. Should they vote for the deceased candidate? Should they instead vote for his running mate? Does state law always allow them to do so? Whom should they choose as a replacement vice president? Presumably, the candidate's political party would designate a replacement (if there is time), but the party and its electors must act in a coordinated fashion in all these matters or they risk losing the election. State legislatures could also help in advance by providing guidelines for their electors. Perhaps state legislatures want their electors to follow the guidance of the political parties. Or perhaps they want their electors to vote for the vice presidential candidate and then follow the presidential line of succession, as needed.

What if the candidate dies or becomes ineligible after the meetings of the Electoral College but before the congressional counting of votes? Difficulties still arise. Remember, the winning candidate is not officially the president-elect until he has been formally declared the winner by Congress.[86] Congress would need to decide whether to count votes for someone who is not otherwise eligible under the Constitution.

A difficult situation is created, no matter what Congress decides. On the one hand, counting the votes enables an otherwise ineligible candidate to become president-elect long enough to pass the baton to the next person in the presidential line of succession. On the other hand, if Congress chooses not to count these ballots, then no candidate will have a majority of electors, and the House will choose a new president from the remaining presidential candidates. In this scenario, remember, the House does not have the option of choosing the vice president-elect because he is not one of the remaining *presidential* candidates. The House might hold a contingent election in which it had only one choice: the major-party candidate who had *lost* the election.

As an example, imagine the outcome in 1872 but with a twist—Ulysses S. Grant dies after 286 electors have voted for him and sixty-six electors have voted for Greeley. Congress decides that the 286 Grant votes cannot be counted because of his death and subsequent ineligibility. Without those votes, no candidate has a majority of electors, so the House moves to a contingent election. Here's the catch: representatives will be left with only one option in that election—Greeley, who'd otherwise lost the election. Voters would surely be wishing that one faithless elector had voted for Grant's running mate, giving them another option during the contingent election.

Many of these timing problems could be resolved without much effort. For instance, a simple federal statute could shorten the time between the meetings of the Electoral College and the counting of those votes by Congress. Alternatively, a constitutional amendment could establish a line of succession for the interval between the meetings of the Electoral College and the counting of the electoral votes by Congress. Perhaps an otherwise ineligible candidate could be deemed eligible for election purposes—just long enough to pass the baton to the vice president or the next person in the line of succession.

Until such changes are made to federal law or the Constitution, however, states and political parties might consider working together to ensure that in each presidential election, one elector from each party deviates from the popular vote. Perhaps one elector from each vice presidential candidate's home state could cast a presidential ballot for his own hometown favorite.[87] In 2016, for example, twelve of Virginia's thirteen electors could have cast presidential ballots for Clinton, who carried the state, and one Virginia elector could have cast a presidential ballot for her running mate, Tim Kaine. Likewise, ten of Indiana's eleven electors could have cast their presidential ballots for Trump, while one cast a ballot for his running mate, Mike Pence.

One other constitutional amendment has been proposed as a solution to this timing problem. The so-called "Automatic Plan" would eliminate the office of elector and award a state's electoral votes automatically, based upon certified election returns within each state. It could even provide that the votes be automatically awarded to the vice presidential candidate if a presidential candidate becomes ineligible. The idea isn't a new one. A constitutional amendment along these lines was proposed as early as the 1820s.[88] At the time, a Senate report blasted the concept of electors: "They have degenerated into mere agents, in a case which requires no agency, and where the agent must be useless, if he is faithful, and dangerous, if he is not."[89]

A solution such as the Automatic Plan would have the benefit of avoiding some of the logistical tangles discussed above, but it would have a downside, too. Some states might prefer to leave open the possibility that an elector could be one last, republican safeguard in the presidential election system—or one last opportunity for a state to make its voice heard. The Automatic Plan, if adopted as a constitutional amendment, would eliminate this possibility.

If such a plan is to be considered, perhaps it's also worth remembering a letter written by the Father of the Constitution, James Madison, after he'd had the benefit of living through several presidential elections. In 1826, he wrote a letter in which he spoke of the advantages of main-

taining the office of elector: he thought it a benefit that electors are real
people who can intervene in the election if needed. He concluded:

> [A]nother advantage [of electors] is, that altho' generally the
> mere mouths of their Constituents, they may be intentionally
> left sometimes to their own judgment, guided by further
> information that may be acquired by them: and finally, what
> is of material importance, they will be able, when ascertain-
> ing, which may not be till a late hour, that the first choice of
> their constituents is utterly hopeless, to substitute in the elec-
> toral vote the name known to be their second choice.[90]

Madison would doubtless be pleased with America's long history of
electors who are generally faithful to the outcome of states' popular
votes—electors who serve as the "mere mouths of their Constituents."
But maybe he would also wonder why modern Americans have so casu-
ally rejected the notion of elector independence, without at least taking
time to discuss it.

***

As the Constitutional Convention came to a close, one delegate made
a remark that would prove to be prophetic. "This subject [of presidential
elections] has greatly divided the House," James Wilson observed, "and
will also divide people out of doors. It is in truth the most difficult of all
on which we have had to decide."[91] Nevertheless, he pronounced himself
happy with the compromise that had been struck.

Others would join in his approval. Alexander Hamilton noted the
general satisfaction with the plan and declared that "if the manner of it
be not perfect, it is at least excellent."[92] The system, he thought, would
allow the "sense of the people" to be expressed, even as it encouraged
thoughtful deliberation about the qualities of presidential candidates.[93]
He concluded:

> This process of election affords a moral certainty that the
> office of President will seldom fall to the lot of any man who

is not in an eminent degree endowed with the requisite qualifications. Talents for low intrigue, and the little arts of popularity, may alone suffice to elevate a man to the first honors
in a single State; but it will require other talents, and a different kind of merit, to establish him in the esteem and confidence of the whole Union, or of so considerable a portion of
it as would be necessary to make him a successful candidate
for the distinguished office of President of the United States.[94]

Perhaps Wilson would be unsurprised to discover that the prospect
of independent electors has become controversial over time. On the other
hand, Hamilton might be puzzled to learn that modern Americans don't
take advantage of the constitutional safeguard that he praised with such
fervor. He would certainly be surprised to learn that most Americans no
longer even know the names of their electors.

If nothing else, the 2016 election revealed that too many Americans
fail to appreciate the importance of electoral independence. A serious
public discussion, free of the emotion of a particular election, would be
beneficial. There are arguments for and against various courses of action,
of course, but the electors' responsibilities are serious. Their duties—and
identities—have been treated too flippantly for too long.

CHAPTER NINE

THE HOUSE CONTINGENT ELECTION AND THE SMALL STATES

"The third-most likely person to be the next president of the United States," a political commentator wrote for the popular *FiveThirtyEight* blog in October 2016, "[is] Evan McMullin."[1] At the time, most Americans had no idea who Evan McMullin was. The former investment banker and CIA agent had jumped into the presidential race relatively late in the process. In fact, he joined so late that he was able to get on the ballot in only eleven states. Those eleven states held eighty-four electoral votes, not nearly enough to win the presidency.[2]

McMullin's supporters were under no illusions: they knew they couldn't obtain the 270 electoral votes needed to win the White House, but they hoped to win Utah and maybe one or two other states. If events played out right, they hoped it would be enough to hold both Hillary Clinton and Donald Trump under 270. In that scenario, the election would move to a secondary election process in the House of Representatives. In this House contingent election, McMullin would be one of only three options. Many of his supporters felt that he stood a good chance

133

of victory in the House. Not only was McMullin well-known among congressmen because of his work as policy director of the House Republican Conference, but he would also provide an outlet for anyone discontent with the Trump-Clinton choice.[3]

Historically speaking, no third-party candidate has ever successfully run on such a strategy. For a time, though, it seemed possible that McMullin could succeed where others had failed. In mid-October, at least two polls showed him in a statistical tie with the major-party candidates in Utah.[4] Commentators began writing of "plausible scenarios" that would leave all candidates under 270.[5] Would the small state single-handedly force the country into considering a third option?

In the end, of course, the long-shot strategy did not work, despite the unusual opportunity created by the divisive election year. Nevertheless, the McMullin candidacy highlighted the ability of small states to make their voices heard in a way that no one had previously anticipated. It also showed the degree to which political parties ultimately care about even their very safe small states.

Consider what happened in late October 2016. A vice presidential candidate might typically find himself visiting a variety of swing states in the final days of a campaign, but on October 26, Republican vice presidential candidate Mike Pence found himself in Utah instead. He was needed to shore up support in the previously safe little red state. "It is a rarity for such a high-profile figure to appear in Utah so near the election," the *Salt Lake Tribune* reported, "because Democrats have long conceded the state—but this year is different."[6] Without the Electoral College, it's hard to imagine any scenario that would prompt a major-party candidate to zip off to a small state like Utah in the last few days before a presidential election. With the Electoral College, however, the GOP couldn't afford to lose Utah's six electoral votes.

Pence's visit proved to be enough, perhaps in combination with the concerns of some Utahns that a vote for McMullin would inadvertently hand the election to Clinton. But what would have happened if Utah's six votes had gone to McMullin and forced a contingent election instead? Would it have ripped the country apart, creating some type of crisis situation? Academics have long supposed that such an election would be a "horror,"[7] but such an assumption should be re-visited in the wake of the 2016 election. After all, a surprisingly high number of people from both sides of the political aisle were working toward exactly that outcome at various points during the election cycle. It suggests that voters will accept the winner of a contingent election, at least under the right set of circumstances.

Either way, the Founders' views on the matter are worth exploring. What were the Founders' expectations of their back-up election procedure? Has the process become outdated over time or could it serve as yet another attention-grabbing tool for states when they are feeling too ignored by national forces?

THE FOUNDERS' CONTINGENCY PLAN

Modern Americans are used to a presidential election system that routinely produces majority winners in the Electoral College, but this experience is the opposite of what many of the Founders would have expected. In fact, one delegate to the Constitutional Convention, George Mason of Virginia, felt sure that the contingent election would be used in as many as nineteen out of twenty elections.[8]

Would he and other Founders be surprised to learn that his prediction did not come to fruition?

Mason's statement is one of the few to be recorded while the contingent election was being proposed and debated at the Convention. As with the issue of elector independence, the legislative record is incomplete because the secondary election procedure has its roots in the Committee on Postponed Matters.[9] No minutes were taken in that Committee, although one delegate later described a moment when James Madison "took a Pen and Paper, and sketched out a Mode for Electing the President . . . ."[10] Details of the Committee's deliberations might be scant, but more evidence exists as to how and why the plan was changed after it came out of that Committee.

The plan presented to the Convention on September 4 provided for a contingent election to be held in the Senate if no presidential candidate were to obtain a majority of electors.[11] Senators were to choose from the top five vote-getters. In the case of a tie, they could choose which of those two candidates would be president.[12]

Several delegates immediately expressed their concern about the contingent election. The way they saw it, they weren't just debating a random election procedure that would hardly ever be needed. They believed most elections would end up in this secondary process. How could any presidential candidate besides George Washington ever hope to obtain the votes of a majority of electors? "[N]ineteen times in twenty," Mason remarked to the assembled delegates, "the President would be chosen by the Senate."[13] He thought the Senate "an improper body for the purpose."[14]

Charles Pinckney of South Carolina soon jumped in with similar concerns. He believed that Senators would ultimately choose the president once every four years. The system proposed would make the "same body of men which will in fact elect the President his Judges in case of an impeachment."[15] He thought the proposal gave the Senate too much power and the president not enough independence. Hugh Williamson of North Carolina similarly worried that the situation made the president entirely too dependent on the Senate. Could they at least restrain senatorial discretion by limiting the choice to the top two vote-getters?[16]

One Georgia delegate, Abraham Baldwin, appears to have been sitting nearby, just listening and thinking. At this point, he piped in, noting that the plan wasn't so bad, upon reflection. He thought that, over time, the contingent procedure would be used less and less often. "The increasing intercourse among the people of the States," Baldwin remarked, "would render important characters less & less unknown; and the Senate would consequently be less & less likely to have the eventual appointment thrown into their hands."[17]

James Wilson seemed to agree with much of what Baldwin had said, but he still thought it best to give the legislature, rather than the Senate, final responsibility for the appointment.[18] The membership of the House changed more often than that of the Senate; he thought it would be more difficult for improper influences to sway the proceedings if the House were included. Unspoken in his idea, however, was a fact that would have bothered the small state delegates: moving the contingent election from the Senate to the legislature would also give the large states an advantage due to their larger delegations in the House.

No decision was made on that first day—or the next. The decision was too difficult, and the power being discussed was too great. "Months of debate had clearly not weakened the fear of power or the certainty of its abuse," historian Carol Berkin remarks of this time. "These powerful men gathered in Independence Hall, the most likely candidates for the Senate and the presidency, continued to fear themselves."[19]

The problem was finally resolved when the delegates agreed to an idea, proposed by Roger Sherman of Connecticut: first, the contingent election was moved from the Senate to the House of Representatives. The full legislature was not needed. The House, acting alone, could handle the task.[20] The change eased concerns that the president would be the "Minion of the Senate" if the original proposal were adopted.[21] Second, each state would be given a single vote in this House election. The large states already had an advantage in the vote among electors; this would prevent them from also having an advantage in the secondary election procedure.[22]

Once again, the delegates had found a compromise that balanced the needs of the large and small states. James Madison would later describe the deal that had been struck as the "result of a compromise between the larger & smaller States, giving to the latter the advantage in selecting a president from the Candidates, in consideration of the advantage possessed by the former in selecting the Candidates from the people."[23]

The process approved by the Convention on that day was still slightly different from the process that modern Americans use today. Their Electoral College did not allow electors to distinguish between their votes for president and their votes for vice president. Instead, electors cast two ballots. The winner was president; the second-place winner was vice president. The back-up election process, therefore, would be needed in either of two situations: first, if no candidate won a majority of the electors.[24] In this situation, the House was to choose a president from the top five candidates. The new vice president would be the top electoral vote-getter of the four remaining candidates. Second, if two candidates obtained votes from a majority of electors (remember that each elector could cast two ballots), but each candidate had an equal number of votes.[25] In this case, the House chose from the two candidates who had tied. The person who placed second in this House election would be vice president, since he would also have the most electoral votes of the remaining presidential candidates.

This contingent election procedure was used only one time before it was changed. The fourth presidential election in 1800 ended in an electoral tie between Thomas Jefferson and Aaron Burr. A contentious House contingent election followed, although it really should have been unnecessary. The electors knew that they wanted Jefferson for president and Burr for vice president, but they hadn't been allowed to indicate this preference on their ballots. The events in 1800 apparently didn't sit too well with many people, and Congress soon adopted a slight modification to the Constitution's presidential election provisions. The changes were ratified as the Twelfth Amendment to the U.S. Constitution in June 1804, with mere months to go before the next election. That amendment left the basic structure of the Electoral College in place, but it also made a few changes to avoid a repeat of the problems in 1800.

The amendment began by separating the voting for president and vice president, enabling presidential electors to identify which candidate should hold which office. There would be no more accidental ties between a presidential candidate and his running mate. Next, the amendment also separated the voting in the back-up election process. This revised process for the contingent election was used once after the 1824 election, and it remains in place today.

As the system currently operates, the House of Representatives is to choose from the top three presidential candidates if no candidate achieves a majority of electors in the Electoral College vote. In this House election for president, each state delegation still has one vote, just as it did in the original constitutional provision. Similarly, if no vice presidential candidate receives a majority of electors, then a separate contingent election is held in the Senate. Senators may choose a vice president from the top two vice presidential contenders. In the Senate election for vice president, each Senator has one vote.[26]

Further adjustments were made to these processes by the Twentieth Amendment and by federal statute: if the House of Representatives fails to make a choice before Inauguration Day, then the vice president-elect acts as president until such time as a choice is made.[27] If the vice president has not yet been chosen, then the Presidential Succession Act should apply,[28] making the speaker of the House of Representatives acting president until a choice can be made.

The House contingent election has not been used since Andrew Jackson failed to achieve an electoral majority in 1824. In the meantime, the Senate contingent election has been used only once: in 1836, when Virginia's electors refused to vote for the Democratic vice presidential candidate, Richard M. Johnson, preventing him from winning an outright majority. The rare usage has not eased the minds of some critics. Instead, they worry that several features of the system could lead to problems in future years.

CRITICISMS OF THE SYSTEM

"To hear George Wallace tell it," *Life* magazine reported in September 1968, "he's on his way to the White House."[29] The former Alabama governor, a segregationist, was running as a third-party candidate against Republican Richard Nixon and Democrat Hubert Humphrey.[30] He'd earned a place on the ballot in every state—a huge accomplishment for a third-party candidate.[31] Nevertheless, his strategy wasn't to win. He was mostly hoping to hold both Nixon and Humphrey under 270.[32] A third-place finish would give him exactly what he wanted: a position from which to bargain. He wanted concessions on civil rights and other issues.[33]

Wallace had even gone so far as to obtain signed pledges from his electors: they were committed to voting for him—or any other candidate that he chose.[34] "I don't believe it is going to go to the House of Representatives," he told a reporter at the *Miami Herald*. "I'd say the electoral college would settle the presidency before it gets to the House."[35] He spoke of "covenanting" with the two major-party candidates after Election Day but before the meetings of the Electoral College. The candidate that would give his ideas "some representation in the attitude of the new administration" could count on obtaining the votes of Wallace's electors when it came time for the Electoral College vote.[36]

In other words, he'd sidestep the House contingent election altogether, if he could. He would simply use his electors as bargaining chips and give them to the candidate that made the best offer.

But, as they say, the best-laid plans of mice and men often go awry. Wallace's plans didn't work out. Actually, he didn't really even come close.

RESULTS: ELECTION OF 1968

	Political Party	Electoral Votes		Popular Votes	
		Actual	*Percent*	*Actual*	*Percent*
Richard M. Nixon	Republican	301	55.9%	31,785,480	43.4%
Hubert H. Humphrey	Democrat	191	35.5%	31,275,166	42.7%
George C. Wallace	American Independent	46	8.6%	9,906,473	13.5%

On Election Day, he won only five states and forty-five pledged electoral votes.[37] Nixon had won by a comfortable margin, with 302 pledged electoral votes. Wallace wouldn't have any bargaining power that year after all. Nixon won on his own, despite the fact that a faithless elector dropped his final tally from 302 to 301.

Wallace failed in his attempt to manipulate the system, but the mere fact that he tried is enough to raise the concerns of some critics. One of their worst fears is that the contingent election will devolve into a revolting exhibition of political, partisan, or self-interested deal-making. If George Wallace can use his electors like bargaining chips, then what can't be traded? What couldn't a representative from an evenly-divided state delegation demand in exchange for his vote? Indeed, during the 1825 contingent election, these types of allegations swirled around the process, with many people alleging that Henry Clay had used his influence to sway votes in return for an appointment as secretary of state. The "corrupt bargain" outraged voters who thought that Andrew Jackson had been cheated out of his victory.[38]

The rumors in 1825 surely didn't surprise at least two Founders. They'd already come to the conclusion that the contingent election process needed to be changed. In 1823, Thomas Jefferson wrote that he "considered the constitutional mode of election ultimately by the legislature voting by states as the most dangerous blot in our constn, and one which some unlucky chance will some day hit, and give us a pope & anti-pope."[39]

Jefferson's statement about the "legislature voting by states" is a reference to the House contingent election, but Jefferson may not have been the most unbiased observer when it came to that particular constitutional institution. He was a candidate in the nation's first contingent election. In that election, Jefferson was tied with Aaron Burr, the man who was supposed to be the vice presidential candidate. Burr refused to bow out gracefully, as he should have, and some congressmen tried to take advantage of the situation. The House eventually chose Jefferson, but it took thirty-six votes before Jefferson obtained a majority of state delegations.[40]

How unsurprising that Jefferson didn't particularly like the process. Also not surprising is that one of his good friends, James Madison, grew to dislike the institution as well.[41] Both men had seen a contingent election in action, so their words shouldn't be dismissed too lightly. On the other hand, both men may have had difficulty remaining objective about this particular issue, given the way Jefferson had been treated.[42] Perhaps Madison's original assessment of the institution was more impartial: the process was simply a "compromise between the larger & smaller States" in which both sides get something at some point in the process.[43]

Despite the country's experiences following the contingent elections in 1801 and 1825, a reasonable argument can be made that the danger from deal making is not quite as great today as it was during the country's early years. Improved communications have enhanced the ability of voters to quickly obtain information about the actions of their elected officials. Even in 1968, when George Wallace worked to win enough electors to sway the election, any deal that he brokered with Humphrey or Nixon would have been known to the public. Imagine how much faster information (and, admittedly, even misinformation) would spread today, given the advent of Twitter and other types of social media.

If a third-party candidate cuts an inappropriate deal with a major-party candidate before the meetings of the Electoral College, then the electorate will know that something is awry fairly quickly.[44] The possibility of being discovered is its own disincentive to any candidate who is thinking about cutting a dishonest deal. And wouldn't any other type of deal fall into the category of coalition building, which the system seeks to encourage anyway?

After the meetings of the Electoral College, the same incentive structure remains during the House contingent election. The vote for president will obviously be a high-profile event in which voters are keeping tabs on how their congressmen and state delegations voted. Voter attention should act as a disincentive to inappropriate deal making because congressional members hope to be re-elected someday. Congressmen are imperfect human beings who may wish to act for political or selfish advantage, but they cannot do all their deal making behind closed doors. They must be able to explain their actions to the public. In all likelihood, congressmen will probably vote fairly predictably: for their party candidate, the popular vote winner, or the state's popular vote winner. Voters can act in reliance upon this expectation when they vote for their congressional candidate—an election that will always occur at the same time as presidential elections because congressmen run for re-election every two years.

Critics have other complaints that stem from the separated voting for president and vice president.[45] Remember, the House selects a president from the top three candidates, while the Senate selects a vice president from the top two candidates. By definition, one presidential candidate will not have the option of working with his preferred vice president if he is elected. In a hypothetical 2016 contingent election, for instance, the House could have selected Evan McMullin as president, but the Senate could not have selected his preferred running mate, Mindy Finn. It would have instead been limited to a choice between Tim Kaine (D) and Mike Pence (R). Even without a third-party candidate in the mix, the House could choose a president from one party while the Senate chooses a vice president from another party. Many critics find this situation unacceptable.

The concern is reasonable. Arguably, the contingent election process would serve the country better if it simply endorsed a single ticket, instead of expecting two candidates from opposite parties to work together.[46] As early as 1796, when President John Adams (Federalist Party) was required to work with Thomas Jefferson (Democratic-Republican Party) as his vice president, the two had difficulty working together productively. To the contrary, the relationship between Jefferson and Adams broke down soon after the two men had been inaugurated. Afterwards, Jefferson recalled, Adams never again "consulted me as to any measures of the government."[47]

On the other hand, the separated voting gives Congress latitude to make decisions that suit specific situations. Perhaps a split ticket does more to unify the country in some circumstances. In November 2016, one political commentator hoped for exactly this scenario if a House contingent election were needed. He urged Congress to consider selecting the conservative McMullin as president, along with the more liberal Kaine as vice president. "[A]s a bipartisan team," he concluded, "they could unite the country in a way neither Trump nor Clinton ever will."[48]

Electoral College critics throw one last complaint at the contingent election procedure. They dislike the fact that all states, large or small, each get one vote in this special election. The objection, of course, is simply a variation on the argument that Electoral College opponents have made to the presidential election system as a whole. Votes are cast by state delegations in the Electoral College for the same reason that states are given two extra electoral votes, regardless of population. These devices ensure that small states are not forgotten in the process of selecting a chief executive. They buttress federalist principles and reinforce the need of presidential candidates to build a national coalition as they campaign for the presidency.

One Electoral College opponent nevertheless complains that the process is even more "'democratically' problematic than is choice by the electoral college itself."[49] He notes that the twenty-six least populous states contain less than 20 percent of the population.[50] Why should these states get to choose the next president, without the support of more heavily populated states? The list of small states that he cites, however, includes states as different from each other as Rhode Island and Wyoming. It is hard to imagine a candidate that could achieve the support of "blue" Rhode Island and "red" Wyoming without also achieving the support of at least some of the other large states. The contingent election itself is rare. Rarer still would be a contingent election with an outcome dictated solely by the twenty-six smallest states.

THE DEVIL'S ADVOCATE

The 2016 presidential election seemed to be the "perfect storm" that could finally produce a House contingent election, despite the fact that the nation had managed to avoid one for nearly two centuries. Even then, the fear of such an election turned out to be much ado about nothing. The meetings of the Electoral College occurred with relatively little drama, all things considered. Instead, the nation moved on to a certain and stable electoral outcome.

Secondary election procedures are rare in the United States. The Electoral College, by design, prevents the need for them most of the time.[51] It instead tends to magnify the margin of victory, providing the country with a clear winner even when popular vote totals are close. This state of affairs has held true, even when candidates specifically seek to trigger a contingent election procedure, as George Wallace did in 1968 or Evan McMullin did in 2016.

Those who fear the specter of a House contingent election don't need to worry so much. The elections in which such procedures are necessary are few and far between. Most people would probably consider the need for a future contingent election less than ideal, but it wouldn't be a crisis, either. Constitutional provisions would simply go into effect and work as intended.

After the election of 1800, the House voted thirty-six times before it elected Jefferson. Representatives did this at a time when the Constitution was still relatively new, yet that document was—and is—strong enough to withstand the situation. Jefferson was not only elected, but he was accepted by the country. He went on to serve so successfully that the manner in which he was elected is nothing more than a footnote in history. John Quincy Adams had a similar experience, despite the rumors about deal making at the time. In all likelihood, America can continue to rely on its current back-up election process without too much harm— which is, in and of itself, a good argument for leaving the current system largely as it stands.

Moreover, given how many voters were actively working toward this situation in 2016, perhaps the conventional wisdom about contingent elections should be reconsidered: is such a situation entirely bad? Or could there be a few benefits that are actively worth preserving? A reasonable argument can be made that the House contingent election simply presents one last opportunity for the states to make themselves heard. It serves as one final, republican safeguard in America's system of checks and balances. True, such opportunities don't exist and aren't needed in most election years. Most Americans undoubtedly remain grateful for that state of affairs. On the other hand, perhaps the contingent election provides one last outlet when both political parties simultaneously nominate candidates that have left the electorate generally unhappy with their choices.

Consider the unique position of Utah in 2016: the little red state was nearly in a situation, with its small allocation of only six electoral votes, to reject both the DNC's and the RNC's choices of candidate and to insert a third option into the mix. Moreover, blue states had more options than they seem to have realized in November 2016, once it became clear that Hillary Clinton could not win the election.

In the real election, of course, liberals and blue state protestors hit the streets, marching and protesting and even destroying private property. How much more productive it would have been for them to take one last stab at using their state's authority to reach across the aisle and ask for compromise. Instead of destroying things, they could have sought to build a coalition, as the Electoral College always encourages.

Some Californians began discussing secession, but they could have instead asked their legislature to meet and consider other options. It was a known quantity that their votes for Hillary Clinton would not make her president. The legislature could have considered a resolution asking its electors to vote for a third, compromise candidate. They could have issued a public appeal to a conflicted state like Utah to join them in voting for a respected U.S. Army general or a statesman who was perceived as being above the fray. They could have asked Texas to join the effort, knowing that the thirty-eight Texas electors, acting alone, could trigger a contingent election.[52]

There are pros and cons to such measures, of course. Perhaps Californians would decide that they are too wedded to the results of their popular vote. Or maybe they would decide that the chances of getting a red state to join them are far too remote. The state will choose its priorities, as anticipated and celebrated in America's federalist system. But certainly it would have been better for state legislatures to instigate a discussion of these issues, soliciting feedback from constituents, as opposed to random, unknown electors attempting to make such decisions on their own. Regardless of what states decide, the mere *discussion* of other options would surely have been more unifying and productive than nightly protests and violence around the country.

***

America has changed since those days in Philadelphia when delegates to the Constitutional Convention contemplated the best form of presidential selection. At that time, some of those delegates worried that America would end up using its back-up contingent election process too often. They felt sure that most elections would be decided in the House.

Perhaps some delegates soon felt that they'd been proven right. Two House contingent elections were held before the nation's fiftieth birthday. Since that time, however, the system has stabilized, partly because "Continental Characters" have come to be known across the country, as James Wilson predicted they would.[53] Indeed, since 1825, contingent elections have become extraordinarily rare—almost entirely absent from the process. Arguably, modern Americans have hit a nice balance: the Electoral College pretty much always selects a president based on the popular vote within states. Yet a small, narrow path toward a contingent election might be found in extraordinary election years when voters choose to make use of it.

With more than two hundred years' experience under their belt, perhaps it is time for modern Americans to reconsider their skepticism toward the House contingent election process: at worst, it's an anomaly that has been used once every two hundred years or so, without disrupting the overall stability of the presidential election system. At best, however, it could be viewed as just one more tool for those states that are feeling too ignored or forgotten by the major political parties.

CONCLUSION

"The Electoral College is actually genius in that it brings all states, including the smaller ones, into play," Donald Trump tweeted in November 2016 when it became apparent that he would win the electoral vote but lose the popular vote.[1] A few weeks later, he elaborated on the sentiment: "It would have been much easier for me to win the so-called popular vote than the Electoral College in that I would only campaign in 3 or 4 states instead of the 15 states that I visited."[2] "Campaigning to win the Electoral College is much more difficult & sophisticated than the popular vote," he concluded. "Hillary focused on the wrong states!"[3]

His observations were true, although his views on the matter had surely evolved since his November 2012 tweet that the "electoral college is a disaster for a democracy."[4] The truth, of course, is almost the exact opposite: a pure democracy would be a disaster for a large, diverse country such as America.

The Founders understood this truth all too well, even if modern Americans have forgotten it. They recognized that a simple democracy would not suffice. Instead, their new government would need to incorporate safeguards against the flaws of human nature. After all, power corrupts. People make mistakes. Emotion can overtake a mob. Personal ambition has a tendency to take over, undermining the public good. Bare majorities will too often tyrannize minority voting blocks, given the opportunity to do so.

How could the delegates to the Constitutional Convention create a self-governing society, even as they created protections against these human shortcomings? How could they ensure that minorities would be protected from unreasonable or mob rule? How could they enable a nation composed of both large and small states to live together in peace? Delegates deliberated these questions at length before answering their dilemma with a unique solution. An "experiment," as George Washington would later say, "entrusted to the hands of the American people."[5]

Convention delegates proposed a new system of governance that would blend democratic, self-governing principles with republican and federalist ones. Then they added a unique presidential election system to the mix: the Electoral College system echoed the choices and compromises that had already been made in the general structure of the Constitution. Liberty would be protected by a multitude of safeguards and checks and balances. The election system would be decentralized, leaving states with enough power to express their concerns when things seem to be going awry.

The Founders might have crafted a careful balance and left the bulk of the power to the states, but modern Americans have mostly forgotten it. Instead, voters and states have been slowly giving their power away in recent decades. A presidential election process that was meant to be decentralized has too often become the opposite: power has become too heavily focused in a handful of places. The mainstream media, the Republican National Committee, and the Democratic National Committee wield power over the process in many ways, as most Americans doubtless recognize. However, the process has become centralized in other, less obvious ways as well.

Consider that a handful of pollsters effectively tell Americans who is (or isn't) a serious candidate, simply by determining whom they will or will not include in polls. The Commission on Presidential Debates makes similar judgments, communicating comparable messages to voters, based upon which candidates they include in the presidential debates. To some degree this situation is unavoidable. Dozens of presidential candidates can't appear on the national debate stage every year. On the other hand, both pollsters and CPD too often act under a misimpression about the presidential election system. They craft their selection criteria for polls and debates as if the presidential election were a national election between two national candidates. Such a perspective doesn't reflect the reality of the Electoral College, which is, at its heart, an election driven by a series of state-by-state actions.[6]

In 2016, four candidates were competitive in state races at various points during the fall. The two major-party contenders could have lost electoral votes to Gary Johnson (New Mexico) and to Evan McMullin (Utah). Nevertheless, CPD looked to national polling, entirely dismissing state polls, to determine whether Johnson and McMullin would be allowed on the debate stage. Pollsters treated McMullin with similar disdain, rarely including him in national polling, even when analysts were speculating about the possibility of a McMullin win in Utah and a subsequent House contingent election. In the meantime, Johnson was included in the polling based upon national considerations, despite the fact that his chances of winning New Mexico had become more remote than McMullin's chances of winning Utah.

As the process becomes more and more centralized, is it any wonder that Americans are becoming increasingly dissatisfied with their choices of presidential candidates? The Constitution ultimately leaves the states in charge of the presidential election process. Elections will go best when states remain mindful of their duty.

None of this is to suggest that the states should suddenly become deliberately stubborn and contrary, refusing to cooperate with other states. As this book has discussed, the American presidential election system has historically been characterized by coalition building. States and political parties have worked together to find candidates who can unify the electorate. Such a state of affairs is healthy and one of the best benefits of America's unique presidential election system. States have the power to express concern when they see things going awry, but they serve their voters best if they use that power wisely.

American politics works in cycles, like a pendulum that swings slowly back and forth. In many ways, Americans in the early twenty-first century are in a position similar to the one that existed at the end of the nineteenth century. In those post-Civil War years, the political parties had worked themselves into a pretty unhealthy situation. Republicans potentially weren't so much working on coalition building as they were simply relying on their electoral strength in the northern and western regions of the country.[7] By contrast, Democrats could not rely solely on their home base in the South. There weren't enough electoral votes in those states. Instead, Democrats had to flip a few Republican-leaning states if they wanted to win a presidential election.

The Electoral College served the country well in those years. Over the course of a few election cycles, the system gently forced people on opposite sides of the political aisle to work together, whether they wanted to or not. Lessons about working together in a diverse country were learned, and the political pendulum eventually swung back to a healthier place.

The pendulum has once again swung too far in an unhealthy direction. The best response to the situation would be for the political parties to focus on where they have gone awry. Why has coalition building become so difficult? How can they focus less on winning, at any cost, and focus more on speaking to the concerns of the American people? How can the presidential primaries be adjusted to encourage coalition building, as the general election system does? If the political parties refuse to get a hold of themselves, what can the states do to force their hand?

The Electoral College has served the nation well for more than two centuries because it has historically forced political parties, candidates, and voters to focus on these types of questions, even when it would be easier not to do so. As a result, the system has seen the nation through other politically difficult times—and it can do so again.

History has vindicated Alexander Hamilton's assessment of the system. A perfect presidential election system is perhaps unachievable in a government composed of flawed human beings. But the Founders' Electoral College has proven itself "at least excellent."[8]

APPENDIX A

U.S. CONSTITUTION

ARTICLE II, SECTION 1, CLAUSES 1–4

The executive Power shall be vested in a President of the United States of America. He shall hold his Office during the Term of four Years, and, together with the Vice President, chosen for the same Term, be elected, as follows

Each State shall appoint, in such Manner as the Legislature thereof may direct, a Number of Electors, equal to the whole Number of Senators and Representatives to which the State may be entitled in the Congress: but no Senator or Representative, or Person holding an Office of Trust or Profit under the United States, shall be appointed an Elector.

The Electors shall meet in their respective States, and vote by Ballot for two Persons, of whom one at least shall not be an Inhabitant of the same State with themselves. And they shall make a List of all the Persons voted for, and of the Number of Votes for each; which List they shall sign and certify, and transmit sealed to the Seat of the Government of the United States, directed to the President of the Senate. The President of the Senate shall, in the Presence of the Senate and House of Representatives, open all the Certificates, and the Votes shall then be counted. The Person having the greatest Number of Votes shall be the President, if such Number be a Majority of the whole Number of Electors appointed; and if there be more than one who have such Majority, and have an equal Number of Votes, then the House of Representatives shall immediately chuse by Ballot one of them for President; and if no Person have a Majority, then from the five highest on the List the said House shall in like Manner chuse the President. But in chusing the President, the Votes shall be taken by States, the Representation from each State having one Vote; A quorum for this Purpose shall consist of a Member or Members from two thirds of the States, and a Majority of all the States shall be necessary to a Choice. In every Case, after the Choice of the President, the Person having the greatest Number of Votes of the Electors shall be the Vice President. But if there should remain two or more who have equal Votes, the Senate shall chuse from them by Ballot the Vice President.

The Congress may determine the Time of chusing the Electors, and the Day on which they shall give their Votes; which Day shall be the same throughout the United States.

U.S. CONSTITUTION 12TH AMENDMENT

The Electors shall meet in their respective states and vote by ballot for President and Vice-President, one of whom, at least, shall not be an inhabitant of the same state with themselves; they shall name in their ballots the person voted for as President, and in distinct ballots the person voted for as Vice-President, and they shall make distinct lists of all persons voted for as President, and of all persons voted for as Vice-President, and of the number of votes for each, which lists they shall sign and certify, and transmit sealed to the seat of the government of the United States, directed to the President of the Senate;—the President of the Senate shall, in the presence of the Senate and House of Representatives, open all the certificates and the votes shall then be counted;—The person having the greatest number of votes for President, shall be the President, if such number be a majority of the whole number of Electors appointed; and if no person have such majority, then from the persons having the highest numbers not exceeding three on the list of those voted for as President, the House of Representatives shall choose immediately, by ballot, the President. But in choosing the President, the votes shall be taken by states, the representation from each state having one vote; a quorum for this purpose shall consist of a member or members from two-thirds of the states, and a majority of all the states shall be necessary to a choice. And if the House of Representatives shall not choose a President whenever the right of choice shall devolve upon them, before the fourth day of March next following, then the Vice-President shall act as President, as in the case of the death or other constitutional disability of the President.—The person having the greatest number of votes as Vice-President, shall be the Vice-President, if such number be a majority of the whole number of Electors appointed, and if no person have a majority, then from the two highest numbers on the list, the Senate shall choose the Vice-President; a quorum for the purpose shall consist of two-thirds of the whole number of Senators, and a majority of the whole number shall be necessary to a choice. But no person constitutionally ineligible to the office of President shall be eligible to that of Vice-President of the United States.

APPENDIX B

ELECTION RESULTS: 1789–2016[1]

Candidate	Party	Electoral Votes		Popular Vote[2]	
		Actual[3]	Percent[4]	Actual	Percent
1789					
George Washington	F	69			
John Adams	F	34			
Others (10 candidates)	Misc.	35 (total)			
1792					
George Washington	F	132			
John Adams	F	77			
Others (3 candidates)	Misc.	55 (total)			

| Candidate | Party | Electoral Votes | | Popular Vote[2] | |
		Actual[3]	Percent[4]	Actual	Percent
1796					
John Adams	F	71			
Thomas Jefferson	DR	68			
Others (11 candidates)	Misc.	137 (total)			
1800					
Thomas Jefferson	DR	73			
Aaron Burr	DR	73			
John Adams	F	65			
Others (2 candidates)	Misc.	65 (total)			
1804					
Thomas Jefferson	DR	162	92.0%		
Charles C. Pinckney	F	14	8.0%		
1808[5]					
James Madison	DR	122	69.3%		
Charles C. Pinckney	F	47	26.7%		
George Clinton	IDR	6	3.4%		
1812[6]					
James Madison	DR	128	58.7%		

Candidate	Party	Electoral Votes		Popular Vote[2]	
		Actual[3]	Percent[4]	Actual	Percent
DeWitt Clinton	F / IDR	89	40.8%		
1816[7]					
James Monroe	DR	183	82.8%		
Rufus King	F	34	15.4%		
1820[8]					
James Monroe	DR	231	98.3%		
John Quincy Adams	IDR	1	0.4%		
1824[9]					
John Quincy Adams	DR	84	32.2%	113,122	30.9%
Andrew Jackson	DR	99	37.9%	151,271	41.3%
William H. Crawford	DR	41	15.7%	40,856	11.2%
Henry Clay	DR	37	14.2%	47,531	13.0%
1828					
Andrew Jackson	DR	178	68.2%	642,553	56.0%
John Quincy Adams	NR	83	31.8%	500,897	43.6%
1832[10]					
Andrew Jackson	D	219	76.0%	701,780	54.2%

| Candidate | Party | Electoral Votes | | Popular Vote[2] | |
		Actual[3]	Percent[4]	Actual	Percent
Henry Clay	NR	49	17.0%	484,205	37.4%
John Floyd	ID	11	3.8%	—	—
William Wirt	AM	7	2.4%	100,715	7.8%
1836					
Martin Van Buren	D	170	57.8%	764,176	50.8%
William H. Harrison	W	73	24.8%	550,816	36.6%
Hugh L. White	W	26	8.8%	146,107	9.7%
Daniel Webster	W	14	4.8%	41,201	2.7%
W.P. Mangum	ID	11	3.7%	—	—
1840					
William H. Harrison	W	234	79.6%	1,275,390	52.9%
Martin Van Buren	D	60	20.4%	1,128,854	46.8%
1844					
James K. Polk	D	170	61.8%	1,339,494	49.5%
Henry Clay	W	105	38.2%	1,300,004	48.1%
1848					
Zachary Taylor	W	163	56.2%	1,361,393	47.3%
Lewis Cass	D	127	43.8%	1,223,460	42.5%

Candidate	Party	Electoral Votes		Popular Vote[2]	
		Actual[3]	Percent[4]	Actual	Percent
1852					
Franklin Pierce	D	254	85.8%	1,607,510	50.8%
Winfield Scott	W	42	14.2%	1,386,942	43.9%
1856					
James Buchanan	D	174	58.8%	1,836,072	45.3%
John C. Fremont	R	114	38.5%	1,342,345	33.1%
Millard Fillmore	WA	8	2.7%	873,053	21.5%
1860					
Abraham Lincoln	R	180	59.4%	1,865,908	39.9%
John C. Breckinridge	SD	72	23.8%	848,019	18.1%
John Bell	CU	39	12.9%	590,901	12.6%
Stephen A. Douglas	D	12	4.0%	1,380,202	29.5%
1864[11]					
Abraham Lincoln	R	212	90.6%	2,220,846	55.1%
George B. McClellan	D	21	9.0%	1,809,445	44.9%
1868					
Ulysses S. Grant	R	214	72.8%	3,013,650	52.7%

Candidate	Party	Electoral Votes		Popular Vote[2]	
		Actual[3]	Percent[4]	Actual	Percent
Horatio Seymour	D	80	27.2%	2,708,744	47.3%
1872[12]					
Ulysses S. Grant	R	286	78.1%	3,598,468	55.6%
Thomas Hendricks	D	42	11.5%	—	—
B. Gratz Brown	D	18	4.9%	—	—
Charles J. Jenkins	D	2	0.5%	—	—
David Davis	D	1	0.3%	—	—
1876					
Rutherford B. Hayes	R	185	50.1%	4,033,497	48.0%
Samuel J. Tilden	D	184	49.9%	4,288,191	51.0%
1880					
James A. Garfield	R	214	58.0%	4,453,611	48.3%
Winfield S. Hancock	D	155	42.0%	4,445,256	48.2%
1884					
Grover Cleveland	D	219	54.6%	4,915,586	48.9%
James G. Blaine	R	182	45.4%	4,852,916	48.2%

| Candidate | Party | Electoral Votes | | Popular Vote[2] | |
		Actual[3]	Percent[4]	Actual	Percent
1888					
Benjamin Harrison	R	233	58.1%	5,449,825	47.8%
Grover Cleveland	D	168	41.9%	5,539,118	48.6%
1892					
Grover Cleveland	D	277	62.4%	5,554,617	46.0%
Benjamin Harrison	R	145	32.7%	5,186,793	43.0%
James B. Weaver	PO	22	5.0%	1,024,280	8.5%
1896					
William McKinley	R	271	60.6%	7,105,144	51.1%
William J. Bryan	D / PO	176	39.4%	6,370,897	45.8%
1900					
William McKinley	R	292	65.3%	7,219,193	51.7%
William J. Bryan	D	155	34.7%	6,357,698	45.5%
1904					
Theodore Roosevelt	R	336	70.6%	7,625,599	56.4%
Alton B. Parker	D	140	29.4%	5,083,501	37.6%

Candidate	Party	Electoral Votes		Popular Vote[2]	
		Actual[3]	Percent[4]	Actual	Percent
1908					
William H. Taft	R	321	66.5%	7,676,598	51.6%
William J. Bryan	D	162	33.5%	6,406,874	43.0%
1912					
Woodrow Wilson	D	435	81.9%	6,294,326	41.8%
Theodore Roosevelt	P	88	16.6%	4,120,207	27.4%
William H. Taft	R	8	1.5%	3,486,343	23.2%
1916					
Woodrow Wilson	D	277	52.2%	9,126,063	49.2%
Charles E. Hughes	R	254	47.8%	8,547,039	46.1%
1920					
Warren G. Harding	R	404	76.1%	16,151,916	60.3
James M. Cox	D	127	23.9%	9,134,074	34.1
1924					
Calvin Coolidge	R	382	71.9%	15,724,310	54.0%
John W. Davis	D	136	25.6%	8,386,532	28.8%

Candidate	Party	Electoral Votes		Popular Vote[2]	
		Actual[3]	Percent[4]	Actual	Percent
Robert M. La Follette	P	13	2.4%	4,827,184	16.6%
1928					
Herbert C. Hoover	R	444	83.6%	21,432,823	58.2%
Alfred E. Smith	D	87	16.4%	15,004,336	40.8%
1932					
Franklin D. Roosevelt	D	472	88.9%	22,818,740	57.4%
Herbert C. Hoover	R	59	11.1%	15,760,425	39.6%
1936					
Franklin D. Roosevelt	D	523	98.5%	27,750,866	60.8%
Alfred M. Landon	R	8	1.5%	16,679,683	36.5%
1940					
Franklin D. Roosevelt	D	449	84.6%	27,343,218	54.7%
Wendell Willkie	R	82	15.4%	22,334,940	44.8%
1944					
Franklin D. Roosevelt	D	432	81.4%	25,612,610	53.4%
Thomas E. Dewey	R	99	18.6%	22,021,053	45.9%

Candidate	Party	Electoral Votes		Popular Vote[2]	
		Actual[3]	Percent[4]	Actual	Percent
1948					
Harry S. Truman	D	303	57.1%	24,105,810	49.5%
Thomas E. Dewey	R	189	35.6%	21,970,064	45.1%
J. Strom Thurmond	SRD	39	7.3%	1,169,114	2.4%
1952					
Dwight Eisenhower	R	442	83.2%	33,777,945	54.9%
Adlai Stevenson	D	89	16.8%	27,314,992	44.4%
1956					
Dwight Eisenhower	R	457	86.1%	35,590,472	57.4%
Adlai Stevenson	D	73	13.7%	26,022,752	42.0%
Walter B. Jones	D	1	0.2%	—	—
1960					
John F. Kennedy	D	303	56.4%	34,226,731	49.7%
Richard M. Nixon	R	219	40.8%	34,108,157	49.5%
Harry F. Byrd	D	15	2.8%	—	—
1964					
Lyndon B. Johnson	D	486	90.3%	43,129,566	61.1%

Candidate	Party	Electoral Votes		Popular Vote[2]	
		Actual[3]	Percent[4]	Actual	Percent
Barry M. Goldwater	R	52	9.7%	27,178,188	38.5%
1968					
Richard M. Nixon	R	301	55.9%	31,785,480	43.4%
Hubert H. Humphrey	D	191	35.5%	31,275,166	42.7%
George C. Wallace	AI	46	8.6%	9,906,473	13.5%
1972					
Richard M. Nixon	R	520	96.7%	47,169,911	60.7%
George S. McGovern	D	17	3.2%	29,170,383	37.5%
John Hospers	L	1	0.2%	3,673	<0.1%
1976					
Jimmy Carter	D	297	55.2%	40,830,763	50.1%
Gerald R. Ford	R	240	44.6%	39,147,793	48.0%
Ronald Reagan	R	1	0.2%	—	—
1980					
Ronald Reagan	R	489	90.9%	43,904,153	50.7%
Jimmy Carter	D	49	9.1%	35,483,883	41.0%

| Candidate | Party | Electoral Votes | | Popular Vote[2] | |
		Actual[3]	Percent[4]	Actual	Percent
1984					
Ronald Reagan	R	525	97.6%	54,455,075	58.8%
Walter F. Mondale	D	13	2.4%	37,577,185	40.6%
1988					
George H.W. Bush	R	426	79.2%	48,886,097	53.4%
Michael S. Dukakis	D	111	20.6%	41,809,074	45.6%
Lloyd Bentsen	D	1	0.2%	—	—
1992					
Bill Clinton	D	370	68.8%	44,909,326	43.0%
George H.W. Bush	R	168	31.2%	39,103,882	37.4%
1996					
Bill Clinton	D	379	70.4%	47,402,357	49.2%
Bob Dole	R	159	29.6%	39,198,755	40.7%
2000					
George W. Bush	R	271	50.4%	50,455,156	47.9%
Albert Gore, Jr.	D	266	49.4%	50,992,335	48.4%
2004					
George W. Bush	R	286	53.2%	62,040,610	50.7%

Candidate	Party	Electoral Votes		Popular Vote[2]	
		Actual[3]	Percent[4]	Actual	Percent
John Kerry	D	251	46.7%	59,028,439	48.3%
John Edwards[13]	D	1	.2%	—	—
2008					
Barack Obama	D	365	67.8%	69,498,516	52.9%
John McCain	R	173	32.2%	59,948,323	45.7%
2012					
Barack Obama	D	332	61.7%	65,446,032	50.9%
Mitt Romney	R	206	38.3%	60,589,084	47.1%
2016[14]					
Donald Trump	R	304	56.5%	62,985,106	45.94%
Hillary Clinton	D	227	42.2%	65,853,625	48.03%
Colin Powell	R	3	0.6%	—	—
John Kasich	R	1	0.2%	—	—
Ron Paul	R	1	0.2%	—	—
Bernie Sanders	I	1	0.2%	—	—
Faith Spotted Eagle	D	1	0.2%	—	—

AI = American Independent
ID = Independent Democrat
R = Republican
AM = Anti-Mason
IDR = Ind. Dem.-Republican
SRD = States' Right Democrat
CU = Constitutional Union
L = Libertarian
SD = Southern Democrat
D = Democrat
NR = National-Republican
W = Whig
DR = Democratic-Republican
P = Progressive
WA = Whig-American
F = Federalist
PO = Populist

APPENDIX C

FAITHLESS ELECTORS

1796 TO 2016[1]

Year	Name of Elector	Pledged to:	Cast Ballot For:
2016	David Mulinix (HI)	Hillary Clinton (D)	Bernie Sanders (I)
2016	Chris Suprun (TX)	Donald Trump (R)	John Kasich (R)
2016	Bill Greene (TX)	Donald Trump (R)	Ron Paul (R)
2016	Bret Chiafalo (WA)	Hillary Clinton (D)	Colin Powell (R)
2016	Esther John (WA)	Hillary Clinton (D)	Colin Powell (R)
2016	Levi Guerra (WA)	Hillary Clinton (D)	Colin Powell (R)
2016	Robert Satiacum (WA)	Hillary Clinton (D)	Faith Spotted Eagle (D)
2004	Anonymous (MN)	John Kerry (D)	John Edwards (D)

Year	Name of Elector	Pledged to:	Cast Ballot For:
2000	Barbara Lett-Simmons (D.C.)	Al Gore (D)	Abstained
1988	Margaret Leach (WV)	Michael Dukakis (D)	Lloyd Bentsen (D)
1976	Mike Padden (WA)	Gerald Ford (R)	Ronald Reagan (R)
1972	Roger MacBride (VA)	Richard Nixon (R)	John Hospers (L)
1968	Lloyd W. Bailey (NC)	Richard Nixon (R)	George Wallace (AI)
1960	Henry D. Irwin (OK)	Richard Nixon (R)	Harry F. Byrd (D)
1956	W.F. Turner (AL)	Adlai Stevenson (D)	Walter B. Jones (D)
1948	Preston Parks (TN)[2]	Harry Truman (D)	Strom Thurmond (SR)
1824	5 of 15 electors (NC)	John Q. Adams (DR)	Andrew Jackson (DR)
1824	3 of 36 electors (NY)	Henry Clay (DR)	J.Q. Adams (DR) W.H. Crawford (DR) A. Jackson (DR)
1820	William Plumer (NH)	James Monroe (DR)	John Q. Adams (IDR)
1796	Samuel Miles (PA)	John Adams (F)	Thomas Jefferson (DR)

APPENDIX D

STATUS OF STATE LAWS ATTEMPTING TO BIND ELECTORS

CURRENT AS OF SPRING 2017

State	Electors Bound?	Penalty imposed?	State code
Alabama	Yes	No	ALA. CODE § 17-14-31
Alaska	Yes	No	ALASKA STAT. § 15.30.040 § 15.30.090
Arizona	No	N/A	
Arkansas	No	N/A	
California	Yes, "if both candidates are alive"	No	CAL. ELEC. CODE § 6906

State	Electors Bound?	Penalty imposed?	State code
Colorado	Yes	Vote invalidated; Elector replaced; Possibly treated as misdemeanor[1]	COLO. REV. STAT. § 1-4-304
Connecticut	Yes	No	CONN. GEN. STAT. § 9-176
Delaware	Yes	No	DEL. CODE ANN. tit. 15, § 4303(b)
D.C.	Yes	No	D.C. CODE § 1-1001.08(g)
Florida	Yes	No	FLA. STAT. § 103.021(1) § 103.021(5)
Georgia	No	N/A	
Hawaii	Yes, "if both candidates are alive"	No	HAW. REV. STAT. § 14-28
Idaho	No	N/A	
Illinois	No	N/A	
Indiana	No	N/A	
Iowa	No	N/A	
Kansas	No	N/A	
Kentucky	No	N/A	

State	Electors Bound?	Penalty imposed?	State code
Louisiana	No	N/A	
Maine	Yes	An independent vote was rejected in 2016[2]	ME. STAT. tit. 21-A, § 805(2)
Maryland	Yes	No	MD. CODE ANN., Elec. Law § 8-505
Massachusetts	Yes	No	MASS GEN. LAWS ch. 53, § 8
Michigan	Yes	Vote invalidated; Elector replaced	MICH. COMP. LAWS § 168.47
Minnesota	Yes	Vote invalidated; Elector replaced	MINN. STAT. § 208.43 § 208.45 § 208.46
Mississippi	Yes	No	MISS. CODE ANN. § 23-15-771 § 23-15-785
Missouri	No	N/A	

State	Electors Bound?	Penalty imposed?	State code
Montana	Yes	Vote invalidated; Elector replaced	MONT. CODE ANN. § 13-25-304 § 13-25-306 § 13-25-307
Nebraska	Yes	Vote invalidated; Elector replaced	NEB. REV. STAT. § 32-713 § 32-714
Nevada	Yes	Vote invalidated; Elector replaced	NEV. REV. STAT. § 298.045 § 298.065 § 298.075
New Hampshire	No	N/A	
New Jersey	No	N/A	
New Mexico	Yes	Considered guilty of a 4th degree felony	N.M. STAT. ANN. § 1-15-9
New York	No	N/A	
North Carolina	Yes	Vote invalidated; Elector replaced; $500 fine	N.C. GEN. STAT. § 163-212
North Dakota	No	N/A	

State	Electors Bound?	Penalty imposed?	State code
Ohio	Yes	No	OHIO REV. CODE ANN. § 3505.40
Oklahoma	Yes	Vote invalidated; Elector replaced; Misdemeanor; Fined up to $1,000	OKLA. STAT. tit. 26, § 10-102 § 10-109
Oregon	Yes	No[3]	OR. REV. STAT. § 248.355(2)
Pennsylvania	No	N/A	
Rhode Island	No	N/A	
South Carolina	Yes, unless party releases elector	"Attorney General shall institute criminal action"	S.C. CODE ANN. § 7-19-80
South Dakota	No	N/A	
Tennessee	Yes, "if both candidates are alive"[4]	No	TENN. CODE ANN. § 2-15-104(c)
Texas	No	N/A	
Utah	Yes, "except in the cases of death or felony conviction"	Vote invalidated; Elector replaced	UTAH CODE ANN. § 20A-13-304

State	Electors Bound?	Penalty imposed?	State code
Vermont	Yes	No[5]	VT. STAT. ANN. tit. 17, § 2732
Virginia	Yes	No[6]	VA. CODE ANN. § 24.2-203
Washington	Yes	Fined up to $1,000[7]	WASH. REV. CODE § 29A.56.320 § 29A.56.340
West Virginia	No	N/A	
Wisconsin	Yes, but "not required to vote for a candidate who is deceased"	No[8]	WIS. STAT. § 7.75(2)
Wyoming	Yes	No	WYO. STAT. ANN. § 22-19-108

APPENDIX E

RULES GOVERNING HOUSE CONTINGENT ELECTION

ADOPTED BY THE HOUSE OF REPRESENTATIVES

FEBRUARY 9, 1801[1]

1st. In the event of its appearing, upon the counting and ascertaining of the votes given for President and Vice President, according to the mode prescribed by the Constitution, that no person has a Constitutional majority, and the same shall have been duly declared and entered on the Journals of this House, the Speaker, accompanied by the members of the House, shall return to their chamber.

2d. Seats shall be provided in this House for the President and members of the Senate; and notification of the same shall be made to the Senate.

3d. The House, on their return from the Senate Chamber, it being ascertained that the Constitutional number of States were present, shall immediately proceed to choose one of the persons from whom the choice is to be made for President; and in case upon the first ballot there shall not appear to be a majority of the States in favor of one of them, in such case the House shall continue to ballot for a President, without interruption by other business, until it shall appear that a President is duly chosen.

4th. After commencing the balloting for President, the House shall not adjourn until a choice be made.

5th. The doors of the House shall be closed during the balloting, except against the officers of the House.

6th. In balloting, the following mode shall be observed, to wit: The representatives of the respective States shall be so seated that the delegation of each State shall be together. The representatives of each State, shall, in the first instance, ballot among themselves, in order to ascertain the votes of the State; and it shall be allowed, where deemed necessary by the delegation, to name one or more persons of the representation, to be tellers of the ballots. After the vote of each State is ascertained, duplicates thereof shall be made; and in case the vote of the State be for one person, then the name of that person shall be written on each of the duplicates; and in case the ballots of the State be equally divided, then the word "*divided*" shall be written on each duplicate, and the said duplicates shall be deposited in manner hereafter prescribed, in boxes to be provided. That, for the conveniently taking the ballots of the several representatives of the respective States, there be sixteen ballot boxes provided; and that there be, additionally, two boxes provided for the purpose of receiving the votes of the States; that after the delegation of each State shall have ascertained the vote of the State, the Sergeant-at-Arms shall carry to the respective delegations the two ballot boxes, and the delegation of each State, in the presence and subject to the examination of all the members of the delegation, shall deposit a duplicate of the vote of the State in each ballot box; and where there is more than one representative of a State, the duplicates shall not both be deposited by the same person. When the votes of the States are all thus taken in, the Sergeant-at-Arms shall carry one of the general ballot boxes to one table, and the other to a second and separate table. Sixteen members shall then be appointed as tellers of the ballots; one of whom shall be taken from each State, and be nominated by the delegation of the State from which he was taken. The said tellers shall be divided into two equal sets, according to such agreement as shall be made among themselves; and one of the said sets of tellers shall proceed to count the votes in one of the said boxes, and the other set the votes in the other box; and in the event of no appointment of teller by any delegation, the Speaker shall in such case appoint. When the votes of the States are counted by the respective sets of tellers, the result shall be reported to the House; and if the reports agree, the same shall be accepted as the true votes of the States; but if the reports disagree, the States shall immediately proceed to a new ballot, in manner aforesaid.

7th. If either of the persons voted for, shall have a majority of the votes of all the States, the Speaker shall declare the same; and official notice thereof shall be immediately given to the President of the United States, and to the Senate.

8th. All questions which shall arise after the balloting commences, and which shall be decided by the House voting *per capita* to be incidental to the power of choosing the President, and which shall require the decision of the House, shall be decided by States, and without debate; and in case of an equal division of the votes of States, the question shall be lost.

RULES GOVERNING HOUSE CONTINGENT ELECTION ADOPTED BY THE HOUSE OF REPRESENTATIVES FEBRUARY 7, 1825[2]

1st. In the event of its appearing, on opening all the certificates, and counting the votes given by the electors of the several states for President, that no person has a majority of the votes of the whole number of the electors appointed, and the result shall have been declared, the same shall be entered on the journals of this House.

2d. The roll of the House, shall then be called, by states, and, on its appearing that a member or members from two-thirds of the states are present, the House shall immediately proceed, by ballot, to choose a President from the persons having the highest numbers, not exceeding three, on the list of those voted for as President; and in case neither of those persons shall receive the votes of a majority of all the states on the first ballot, the House shall continue to ballot for a President, without interruption by other business, until a President be chosen.

3d. The doors of the Hall shall be closed during the balloting, except against members of the Senate, Stenographers, and the officers of the House.

4th. From the commencement of the balloting, until an election is made, no proposition to adjourn shall be received, unless on the motion of one state, seconded by another state; and the question shall be decided by states. The same rule shall be observed in regard to any motion to change the usual hour for the meeting of the House.

5th. In balloting, the following mode shall be observed, to wit:

The Representatives of each state shall be arranged and seated together, beginning with the seat at the right hand of the Speaker's chair, with the members from the state of Maine; thence, proceeding with the members from the states in the order the states are usually named for receiving petitions, around the Hall of the House, until all are seated;

A ballot box shall be provided for each state;

The Representatives of each state shall, in the first instance, ballot among themselves, in order to ascertain the vote of their state, and they may, if necessary, appoint tellers of their ballots;

After the vote of each state is ascertained, duplicates thereof shall be made out, and, in case any one of the persons from whom the choice is to be made, shall receive a majority of the votes given, on any one balloting, by the Representatives of a state, the *name* of that person shall be written on each of the duplicates; and, in case the votes so given shall be divided, so that neither of said persons shall have a majority of the whole number of votes given by such state on any one balloting, then the word "*divided*," shall be written on each duplicate;

After the delegation from each state shall have ascertained the vote of their state, the Clerk shall name the states in the order they are usually named for receiving petitions; and, as the name of each is called, the Sergeant-at-Arms shall present to the delegation of each two ballot boxes, in each of which shall be deposited, by some Representative of the state, one of the duplicates made as aforesaid, of the vote of said state, in the presence, and subject to the examination, of all the members from said state then present; and, where there is more than one Representative from a state, the duplicates shall not both be deposited by the same person.

When the votes of the states are thus all taken in, the Sergeant-at-Arms shall carry one of said ballot boxes to one table, and the other to a separate and distinct table;

One person from each state, represented in the balloting, shall be appointed by its Representative[s], to tell off said ballots; but, in case the Representatives fail to appoint a teller, the Speaker shall appoint;

The said Tellers shall divide themselves into two sets, as nearly equal in number as can be, and one of the said sets of Tellers shall proceed to count the votes in one of said boxes, and the other set the votes in the other box.

When the votes are counted by the different sets of Tellers, the result shall be reported to the House, and, if the reports agree, the same shall be accepted as the true votes of the states; but, if the reports disagree, the states shall proceed, in the same manner as before, to a new ballot.

6th. All questions arising after the balloting commences, requiring the decision of the House, which shall be decided by the House voting per capita, to be incidental to the power of choosing a President, shall be decided by states, without debate; and, in case of an equal division of the votes of states, the question shall be lost.

7th. When either of the persons from whom the choice is to be made, shall have received a majority of all the states, the Speaker shall declare the same, and that that person is elected President of the United States.

8th. The result shall be immediately communicated to the Senate by Message; and a committee of three persons shall be appointed to inform the President of the United States, and the President elect, of said election.

NOTES

Introduction

1. Henry F. DePuy, *Some Letters of Andrew Jackson, in* 31 AM. ANTIQUARIAN SOC'Y, PROCEEDINGS OF THE AMERICAN ANTIQUARIAN SOCIETY 70, 78 (1922) (reprinting a December 1824 letter from Andrew Jackson to Samuel Swartwout).

2. The accusations thrown around were so numerous that one contemporary remarked upon the impossibility of believing them all. Otherwise, he concluded, "our Presidents, Secretaries, Senators, and Representatives, are all traitors and pirates, and the government of this people [are all] committed to the hands of public robbers." CHASE C. MOONEY, WILLIAM H. CRAWFORD: 1772–1834, at 287 (1974).

3. Letter from Henry Clay to Francis Preston Blair (Jan. 8, 1824), *in* 4 THE PAPERS OF HENRY CLAY 9, 9 (James F. Hopkins et al. eds., 1825).

4. *Mr. Clay's Affair*, MD. GAZETTE (Annapolis), Feb. 10, 1825, at 2.

5. More information on the 1824 election can be found at PAUL F. BOLLER, JR., PRESIDENTIAL CAMPAIGNS 33–41 (rev. ed. 1996); H.W. BRANDS, ANDREW JACKSON: HIS LIFE AND TIMES 382–88 (2005); James F. Hopkins, *Election of 1824, in* 1 HISTORY OF AMERICAN PRESIDENTIAL ELECTIONS: 1789–2008, at 170, 190–97 (Gil Troy et al. eds., 4th ed. 2012).

6. CQ PRESS, PRESIDENTIAL ELECTIONS: 1789–2008, at 192–93, 215 (2010).

7. DePuy, *supra* note 1, at 78.

8. LAWRENCE D. LONGLEY & NEAL R. PEIRCE, THE ELECTORAL COLLEGE PRIMER 2000, at 111–12 (1999). One elector was elected to Congress and thus did not cast his ballot. His replacement defected from the expected vote, voting for Adams instead. One of the other electors voted for William Crawford. The other voted for Andrew Jackson. These votes are not always considered "faithless" because the electors already knew that Clay could not win by the time they cast their ballots. *Id.*

9. The final tally was John Quincy Adams (13 states), Andrew Jackson (7 states), and William Crawford (4 states). CQ PRESS, *supra* note 6, at 26.

10. Cleveland's win is commonly accepted, but not universally so. Some historians and commentators question whether fraud affected the outcome in 1888, just as it did in 1876. *See, e.g.*, George Will, *The Electoral College is an Excellent System*, WASH. POST (Dec. 16, 2016), https://www.washingtonpost. com/opinions/the-electoral-college-is-an-excellent-system/2016/12/16/30480790-c2ef-11e6-9a51-cd56ea1c2bb7_story.html?utm_term=.825cac97b5b6.

11. *E.g.*, Lydia Saad, *Trump Leads Clinton in Historically Bad Image Ratings*, GALLUP (July 1, 2016), http://www.gallup.com/poll/193376/trump-leads-clinton-historically-bad-image-ratings.aspx.

12. Ian Schwartz, *Obama: It Is Now the Electors' Job to Determine My Successor; Electoral College a "Vestige,"* REALCLEARPOLITICS (Dec. 17, 2016), http://www.realclearpolitics.com/video/2016/12/17/obama_it_is_now_the_electors_job_to_determine_my_successor.html ("The Electoral College is a vestige. It's a carry-over from an earlier vision of how our federal government was going to work that put a lot of premium on states . . . . [T]here are some structures in our political system, as envisioned by the Founders, that sometimes are going to disadvantage Democrats.").

13. *Id.*

14. Chris Cillizza, *Electoral College Gives Democrats a 2016 Edge*, WASH. POST, Mar. 16, 2015, at A2.

15. Ben Highton, *The Electoral College Challenge Facing the Republicans in 2016*, WASH. POST: MONKEY CAGE (May 7, 2014), https://www.washingtonpost.com/news/monkey-cage/wp/2014/05/07/the-electoral-college-challenge-facing-the-republicans-in-2016.

16. This book was written quickly in the wake of the 2016 presidential election and official sources from the National Archives were only partially available. This author relied on a variety of news sources to compile final election results from the 2016 election. In addition to states' election websites, two other websites were especially helpful. *See* CQ PRESS, VOTING AND ELECTIONS COLLECTION, http://library.cqpress.com/elections/index.php (last visited Apr. 27, 2017); DAVE LEIP'S

ATLAS OF U.S. PRESIDENTIAL ELECTIONS, http://
uselectionatlas.org (last visited Apr. 27, 2017).

17. *See, e.g.*, Thomas Brunell & Bernard Grofman, *The 1992 and
1996 Presidential Elections: Whatever Happened to the
Republican Electoral College Lock?*, 27 PRESIDENTIAL STUD.
Q. 134 (1997); Nate Silver, *There Is No 'Blue Wall,'*
FIVETHIRTYEIGHT (May 12, 2015, 1:32 PM), https://
fivethirtyeight.com/features/there-is-no-blue-wall.

18. States turning blue for the first time included California,
Colorado, Illinois, Montana, Nevada, New Hampshire, New
Jersey, New Mexico, and Vermont. *See* Silver, *supra* note 17.

19. The states that hadn't voted Republican since 1928 were:
Arizona, California, Florida, Idaho, Illinois, Minnesota,
Missouri, Montana, Nevada, New Mexico, Oklahoma,
Tennessee, Texas, Utah, Virginia, and Washington.
Massachusetts and Rhode Island voted for the Democratic
candidate in 1928, but they had voted for Republican Calvin
Coolidge in 1924.

20. Schwartz, *supra* note 12.

21. *See, e.g., General Election: Trump vs. Clinton,*
REALCLEARPOLITICS: POLLS, http://www.realclearpolitics.
com/epolls/2016/president/us/general_election_trump_vs_
clinton-5491.html (last visited Mar. 8, 2017).

22. *E.g.*, Philip Bump, *Donald Trump Now Leads in Two of His
Three Must-Win States—But the Path Forward Is Grim,*
WASH. POST: THE FIX (Nov. 1, 2016), http://www.
washingtonpost.com/news/the-fix/wp/2016/11/01/donald-
trump-now-leads-in-two-of-his-three-must-win-states-but-the-
path-forward-is-grim.

23. For instance, one poll showed that 58 percent of voters were
dissatisfied with the choice. *Clinton Lead Over Trump
Narrows, Public Broadly Dissatisfied with Candidates,*

WASH. POST (July 25, 2016), https://www.washingtonpost.
com/page/2010-2019/WashingtonPost/2016/07/17/National-
Politics/Polling/release_433.xml.

24. *See, e.g.,* Jonah Goldberg, *The Perfect Presidential Candidate
for an Imperfect Time*, CHI. TRIB. (Dec. 28, 2015), http://
www.chicagotribune.com/news/nationworld/ct-perfect-
presidential-candidate-for-an-imperfect-time-20151228-
column.html; *Disgruntled Voters Cast Write-In Ballot for
'Sweet Meteor O'Death' for President*, CBS LOS ANGELES
(Nov. 8, 2016, 9:14 AM), http://losangeles.cbslocal.
com/2016/11/08/disgruntled-voters-cast-write-in-ballot-for-
sweet-meteor-odeath-for-president; *see also* Douglas Ernst,
*"Giant Meteor" of Death Tied with Hillary Clinton, Donald
Trump Among Independents: Poll*, WASH. TIMES (June 30,
2016), http://www.washingtontimes.com/news/2016/jun/30/
giant-meteor-of-death-tied-with-hillary-clinton-do.

25. Google "Anyone Else 2016" and look in the images section for
a small sampling of this sentiment.

26. Gov. Gary Johnson (@GovGaryJohnson), TWITTER (June 29,
2016, 8:00 PM), https://twitter.com/GovGaryJohnson/
status/748320273754165249.

27. The total number of votes cast for a third-party candidate was
higher than it had been since Ross Perot's campaigns in 1992
and 1996. For more on election results, see discussion *supra*
note 16.

28. The Democratic nomination process went through many
reforms between 1969 and 1982, but most of those details are
beyond the scope of this book.

29. Soon after Carter's loss in 1980, the Hunt Commission
proposed reforms that were adopted by the Democratic Party.
Its written recommendations emphasized the need to "reduce
the party's fragmentation" and to "place a premium on

coalition-building." *Excerpts from Democratic Commission's Report on New Convention Rules*, N.Y. TIMES, Mar. 27, 1982, at 10; *see also* Adam Clymer, *Democrats Alter Delegate Rules, Giving Top Officials More Power*, N.Y. TIMES, Mar. 27, 1982, at 1 ("[Gov. James B. Hunt Jr., chairman] said the changes were necessary if the Democrats were to be controlled by the interests of their party as a whole and not its factions.").

30. *See* Press Release, FBI National Press Office, Statement by FBI Director James B. Comey on the Investigation of Secretary Hillary Clinton's Use of a Personal E-Mail System (July 5, 2016), https://www.fbi.gov/news/pressrel/press-releases/ statement-by-fbi-director-james-b-comey-on-the-investigation-of-secretary-hillary-clinton2019s-use-of-a-personal-e-mail-system.

31. During the primaries, then-candidate Donald Trump spoke of the problems in unifying the party: "I don't think it matters," he told a crowd in Indiana, "but it would be nice to have the Republican Party come together." Then he added: "With that being said, I think I'll win anyway." *The Latest: Trump Predicts Win, with or without United GOP*, BOS. HERALD (May 1, 2016), http://www.bostonherald.com/news/us_ politics/2016/05/the_latest_trump_predicts_win_with_or_ without_united_gop.

32. *See* discussion *infra* notes 60–67 (Ch. 6).

33. *Fox & Friends* (FNC television broadcast Oct. 25, 2016) ("Whatever you think about Trump, he's crude, he's not corrupt. The Clintons are corrupt. Corrupt versus crude occasionally. I'll take 'crude occasionally' any day over a party and a candidate who has methodically lied and dissembled about this issue."); *Fox News Sunday* (Fox television broadcast Oct. 23, 2016) ("I'm willing to concede that Trump

on occasion is crass, but I'd like my opponents to concede that Hillary on occasion is corrupt.").

34. *See supra* note 33.

CHAPTER ONE

1. WILLIAM G. CARR, THE OLDEST DELEGATE: FRANKLIN IN THE CONSTITUTIONAL CONVENTION 122 (1990) (citation omitted).
2. *Id.*
3. An editor of the *Oxford Dictionary of Quotations* notes the frequency with which the misstatement is made in WHAT THEY DIDN'T SAY: A BOOK OF MISQUOTATIONS 26 (Elizabeth Knowles ed., 2006).
4. These issues are discussed in greater detail in Chapters One and Two of TARA ROSS, ENLIGHTENED DEMOCRACY: THE CASE FOR THE ELECTORAL COLLEGE (Colonial Press 2d ed. 2012) (2004).
5. For information on the events that transpired before the Constitutional Convention commenced, see CATHERINE DRINKER BOWEN, MIRACLE AT PHILADELPHIA: THE STORY OF THE CONSTITUTIONAL CONVENTION MAY TO SEPTEMBER 1787 (2d prtg. 1986); CAROL BERKIN, A BRILLIANT SOLUTION: INVENTING THE AMERICAN CONSTITUTION (1st Harvest ed. 2003); ROBERT M. HARDAWAY, THE ELECTORAL COLLEGE AND THE CONSTITUTION: THE CASE FOR PRESERVING FEDERALISM 69–75 (1994); *see also Constitution of the United States—A History: A More Perfect Union: The Creation of the U.S. Constitution*, U.S. NAT'L ARCHIVES & RECORDS ADMIN., https://www.archives.gov/founding-docs/more-perfect-union (last visited Mar. 8, 2017).

6.   *See* JAMES MADISON, NOTES OF DEBATES IN THE FEDERAL
     CONVENTION OF 1787, at 23 (Adrienne Koch ed., W.W.
     Norton & Co. 1987) (1966).

7.   THE FEDERALIST NO. 40, at 244 (James Madison) (Clinton
     Rossiter ed., Signet Classic 2003) (1961); *see also* Robert G.
     Natelson, *Founding-Era Conventions and the Meaning of the
     Constitution's "Convention for Proposing Amendments,"* 65
     FLA. L. REV. 615, 674–79 (2013) (discussing the breadth of the
     powers given to Convention delegates by their states).

8.   Letter from Thomas Jefferson to John Adams (Aug. 30, 1787),
     in 12 THE PAPERS OF THOMAS JEFFERSON 66, 69 (Julian P.
     Boyd et al. eds., 1955); *see also* BOWEN, *supra* note 5, at 4.

9.   JAMES THOMAS FLEXNER, WASHINGTON: THE INDISPENSABLE
     MAN 207 (Back Bay ed. 1974). It could also be that his nature
     made him more prone to reflect than speak during debates, as
     Jefferson once observed of his former colleague's demeanor in
     the Virginia legislature. BOWEN, *supra* note 5, at 29.

10. JOSEPH J. ELLIS, FOUNDING BROTHERS: THE
     REVOLUTIONARY GENERATION 120 (15th prtg. 2001).

11. BOWEN, *supra* note 5, at 30.

12. For detailed discussions of the Convention debates from a
     variety of viewpoints, see BERKIN, *supra* note 5; BOWEN,
     supra note 5; HARDAWAY, *supra* note 5, at 76–89; NEAL R.
     PEIRCE & LAWRENCE D. LONGLEY, THE PEOPLE'S PRESIDENT:
     THE ELECTORAL COLLEGE IN AMERICAN HISTORY AND THE
     DIRECT VOTE ALTERNATIVE 10–30 (Yale Univ. Press rev. ed.
     1981) (1968); DAVID O. STEWART, THE SUMMER OF 1787:
     THE MEN WHO INVENTED THE CONSTITUTION (2007);
     William Josephson & Beverly J. Ross, *Repairing the Electoral
     College*, 22 J. LEGIS. 145, 151–53 (1996).

13. David Stewart, *Abolish the Electoral College*, U.S. NEWS & WORLD REP. (Feb. 6, 2013, 11:25 AM), https://www.usnews.com/opinion/articles/2013/02/06/abolish-the-electoral-college.

14. R. KENT NEWMYER, SUPREME COURT JUSTICE JOSEPH STORY: STATESMAN OF THE OLD REPUBLIC 159 (1985).

15. MICHAEL J. KLARMAN, THE FRAMERS' COUP: THE MAKING OF THE UNITED STATES CONSTITUTION 228 (2016).

16. Letter from James Madison to Thomas Jefferson (Apr. 27, 1785), *in* 8 THE PAPERS OF THOMAS JEFFERSON, *supra* note 8, at 110, 111.

17. The proposal came to be known as the "Virginia Resolves" or the "Virginia Plan" and was presented in Convention by Edmund Randolph, the Governor of Virginia. Madison either drafted most of the resolves or heavily influenced them, however. BOWEN, *supra* note 5, at 37–39; *see also* MADISON, *supra* note 6, at 28–33.

18. THE FEDERALIST NO. 10, *supra* note 7, at 76 (James Madison).

19. MADISON, *supra* note 6, at 39.

20. *Id.* at 42.

21. *Id.* at 110.

22. *Id.* at 233.

23. Letter from James Madison to Thomas Jefferson (Oct. 17, 1788), *in* 11 THE PAPERS OF JAMES MADISON 295, 298 (Robert A. Rutland et al. eds., 1977).

24. 2 THE DEBATES IN THE SEVERAL STATE CONVENTIONS, ON THE ADOPTION OF THE FEDERAL CONSTITUTION, AS RECOMMENDED BY THE GENERAL CONVENTION AT PHILADELPHIA, IN 1787, at 253 (Jonathan Elliot ed., 2d ed. 1836) [hereinafter ELLIOT'S DEBATES].

25. Letter from John Adams to John Taylor (Apr. 15, 1814), *in* 6 THE WORKS OF JOHN ADAMS, SECOND PRESIDENT OF THE

UNITED STATES 447, 484 (Charles Francis Adams ed., 2d prtg. 1969).

26. Letter from Benjamin Rush to John Adams (July 21, 1789), *in* 1 LETTERS OF BENJAMIN RUSH 522, 523 (L. H. Butterfield ed., 1951).

27. JOHN WITHERSPOON, *Lecture XII of Civil Society, in* AN ANNOTATED EDITION OF *LECTURES ON MORAL PHILOSOPHY* 140, 144 (Jack Scott ed., 1982).

28. Fisher Ames, Speech in the Convention of Massachusetts, on Biennial Elections (Jan. 1788), *in* 2 WORKS OF FISHER AMES 3, 7 (Seth Ames ed., 1854).

29. Professor Judith Best also makes this point. *See* JUDITH A. BEST, THE CHOICE OF THE PEOPLE? DEBATING THE ELECTORAL COLLEGE 34–35 (1996). Actually, there were suggestions to give the colonies representation in the House of Commons. These proposals were initially championed by some colonists, including Benjamin Franklin. *See, e.g.,* GORDON S. WOOD, THE AMERICANIZATION OF BENJAMIN FRANKLIN 78, 115–16 (2004).

30. THE DECLARATION OF INDEPENDENCE para. 2 (U.S. 1776).

31. MADISON, *supra* note 6, at 64.

32. *Id.* at 39.

33. *Id.*

34. *Id.*

35. *Id.*

36. *Id.* at 40.

37. *Id.*

38. *Id.* at 306.

39. *Id.* at 307.

40. 1 THE RECORDS OF THE FEDERAL CONVENTION OF 1787, at 500 (Max Farrand ed., rev. ed. 1966) [hereinafter RECORDS].

41. MADISON, *supra* note 6, at 306.

42. *Id.*

43. *Id.* at 307.

44. *Id.* at 326–27.

45. 1 ELLIOT'S DEBATES, *supra* note 24, at 358; *see also* WILLIAM PETERS, A MORE PERFECT UNION 99 (1987).

46. *See* U.S. CONST. art I, § 2, cl. 3; *id.* art. I, § 3, cl. 1; *id.* art II, § 1, cl. 2.

47. *See id.* art II, § 1, cl. 3 (amended 1804).

48. In a similar vein, Derek Muller argues that the ability of states to determine their own elector allocation was an additional important concession—an element of "invisible federalism"—that has had the effect of protecting the stability of American presidential elections. *See* Derek T. Muller, *Invisible Federalism and the Electoral College*, 44 ARIZ. ST. L.J. 1237 (2012).

49. Letter from James Madison to Henry Lee (Jan. 14, 1825), *in* 9 THE WRITINGS OF JAMES MADISON 215, 217 (Gaillard Hunt ed., 1910).

50. Akhil Reed Amar, *The Troubling Reason the Electoral College Exists*, TIME (Nov 8, 2016), http://time.com/4558510/ electoral-college-history-slavery; Sean Illing, *The Real Reason We Have an Electoral College: To Protect Slave States*, VOX (Nov. 12, 2016, 9:30 AM), http://www.vox.com/policy-and-politics/2016/11/12/13598316/donald-trump-electoral-college-slavery-akhil-reed-amar; Mark Joseph Stern, *The Electoral College Is an Instrument of White Supremacy—and Sexism*, SLATE (Nov. 11, 2016, 10:42 AM), http://www.slate.com/ blogs/xx_factor/2016/11/11/the_electoral_college_is_an_ instrument_of_white_supremacy_and_sexism.html.

51. *But see* ANNE FARROW ET AL., COMPLICITY: HOW THE NORTH PROMOTED, PROLONGED, AND PROFITED FROM SLAVERY (2005) (arguing that Northerners were complicit in

the institution of slavery and had just as much motivation to keep it going).

52. First Inaugural Address: Final Version (Apr. 30, 1789), *in* 2 THE PAPERS OF GEORGE WASHINGTON: PRESIDENTIAL SERIES 173, 175 (W.W. Abbot et al. eds., 1987).

53. THE FEDERALIST NO. 39, *supra* note 7, at 236 (James Madison).

54. U.S. CONST. art I, § 2, cl. 3.

55. Elbridge Gerry of Massachusetts, for instance, thought it was inconsistent to count the South's "property" (slaves) for purposes of representation if the North could not also count its property. "The idea of property ought not to be the rule of representation," he told the Convention. "Blacks are property, and are used to the southward as horses and cattle to the northward; and why should their representation be increased to the southward on account of the number of slaves, than horses or oxen to the north?" RECORDS, *supra* note 40, at 205–06; *see also* Erik M. Jensen, *Article I, Section 2, Clause 3: Three-Fifths Clause, in* THE HERITAGE GUIDE TO THE CONSTITUTION 54, 54-55 (David F. Forte & Matthew Spalding eds., 2005) (discussing the compromises made).

56. This point has been made by many, including Dennis Prager. He mentioned it during an interview with this author in November 2016. *See The Dennis Prager Show* (Salem National radio broadcast Nov. 14, 2016), http://www. dennisprager.com/prager-20161114-3-electoral-college.

57. *See* Jensen, *supra* note 55, at 54–55 (discussing the compromises made).

58. MADISON, *supra* note 6, at 327.

59. *See, e.g.,* Amar, *supra* note 50 ("But the Electoral College—a prototype of which Madison proposed in this same speech— instead let each southern state count its slaves, albeit with a

two-fifths discount, in computing its share of the overall count.").

60. Madison, *supra* note 6, at 326.

61. *Id.*

62. *Id.* at 327.

63. Records, *supra* note 40, at 500.

64. The Federalist No. 68, *supra* note 7, at 410 (Alexander Hamilton).

CHAPTER TWO

1. These issues are also discussed in Chapter Three of Tara Ross, Enlightened Democracy: The Case for the Electoral College (Colonial Press 2d ed. 2012) (2004).

2. George Washington announced his retirement in September 1796, shortly before the presidential election. Farewell Address (Sept. 19, 1796), *reprinted in* 35 The Writings of George Washington from the Original Manuscript Sources 1745–1799, at 214, 214–38 (John C. Fitzpatrick ed., 1940). This retirement became effective in March 1797 when John Adams was sworn into office.

3. CQ Press, Presidential Elections: 1789–2008, at 208 (2010).

4. Robert M. Hardaway, The Electoral College and the Constitution: The Case for Preserving Federalism 91 (1994) (discussing the Federalist strategy in 1796); Neal R. Peirce & Lawrence D. Longley, The People's President: The Electoral College in American History and the Direct Vote Alternative 35 (Yale Univ. Press rev. ed. 1981) (1968) (same).

5. Descriptions of the election of 1800 can be found at: David W. Abbott & James P. Levine, Wrong Winner: The Coming Debacle in the Electoral College 13–14

(1991); ROBERT W. BENNETT, TAMING THE ELECTORAL
COLLEGE 22–23 (2006); DAVID P. CURRIE, THE
CONSTITUTION IN CONGRESS: THE FEDERALIST PERIOD,
1789–1801, at 292–93 (1997); THOMAS FLEMING, DUEL:
ALEXANDER HAMILTON, AARON BURR, AND THE FUTURE OF
AMERICA 93–97, 101–02 (1999); HARDAWAY, *supra* note 4, at
91–92; EDWARD J. LARSON, A MAGNIFICENT CATASTROPHE:
THE TUMULTUOUS ELECTION OF 1800, AMERICA'S FIRST
PRESIDENTIAL CAMPAIGN 241–70 (2007); 4 DUMAS
MALONE, JEFFERSON AND HIS TIME: JEFFERSON THE
PRESIDENT; FIRST TERM, 1801–1805, at 3–16 (1970); PEIRCE
& LONGLEY, *supra* note 4, at 36–41.

6. Records of the voting can be found at: 10 ANNALS OF CONG.
1022–30 (1801). The voting ensued from February 11 to
February 17, 1801. The House did not meet on February 15,
which was Sunday. News reports discussing the voting on the
floor are also included in a lengthy footnote in the Annals of
Congress. *See id.* at 1028–33 (citing Feb. 13, 16 and 18 reports
of the *National Intelligencer,* including individual votes cast
by representatives).

7. Letter from Thomas Jefferson to Dr. Benjamin Rush (Jan. 16,
1811), *in* THE LIFE AND SELECTED WRITINGS OF THOMAS
JEFFERSON 607, 610 (Adrienne Koch & William Peden eds.,
1944).

8. A description of these events can be found at MALONE, *supra*
note 5, app. I, at 487.

9. FLEMING, *supra* note 5, at 97 (citation omitted).

10. Donald Lutz et al., *The Electoral College in Historical and
Philosophical Perspective, in* CHOOSING A PRESIDENT: THE
ELECTORAL COLLEGE AND BEYOND 31, 37 (Paul D.
Schumaker & Burdett A. Loomis eds., 2002) (discussing the
negotiations over the 12th Amendment).

11. H.R. Doc. No. 110–50, at 15–16 (2007). Tennessee ratified it later, on July 27, 1804. Three states rejected the amendment. *Id.*

12. U.S. Const. amend. XII. Additional provisions, such as the timing for the Electoral College vote, can be found in Title 3 of the U.S. Code.

13. *See* U.S. Const. art. II, § 1, cl. 3, *amended by* U.S. Const. amend. XII.

14. *See id.* art. II, § 1, cl. 2 & 4; *id.* amend. XII.

15. *Id.* art. II, § 1, cl. 2.

16. *See id.* art. I, § 2, cl. 3; *id.* art. I, § 3, cl. 1.

17. *Id.* amend XXIII, § 1. The District of Columbia is entitled to the same number of electors "to which the District would be entitled if it were a State," but it would never have more than three electoral votes unless the least populous state also had more than three electoral votes. The 23rd Amendment provides that D.C. may have "in no event more than the least populous State." *Id.*

18. *Id.* art. II, § 1, cl. 2.

19. *See* L. Paige Whitaker & Thomas H. Neale, Cong. Research Serv., RL30804, The Electoral College: An Overview and Analysis of Reform Proposals 1–2 (2004). There have been occasional exceptions to the general rule, as detailed at CQ Press, *supra* note 3, at 192.

20. *See, e.g.,* Valerie Richardson, *Group Seeks to Split Colorado Electors,* Wash. Times, June 16, 2004, at A5; George F. Will, *Subverting the Electoral College,* Wash. Post, Oct. 9, 2011, at A25; Jeff Brady, *Pa. May Change Electoral College Allocation Rules,* NPR (Sept. 16, 2011, 3:00 PM), http://www.npr.org/2011/09/16/140543466/pa-may-change-electoral-college-allocation-rules.

21. Me. Rev. Stat. tit. 21-A, § 802 (2009); Neb. Rev. Stat. § 32-1038 (2011).

22. *See, e.g.,* Michael J. Glennon, When No Majority Rules: The Electoral College and Presidential Succession 35–44 (1992) (discussing the "constitutional minefield" that must be navigated when determining where the state's power to select electors ends and where congressional power to count electoral votes begins).

23. The entire slates of electors in South Carolina, Florida, and Louisiana were disputed. One electoral vote was also undecided in Oregon due to a dispute regarding an elector who was deemed ineligible; however, the remainder of the state's vote was decided on Election Day. William H. Rehnquist, Centennial Crisis: The Disputed Election of 1876, at 104–12 (2004).

24. *See id.* at 113–19.

25. Act of Feb. 3, 1887, ch. 90, 24 Stat. 373 (codified at 3 U.S.C. §§ 1–21 (2012)).

26. Some dispute exists regarding the extent of congressional authority in this area. Both the states and Congress have some power, but where do the boundaries of each power lie? The Constitution gives Congress the power to "determine the Time of chusing the Electors, and the Day on which they shall give their Votes." U.S. Const. art. II, § 1, cl. 4. It also gives Congress the authority to "count" the electoral votes. *Id.* amend. XII. The states are explicitly given their own authority as well, to "appoint, in such Manner as the Legislature thereof may direct, a Number of Electors." *Id.* art. II, § 1, cl. 2. For a deeper discussion of this issue, see Vasan Kesavan, *Is the Electoral Count Act Unconstitutional?*, 80 N.C. L. Rev. 1653 (2002); *cf.* Samuel Issacharoff, *Law, Rules, and Presidential Selection*, 120 Pol. Sci. Q. 113, 125 (2005) (questioning

whether one Congress can bind future Congresses to count electoral votes in any particular fashion). One Electoral College opponent states that laws such as the Electoral Count Act should be upheld as "an attempt to bring order to a process that raises serious danger of uncertain and inconsistent outcomes," despite his own admission that the constitutionality of the law is questionable. BENNETT, *supra* note 5, at 148–50, 206 n.57.

27. 3 U.S.C. § 1 (2012).

28. For a listing of state laws on the subject, see NAT'L ASS'N OF SECRETARIES OF STATE, SUMMARY: STATE LAWS REGARDING PRESIDENTIAL ELECTORS (2016); *see also* AFTER THE PEOPLE VOTE: A GUIDE TO THE ELECTORAL COLLEGE 83 app. C (John C. Fortier ed., 3d ed. 2004) (listing the method of nomination in each state).

29. The questions of whether a political party can force a nominee out and how parties would choose a replacement nominee are both beyond the scope of this book.

30. 3 U.S.C. § 6.

31. *Id.* § 7.

32. *Id.* §§ 9–11.

33. *See id.* §§ 12–13.

34. *See id.* § 15.

35. U.S. CONST. amend. XII.

36. There may be some ambiguity if more than three candidates tie for one or more of the top three spots. *See* William Josephson, *Senate Election of the Vice President and House of Representatives Election of the President,* 11 U. PA. J. CONST. L. 597, 630–31, 633–34 (2009).

37. *See id.* at 613 (discussing the considerations if more than two candidates tie for the top spots).

38. A detailed discussion of these logistical issues is beyond the scope of this book, but these questions are discussed at length in *id.*; *see also* HARDAWAY, *supra* note 4, at 55–61.

39. The Constitution makes provision for what constitutes a quorum of states ("a quorum for this purpose shall consist of a member or members from two-thirds of the states"), but it does not address the subject of quorums within state delegations. U.S. CONST. amend. XII; *see also* Josephson, *supra* note 36, at 630, 637–38.

40. The 1825 House Rules are reprinted in Appendix E.

41. For an argument that multiple interpretations can be given to the phrase "a majority of the votes given," see Josephson, *supra* note 36, at 629. Josephson argues that the phrase could mean "the whole number of votes given *to* such state" as opposed to "a majority of those present and voting." *Id.* This author leans toward the latter interpretation, per the examples in the text.

42. U.S. CONST. amend. XII.

43. *But see* Josephson, *supra* note 36, at 602 n.11 ("When the Twelfth Amendment says 'ballot,' it means the identity of each voter is not revealed, i.e., is secret."). Further discussion of the meaning of the "ballot" requirement can be found at HARDAWAY, *supra* note 4, at 58; Josephson, *supra* note 36, at 632.

44. *See, e.g.,* 10 ANNALS OF CONG. 1032–33 (1801) (quoting the *National Intelligencer*); THOMAS H. NEALE, CONG. RESEARCH SERV., R40504, CONTINGENT ELECTION OF THE PRESIDENT AND VICE PRESIDENT BY CONGRESS: PERSPECTIVES AND CONTEMPORARY ANALYSIS 7–8 (2016).

45. U.S. CONST. amend. XX, § 1.

46. 3 U.S.C. § 15 (2012).

47. Hardaway, *supra* note 4, at 56 (discussing House deliberations in 1992).
48. *Cf.* Josephson, *supra* note 36, at 646ff (discussing steps that can be taken, whether by House Rules or by statute, to address unresolved logistical issues with the House contingent election and encouraging discussion of these steps before an immediate need for them arises).

CHAPTER THREE

1. *E.g.*, James P. Pfiffner & Jason Hartke, *The Electoral College and the Framers' Distrust of Democracy*, 3 White House Studies 261, 262 (2003) (citation omitted); *see also* Danny M. Adkison & Christopher Elliott, *The Electoral College: A Misunderstood Institution*, 30 PS: Pol. Sci. & Pol. 77, 77–79 (1997) (discussing errors made in textbooks).
2. These issues are discussed in greater detail in Chapters Five through Seven of Tara Ross, Enlightened Democracy: The Case for the Electoral College (Colonial Press 2d ed. 2012) (2004).
3. 102 Cong. Rec. 5150 (1956) (statement of Senator John F. Kennedy).
4. As an example, passage of the 17th Amendment in 1913 disrupted a careful balance between federal and state governments, and the move had many unintended consequences. Before that amendment was ratified, United States Senators were not elected by popular vote. Instead, state legislatures selected these officials directly, making Senators accountable to state legislators for their votes. In other words, the original constitutional process effectively gave the states themselves, as sovereign entities, a voice in the federal legislative process. They could defend themselves from encroachments upon their power or from unfunded mandates.

Ratification of the 17th Amendment changed all of this. The
Senators no longer care if they create an unfunded state
mandate, leaving state legislators hanging out to dry. They are
much more concerned with satisfying a populist sentiment.
The 17th Amendment, as Senator Zell Miller noted in 2004,
"was the death of the careful balance between State and
Federal Government. . . . Today State governments have to
stand in line because they are just another one of the many
special interests that try to get Senators to listen to them, and
they are at an extreme disadvantage because they have no
PAC." ZELL MILLER, ZELL MILLER: A SENATOR SPEAKS OUT
ON PATRIOTISM, VALUES, *AND* CHARACTER 41 (2005). Now
that the states have one fewer tool with which to defend
themselves against the federal government, perhaps it is
unsurprising that the size and scope of federal government—
to say nothing of federal demands upon the states—have
increased quite a bit in recent decades.

5. *Letters from the Federal Farmer: I* (Oct. 8, 1787), *in* THE
    ANTI-FEDERALIST PAPERS AND THE CONSTITUTIONAL
    CONVENTION DEBATES 257, 264 (Ralph Ketcham ed., Signet
    Classic 2003) (1986) [hereinafter ANTI-FEDERALIST PAPERS].

6. *"Centinel," Number 1* (Oct. 5, 1787), *in* ANTI-FEDERALIST
    PAPERS, *supra* note 5, at 227, 234.

7. *Brutus: I* (Oct. 18, 1787), *in* ANTI-FEDERALIST PAPERS, *supra*
    note 5, at 270, 276.

8. *Id.* at 276–77.

9. Technically, of course, they do not need to win a majority of
    states in order to win the election. (They need a majority of
    electoral votes.) Practically speaking, however, they will need
    to win most states—or close to this majority—in order to
    obtain an electoral majority. Only two Presidents this century

have been elected with less than a majority of states: John F. Kennedy (23 states) and Jimmy Carter (23 states plus D.C.).

10. James MacGregor Burns has described this phenomenon as "the immense widening of the electorate." JAMES MACGREGOR BURNS, THE DEADLOCK OF DEMOCRACY: FOUR-PARTY POLITICS IN AMERICA 251 (1963), *quoted in* JUDITH BEST, THE CASE AGAINST DIRECT ELECTION OF THE PRESIDENT: A DEFENSE OF THE ELECTORAL COLLEGE 66 (1975). Presidential candidates are motivated "to widen and 'flatten out' their vote, [and] to win states by dependable but not wasteful popular majorities." *Id.* The campaigns of presidential candidates stand in sharp contrast to the campaigns of congressional candidates, who are often campaigning in a district that has been specifically drawn to be "safe" for one of the parties. The different campaign strategies required causes many Congressmen (particularly those in safe districts) to be more ideological than the typical Senator or President, who instead tend to be (or must at least appear to be) more moderate. The former are often able to aim their campaigns at individuals who are similar to themselves; the latter must build coalitions, either at the state or national level. *See id.*

11. The elections of Franklin D. Roosevelt and Ronald Reagan are discussed in greater detail in Chapter Seventeen of ROSS, *supra* note 2.

12. *E.g.*, James Pindell, *Will North Carolina Become the New Florida?*, BOS. GLOBE (June 16, 2016), https://www.bostonglobe.com/news/politics/2016/06/16/will-north-carolina-become-new-florida/Ollswvx29EkloAmuAY3hJI/story.html (discussing North Carolina's transformation into a swing state); Scott Horsley & Liz Halloran, *Why New Swing State of Virginia May Determine Presidency*, NPR: SWING

STATE PROJECT (July 13, 2012, 5:02 PM), http://www.npr.org/
sections/itsallpolitics/2012/07/13/156741555/why-new-swing-
state-of-virginia-may-determine-presidency.

13. *See* discussion *infra* notes 1–7 and accompanying text (Ch. 9).

14. Indeed, the George W. Bush campaign spent time in
California in 2000, thinking that it might be able to win the
state after all. KARL ROVE, COURAGE AND CONSEQUENCE:
MY LIFE AS A CONSERVATIVE IN THE FIGHT 164–65 (2010).

15. In this vein, former Federal Election Commission chairman
Bradley Smith points out that battleground states

> form a diverse group indeed . . . . [They include] small
> states and large, east and west, north and south,
> agricultural and industrial, urban and rural, and states
> with large minority populations and states with small
> minority populations. Thus, even on a shrunken
> battleground, it is likely that pandering too strongly to
> parochial concerns will be checked by the need to
> compete in another "battleground" state elsewhere.
> Worse yet, pandering to extreme might antagonize voters
> in other states so as to convert safe states into
> battleground states. Politics is not static.

Bradley A. Smith, *Vanity of Vanities: National Popular Vote
and the Electoral College*, 7 ELECTION L.J. 196, 203–04
(2008).

16. For more on 2016 election results, see discussion *supra* note 16
(Introduction).

17. Churchill said: "Many forms of Government have been tried,
and will be tried in this world of sin and woe. No one pretends
that democracy is perfect or all-wise. Indeed it has been said
that democracy is the worst form of Government except for all
those other forms that have been tried from time to time."

CHURCHILL BY HIMSELF: THE DEFINITIVE COLLECTION OF
QUOTATIONS 573 (Richard M. Langworth ed., 2008).

18. CQ PRESS, PRESIDENTIAL ELECTIONS: 1789–2008, at 161,
251 (2010).

19. *See* discussion *infra* notes 32–37 (Ch. 9) and accompanying
text.

20. For more information on the 1836 election, see MAJOR L.
WILSON, THE PRESIDENCY OF MARTIN VAN BUREN 14–20
(1984); *see also* PAUL F. BOLLER, JR., PRESIDENTIAL
CAMPAIGNS 60–64 (rev. ed. 1996).

21. *See* Norman R. Williams, *Reforming the Electoral College:
Federalism, Majoritarianism, and the Perils of
Subconstitutional Change*, 100 GEO. L.J. 173, 204 (2011)
(discussing the 2002 elections in France). Election totals can
be found at Office for Democratic Institutions and Human
Rights, *Republic of France Presidential Elections, 21 April
and 5 May 2002*, ORG. FOR SECURITY & CO-OPERATION
EUR. (Apr. 21, 2002), http://www.osce.org/odihr/elections/
france/16167?download=true.

22. *See Who's Running for French President*, ASSOCIATED PRESS,
Apr. 20, 2012.

23. Honor Mahony, *France: Hollande Leads, Le Pen Shocks in
Third Place*, EUOBSERVER (Apr. 22, 2012), http://euobserver.
com/843/115976; Greg Keller, *Hollande Enjoys Upper Hand
in French Elections*, ASSOCIATED PRESS (Apr. 23, 2012),
http://news.yahoo.com/hollande-enjoys-upper-hand-french-
elections-103239471.html.

24. Analysis after the election showed that, nationwide, Perot
votes broke fairly equally between Clinton and Bush.
However, the Center for Voting and Democracy reports that
the Perot vote did not split equally in each state. To the
contrary, Perot's candidacy seems to have worked to Bush's

disadvantage in several states that Bush won in 1988 and might otherwise have been expected to win in 1992. *See* Ctr. for Voting & Democracy, *Plurality Wins in the 1992 Presidential Race: Perot's Contribution to Clinton's Victory*, FairVote, http://archive.fairvote.org/plurality/perot.htm (last updated Dec. 10, 2009).

25. CQ Press, *supra* note 18, at 167.
26. Omnibus Budget Reconciliation Act of 1993, Pub. L. No. 103–66, 107 Stat. 312.
27. A copy of the contract can be found at *Republican Contract with America*, McClatchy: D.C. Bureau, http://media.mcclatchydc.com/static/pdf/1994-contract-with-america.pdf (last visited Mar. 8, 2017).
28. For more information on the 1912 election, see Boller, *supra* note 20, at 191–201; James Chace, 1912: Wilson, Roosevelt, Taft and Debs—The Election that Changed the Country (2004); Lewis L. Gould, Four Hats in the Ring: The 1912 Election and the Birth of Modern American Politics (2008); George E. Mowry, *Election of 1912, in* 2 History of American Presidential Elections: 1789–2008, at 877 (Gil Troy et al. eds., 4th ed. 2012).
29. The official name of the party was the Progressive Party.
30. Speech at the Auditorium in Chicago, Illinois (June 17, 1912), *in* 17 The Works of Theodore Roosevelt: Social Justice and Popular Rule 204, 206 (Hermann Hagedorn ed., Charles Scribner's Sons 1926); Edmund Morris, Colonel Roosevelt 197 (2010).
31. David S. Brown, Moderates: The Vital Center of American Politics, from the Founding to Today 169 (2016); *see also* Gould, *supra* note 28, at 21 (discussing Taft's

hesitancy to step down and let Roosevelt run unopposed for President).

32. "[F]or Republicans who supported Taft," historian Lewis Gould writes, "the electoral defeat was worth the ideological victory." Lewis L. Gould, *1912 Republican Convention: Return of the Rough Rider*, SMITHSONIAN MAG. (Aug. 2008), http://www.smithsonianmag.com/history/1912-republican-convention-855607.

33. Letter from Benjamin Franklin to Jean-Baptiste Le Roy (Nov. 13, 1789), *in* 10 THE WRITINGS OF BENJAMIN FRANKLIN 68, 69 (Albert Henry Smyth ed., 1907).

34. *Cf.* BEST, *supra* note 10, at 191–204 (noting the ability of the Electoral College to isolate incidents of fraud); *see also* ROBERT M. HARDAWAY, THE ELECTORAL COLLEGE AND THE CONSTITUTION: THE CASE FOR PRESERVING FEDERALISM 25–28 (1994) (discussing the 1960 election and the uncertainty that could have resulted from the close count and the alleged fraud).

35. A discussion of the 1876 election can be found at WILLIAM H. REHNQUIST, CENTENNIAL CRISIS: THE DISPUTED ELECTION OF 1876 (2004); *see also* BOLLER, *supra* note 20, at 133–41; MICHAEL J. GLENNON, WHEN NO MAJORITY RULES: THE ELECTORAL COLLEGE AND PRESIDENTIAL SUCCESSION 16–17 (1992); HARDAWAY, *supra* note 34, at 128–37.

36. The margin between the two men nationally was 537,179. *See* CQ PRESS, *supra* note 18, at 169. That seems like a big number, and some might argue that the margin wasn't so close as to trigger a national recount under a direct popular vote system. It's a dangerous assumption to make. As Former FEC Commissioner Brad Smith notes, the margin between the two men was only half a percentage point, close enough to trigger a mandatory recount under some state statutes and to allow

an optional recount under others. Smith, *supra* note 15, at
207. Moreover, it's important to remember that the tallies in a
few other states, such as New Mexico and Oregon, were
questioned in 2000. Many of those questions were never
seriously pursued. After all, a changed outcome in those states
would not have changed the outcome of the national election.
If there had been a national popular vote system in place,
perhaps some of those questions would have been pursued
further. The Electoral College served the country in 2000 by
isolating electoral problems to the state of Florida.

37.   Richard Reeves, Op-ed, *There's Always the Option of Giving
      In*, N.Y. TIMES, Nov. 10, 2000, at A33.

38.   RICHARD NIXON, RN: THE MEMOIRS OF RICHARD NIXON
      224 (1978).

39.   *See* CQ PRESS, *supra* note 18, at 159.

40.   Donald J. Trump (@realDonaldTrump), TWITTER (Oct. 16,
      2016, 12:01 PM), https://twitter.com/realdonaldtrump/
      status/787699930718695425.

41.   *See, e.g.*, Trent England & Tara Ross, *No, the Election Wasn't
      Rigged*, DAILY CALLER (Nov. 10, 2016, 1:09 PM), http://
      dailycaller.com/2016/11/10/no-the-election-wasnt-rigged.

42.   U.S. CONST. art II, § 1, cl. 2.

43.   THE FEDERALIST No. 68, at 411 (Alexander Hamilton)
      (Clinton Rossiter ed., Signet Classic 2003) (1961).

44.   *Id.*

45.   MAX FARRAND, THE FRAMING OF THE CONSTITUTION OF
      THE UNITED STATES 175 (7th prtg. 1930).

CHAPTER FOUR

1.   Scott Clement, *One-Third of Clinton Supporters Say Trump
      Election is not Legitimate, Poll Finds*, WASH. POST: THE FIX
      (Nov. 13, 2016), https://www.washingtonpost.com/news/the-

fix/wp/2016/11/13/one-third-of-clinton-supporters-say-trump-election-is-not-legitimate-poll-finds.

2.   Donald J. Trump (@realDonaldTrump), TWITTER (Nov. 27, 2016, 2:30 PM), https://twitter.com/realdonaldtrump/status/802972944532209664.

3.   A large percentage of Republicans (52 percent) believed that Trump won the popular vote, according to one poll. Eric Oliver & Thomas Wood, *A New Poll Shows 52% of Republicans Actually Think Trump Won the Popular Vote*, WASH. POST: MONKEY CAGE (Dec. 18, 2016), https://www.washingtonpost.com/news/monkey-cage/wp/2016/12/18/a-new-poll-shows-an-astonishing-52-of-republicans-think-trump-won-the-popular-vote.

4.   Senator Barbara Boxer, Speech on Senate Floor, YOUTUBE (Nov. 29, 2016), https://www.youtube.com/watch?v=_kqBvcOBgGs&feature=youtu.be. The quote appears at the 0:29 mark.

5.   *Id.* The quote appears at the 8:31 mark.

6.   As for Gore himself, perhaps he couldn't speak out against the Electoral College in 2000, but he wasn't quite so restrained after Clinton's loss in 2016. "Our democracy has been hacked now," he said. "It's pathetic how our system is not working today. And I think that moving to a popular vote for President would be one of the initiatives . . . that could bring our democracy back to life." NBC News, *Al Gore Says He Supports Elimination of Electoral College*, YOUTUBE (Nov. 29, 2016), https://www.youtube.com/watch?v=XUSQXlH4kXo.

7.   Susan Milligan, *The Electoral College: Move Is Afoot for Direct Vote*, BOS. GLOBE, Nov. 12, 2000, at A21. House Democratic Leader Richard Gephardt concurred, "[W]hoever wins the vote should be the next President of the United

States." Carolina Gonzalez, *Electoral College's Time Is Past*, DAILY NEWS (New York), Nov. 13, 2000, at 22.

8. *See, e.g.*, David French, *Hillary's Popular-Vote Win Is (Mostly) Meaningless*, NAT'L REV. (Nov. 14, 2016, 2:37 PM), http://www.nationalreview.com/article/442170/hillary-clintons-popular-vote-victory-meaningless ("My more pressing concern is the absurd notion that Hillary is more legitimate because she won a game that *neither candidate was playing*.").

9. Michael Herz, *How the Electoral College Imitates the World Series*, 23 CARDOZO L. REV. 1191, 1196 (2002) (quoting Albert R. Hunt, *The Electoral College: Legitimate but Anachronistic*, WALL STREET J., Oct. 26, 2000, at A27).

10. Al Gioia, *Our Town Goes Wild Over Pirate Victory: Crowds Yell, Firecrackers Boom, Air Raid Sirens Shriek, Confetti Rains, Church Bells Ring*, PITTSBURGH POST-GAZETTE, Oct. 13, 2010, at P-3 (reprinting the original 1960 news report on the 50th anniversary of the victory).

11. RICK CUSHING, 1960 PITTSBURGH PIRATES: DAY BY DAY: A SPECIAL SEASON, AN EXTRAORDINARY WORLD SERIES 1 (2010).

12. *See, e.g.*, Herz, *supra* note 9, at 1191 (making a similar point about the objective of baseball's rules); *see also* Samuel Issacharoff, *Law, Rules, and Presidential Selection*, 120 POL. SCI. Q. 113, 113–14 (2005). These issues are discussed in greater detail in Chapter Ten of TARA ROSS, ENLIGHTENED DEMOCRACY: THE CASE FOR THE ELECTORAL COLLEGE (Colonial Press 2d ed. 2012) (2004).

13. *Cf.* Issacharoff, *supra* note 12, at 126 ("[I]t is essential that the rules of presidential selection be, insofar as possible, fixed *ex ante*, and that they have the respect of all relevant actors.").

14. Joy McAfee, Comment, *2001: Should the College Electors Finally Graduate?: The Electoral College: An American*

Compromise From Its Inception to Election 2000, 32 CUMB.
L. REV. 643, 662 (2001).

15. *Id.*

16. *See, e.g.,* JUDITH BEST, THE CASE AGAINST DIRECT ELECTION
OF THE PRESIDENT: A DEFENSE OF THE ELECTORAL COLLEGE
46 (1975) ("[M]any critics seem to believe that the objection to
a minority President need only be stated, not argued."); *see
also* ROBERT M. HARDAWAY, THE ELECTORAL COLLEGE AND
THE CONSTITUTION: THE CASE FOR PRESERVING FEDERALISM
13 (1994) ("[Such claims] raise the perfectly legitimate
question of what is a 'majority.' More precisely, one may ask, a
majority of what?").

17. Uncommon Knowledge with Peter Robinson, *The Promise of
Party in a Polarized Age: Interview with Russell Muirhead*,
HOOVER INSTITUTION (Dec. 2, 2016), http://www.hoover.org/
research/promise-party-polarized-age. Such majorities are not
perfect, Muirhead acknowledges, but nothing is in this
imperfect world. *Id.* ("Now, you could get an unjust and a
stupid Constitutional majority, or an erroneous Constitutional
majority, it's happened . . . . Ultimately, without a virtuous
citizenry, you're not going to get good government.").

18. *Id.*

CHAPTER FIVE

1. JOHN R. KOZA ET AL., EVERY VOTE EQUAL: A STATE-BASED
PLAN FOR ELECTING THE PRESIDENT BY NATIONAL POPULAR
VOTE xxx, xxxi (4th ed. 2013).

2. *Id.* at 47, 53.

3. Others have reached similar conclusions about the elections of
1824 and 1876. *E.g.,* JUDITH BEST, THE CASE AGAINST
DIRECT ELECTION OF THE PRESIDENT: A DEFENSE OF THE
ELECTORAL COLLEGE 24–25, 52–54 (1975); *see also* ROBERT

M. Hardaway, The Electoral College and the
Constitution: The Case for Preserving Federalism 4
(1994); Denny Pilant, *NO—The Electoral College Should Not
be Abolished, in* Controversial Issues in Presidential
Selection 216, 219–20 (Gary L. Rose ed., 1991); Grant M.
Dixton, *Book Review: The Electoral College Primer,* 34
Harv. J. on Legis. 293, 298 (1997); Arthur Schlesinger, Jr.,
It's a Mess, But We've Been Through It Before, Time, Nov.
20, 2000, at 64, 65. This author has discussed this issue
before as well. *See, e.g.,* Tara Ross, Enlightened
Democracy: The Case for the Electoral College 192–
93 (Colonial Press 2d ed. 2012) (2004). Others include these
elections as ones in which the will of the people was
"frustrated." *E.g.,* Neal R. Peirce & Lawrence D.
Longley, The People's President: The Electoral
College in American History and the Direct Vote
Alternative 5 (Yale Univ. Press rev. ed. 1981) (1968); *see
also* Akhil Reed Amar, *Presidents Without Mandates (With
Special Emphasis on Ohio),* 67 U. Cin. L. Rev. 375, 391
(1999) (referring to Hayes, along with Harrison, as a "clear
popular loser"); Abner J. Mikva, *Doubting Our Claims to
Democracy,* 39 Ariz. L. Rev. 793, 799 (1997) (discussing the
1876 election). Electoral College opponent George Edwards
concedes that the election of 1824 isn't fairly included on the
list of instances in which a popular vote loser won the White
House. In describing the election, he says that "something
approximating a popular vote for president" occurred and
recognizes that "we must be cautious about interpreting the
vote count as an accurate indicator of public opinion."
George C. Edwards III, Why the Electoral College Is
Bad for America 78 (2d ed. 2011) (internal reference
omitted).

4. This author has previously told a few of these stories in her daily history blog. For Andrew Jackson's inauguration and other, similar stories, see TARA ROSS, http://www.taraross.com (last visited Mar. 21, 2017).

5. More information on Andrew Jackson's inauguration can be found at PAUL F. BOLLER, JR., PRESIDENTIAL ANECDOTES 66–67 (rev. ed. 1996); H.W. BRANDS, ANDREW JACKSON: HIS LIFE AND TIMES 407–13 (2005); JON MEACHAM, AMERICAN LION: ANDREW JACKSON IN THE WHITE HOUSE 57–62 (2008); LYNN HUDSON PARSONS, THE BIRTH OF MODERN POLITICS: ANDREW JACKSON, JOHN QUINCY ADAMS, AND THE ELECTION OF 1828, at xi–xv (2009).

6. Letter to Mrs. Kirkpatrick (Mar. 11, 1829), *in* THE FIRST FORTY YEARS OF WASHINGTON SOCIETY: PORTRAYED BY THE FAMILY LETTERS OF MRS. SAMUEL HARRISON SMITH (MARGARET BAYARD) FROM THE COLLECTION OF HER GRANDSON, J. HENLEY SMITH 290, 290–91 (Gaillard Hunt ed., 1906); *see also* MEACHAM, *supra* note 5, at 58–59.

7. Letter to Mrs. Kirkpatrick, *supra* note 6, at 294.

8. *Id*. at 296.

9. *See* CQ PRESS, PRESIDENTIAL ELECTIONS: 1789–2008, at 125, 215 (2010).

10. Letter from Henry Clay to Francis Preston Blair (Jan. 8, 1825), *in* 4 THE PAPERS OF HENRY CLAY 9, 9 (James F. Hopkins et al. eds., 1972); *see also* BRANDS, *supra* note 5, at 387.

11. Jackson certainly thought so! "So you see, the *Judas* of the West has closed the contract and will receive the thirty pieces of silver," he fumed at the time. "his end will be the same. Was there ever witnessed such a bare faced corruption in any country before?" ROBERT V. REMINI, HENRY CLAY: STATESMAN FOR THE UNION 268 (1991).

12. PAUL JOHNSON, A HISTORY OF THE AMERICAN PEOPLE 331
    (HarperCollins Publishers 1st U.S. ed. 1998) (1997) (citation
    omitted).

13. *Id.* at 332.

14. *See supra* note 3; *see also* Bradley A. Smith, *Vanity of
    Vanities: National Popular Vote and the Electoral College,* 7
    ELECTION L.J. 196, 212 n.109 (2008) ("One quarter of the
    states, representing over one quarter of the population, did not
    vote for president.").

15. Moreover, some states did not include all four candidates on
    their ballots. PAUL F. BOLLER, JR., PRESIDENTIAL CAMPAIGNS
    36 (rev. ed. 1996).

16. *See, e.g.,* Smith, *supra* note 14, at 212 n.109 (discussing where
    the candidates' support was localized in 1824).

17. A discussion of the 1876 election can be found at WILLIAM H.
    REHNQUIST, CENTENNIAL CRISIS: THE DISPUTED ELECTION
    OF 1876 (2004); *see also* BOLLER, PRESIDENTIAL CAMPAIGNS,
    supra note 15, at 133–41; MICHAEL J. GLENNON, WHEN NO
    MAJORITY RULES: THE ELECTORAL COLLEGE AND
    PRESIDENTIAL SUCCESSION 16–17 (1992); HARDAWAY, *supra*
    note 3, at 128–37.

18. The entire slates of electors in South Carolina, Florida, and
    Louisiana were disputed. One electoral vote was also
    undecided in Oregon due to a dispute regarding an elector
    who was deemed ineligible; however, the remainder of the
    state's vote was decided on Election Day. REHNQUIST, *supra*
    note 17, at 104–12.

19. *See id.* at 176–79 (discussing the filibusters); *see also*
    HARDAWAY, *supra* note 3, at 134–35 (same).

20. REHNQUIST, *supra* note 17, at 178–79.

21. PAUL LELAND HAWORTH, THE HAYES-TILDEN DISPUTED
    PRESIDENTIAL ELECTION OF 1876, at 340–41 (1906), *cited by*

BEST, *supra* note 3, at 53; *see also* Smith, *supra* note 14, at 213; Norman R. Williams, *Reforming the Electoral College: Federalism, Majoritarianism, and the Perils of Subconstitutional Change*, 100 GEO. L.J. 173, 201 (2011).

22. KOZA, *supra* note 1, at 11, 47.

23. The election of 1916 between Charles Evans Hughes and Woodrow Wilson is often cited as one example of an election nearly gone awry. Hughes would have won if about 2,000 more votes in California had gone his way. Had he gained these extra votes, a Hughes victory would have occurred despite the fact that Wilson led in the popular vote by more than 500,000 votes. In 1948, Thomas Dewey could have won the election with a shift of less than 30,000 votes across three states, despite the fact that Harry Truman received 2.1 million more votes than Dewey nationwide. Jimmy Carter would have been denied victory in 1976 if Gerald Ford had obtained just 9,300 more votes in two states, although Carter received nearly 1.7 million more votes overall. *See* PEIRCE & LONGLEY, *supra* note 3, at 59, 62, 84; *see also* DAVID W. ABBOTT & JAMES P. LEVINE, WRONG WINNER: THE COMING DEBACLE IN THE ELECTORAL COLLEGE 52–53 (1991) (stating that shifts in California and Ohio would have prevented either Truman or Dewey from gaining an electoral majority, thus throwing the election into the House contingent election); EDWARDS, *supra* note 3, at 72.

24. BEST, *supra* note 3, at 79 ("The shift-in-votes argument fails . . . because it abstracts from political realities and because in many cases it ignores the election laws.").

25. *Id.* at 72–74.

26. Or perhaps he had good ideas that would have served the country well, but he communicated them in a way that failed to gain the trust of voters in many parts of the country.

27. RICHARD NIXON, RN: THE MEMOIRS OF RICHARD NIXON 223 (1978).
28. *See* CQ PRESS, *supra* note 9, at 159.
29. EDWARDS, *supra* note 3, at 67.

CHAPTER SIX

1. Letter from R. C. Drum, Adjutant-General, to Hon. William C. Endicott, Secretary of War (Apr. 30, 1887), *in* NATIONAL DEMOCRATIC COMMITTEE, THE CAMPAIGN TEXT BOOK OF THE DEMOCRATIC PARTY OF THE UNITED STATES, FOR THE PRESIDENTIAL ELECTION OF 1888, at 266, 266 (1888).
2. *Id.*
3. *Id.*
4. *Id.*
5. ALYN BRODSKY, GROVER CLEVELAND: A STUDY IN CHARACTER 190 (2000).
6. *Id.* at 191.
7. *The Captured Flags: General Boynton Asked to Institute Injunction Proceedings*, EVENING TRUTH (Richmond), June 16, 1887, at 1.
8. BRODSKY, *supra* note 5, at 191; HENRY F. GRAFF, GROVER CLEVELAND 84 (American Presidents Series, Arthur M. Schlesinger, Jr. ed., 2002).
9. Letter from Grover Cleveland to the Secretary of War (June 16, 1887), *in* NATIONAL DEMOCRATIC COMMITTEE, *supra* note 1, at 267, 267.
10. *Id.*
11. Cleveland's troubles during 1888 are also discussed in Chapter Sixteen of TARA ROSS, ENLIGHTENED DEMOCRACY: THE CASE FOR THE ELECTORAL COLLEGE (Colonial Press 2d ed. 2012) (2004).

12. Franklin Delano Roosevelt issued more total vetoes, but he
     also served the longest of any President: more than three terms
     in office. A list of presidential vetoes can be found at
     Summary of Bills Vetoed, 1789–present, U.S. Senate, http://
     www.senate.gov/reference/Legislation/Vetoes/vetoCounts.htm
     (last visited Mar. 10, 2017).

13. Horace Samuel Merrill, Bourbon Leader: Grover
     Cleveland and the Democratic Party 107 (1957).

14. *Id.* at 108.

15. Dorothy Burne Goebel & Julius Goebel, Jr., Generals
     in the White House 250 (1945).

16. *See, e.g.*, Homer E. Socolofsky & Allan B. Spetter, The
     Presidency of Benjamin Harrison 12 (1987).

17. For example, Cleveland's campaign even failed to adequately
     highlight instances in which Cleveland had acted against
     southern interests, such as when he vetoed a bill for the
     financial relief of farmers in Texas. He made his decision for
     constitutional reasons: "I can find no warrant for such an
     appropriation in the Constitution, and I do not believe that the
     power and duty of the General Government ought to be
     extended to the relief of individual suffering which is in no
     manner properly related to the public service or benefit. A
     prevalent tendency to disregard the limited mission of this
     power and duty should, I think, be steadfastly resisted, to the
     end that the lesson should be constantly enforced that though
     the people support the Government the Government should
     not support the people." Grover Cleveland, *Veto Message:
     February 16, 1887*, Am. Presidency Project, http://www.
     presidency.ucsb.edu/ws/?pid=71489 (last visited Mar. 10,
     2017).

18. *See* CQ Press, Presidential Elections: 1789–2008, at 141
     (2010). The six states were Alabama, Georgia, Louisiana,

Mississippi, South Carolina, and Texas. In these six states, Cleveland won 690,404 votes to Harrison's 266,158. *See id.*

19. JAMES MANN, GEORGE W. BUSH 39 (American Presidents Series, Arthur M. Schlesinger, Jr. & Sean Wilentz eds., 2015); JEFFREY TOOBIN, TOO CLOSE TO CALL: THE THIRTY-SIX-DAY BATTLE TO DECIDE THE 2000 ELECTION 25 (2001).

20. TOOBIN, *supra* note 19, at 25.

21. A timeline for the evening's events can be found in various sources, including TOOBIN, *supra* note 19, at 16–25; *2000 Events Timeline–Post-Election*, DAVE LEIP'S ATLAS OF U.S. PRESIDENTIAL ELECTIONS, http://uselectionatlas.org/ INFORMATION/ARTICLES/pe2000timeline.php (last visited Mar. 10, 2017).

22. TOOBIN, *supra* note 19, at 18.

23. *See, e.g.*, Matthew Cooper, *College Bound?*, TIME, Nov. 20, 2000, at 42, 42–43 (summarizing the election results as of November 11, 2000).

24. *See* Bush v. Gore, 531 U.S. 98 (2000) (per curiam). The Court's final ruling essentially stopped the Florida Supreme Court from ordering hand recounts in addition to the mechanized recounts that had already been completed. In doing so, it brought a halt to the legal contest in Florida.

25. *See* CQ PRESS, *supra* note 18, at 169.

26. The dynamics behind Bush's victory in 2000 are also discussed in Chapter Sixteen of ROSS, *supra* note 11.

27. *Cf.* JAMES W. CEASER & ANDREW E. BUSCH, THE PERFECT TIE: THE TRUE STORY OF THE 2000 PRESIDENTIAL ELECTION 28 tbl.1.2 (2001) [hereinafter PERFECT TIE] (reporting on exit polls and the national mood).

28. *See* ELECTING THE PRESIDENT, 2000: THE INSIDERS' VIEW 212 (Kathleen Hall Jamieson & Paul Waldman eds., 2001) (quoting Karl Rove) [hereinafter ELECTING THE PRESIDENT].

29. *See, e.g.*, PERFECT TIE, *supra* note 27, at 28–29 (discussing Bush's strategy for competing with Gore on economic issues).

30. *Id.* at 29–31 (discussing the importance of values during the campaign); *see also* DAVID FRUM, THE RIGHT MAN: THE SURPRISE PRESIDENCY OF GEORGE W. BUSH 7–9 (2003) (same).

31. *See* Henry C. Kenski et al., *Explaining the Vote in a Divided Country: The Presidential Election of 2000, in* THE 2000 PRESIDENTIAL CAMPAIGN: A COMMUNICATION PERSPECTIVE 225, 229–30 (Robert E. Denton, Jr. ed., 2002).

32. George W. Bush, Address Accepting the Presidential Nomination at the Republican National Convention in Philadelphia (Aug. 3, 2000), http://www.presidency.ucsb.edu/ws/?pid=25954.

33. PERFECT TIE, *supra* note 27, at 30.

34. John F. Harris, *Scrambling on "Friendly" Turf: In Full Roar, Gore Tries To Rally Tennessee Again*, WASH. POST, Oct. 26, 2000, at A1, *quoted in* Kenski et al., *supra* note 31, at 260.

35. Polls showed that 57 percent of voters believed the country to be on the wrong moral track. Of these people, 62 percent voted for Bush. PERFECT TIE, *supra* note 27, at 28 tbl.1.2. An additional indicator of the importance placed upon moral issues during the 2000 election is the breakdown of the vote according to religious practice. Of those attending religious services more than weekly, 63 percent voted for Bush. The situation was reversed for those who did not attend religious services: 61 percent voted for Gore. *Us Versus Us*, ECONOMIST (Nov. 6, 2003), http://www.economist.com/node/2172019. Additionally, 44 percent of voters thought the Clinton scandals were an important issue in the 2000 election. Of those who rated the scandals "very important," most voted for Bush. *E.g.*, David S. Broder, *One Nation, Divisible:*

Despite Peace, Prosperity, Voters Agree to Disagree, WASH. POST, Nov. 8, 2000, at A1. Moreover, questions about other moral issues, such as stem cell research and abortion, also pulled at the electorate. In the same vein, some people remained concerned about judicial nominations, perceiving that activist judges were leading the nation astray morally. In response, Bush promised to appoint judges who would "strictly interpret the Constitution and not use the bench for writing social policy." Presidential Debate in Boston, AM. PRESIDENCY PROJECT (Oct. 3, 2000), http://www.presidency. ucsb.edu/ws/?pid=29418. Gore instead argued that "[i]t would be likely that [his judges] would uphold *Roe v. Wade*." *Id.*

36. Carter Eskew, *The Lessons of 2000*, WASH. POST, Jan. 30, 2001, at A17, *quoted in* Kenski et al., *supra* note 31, at 257.

37. ELECTING THE PRESIDENT, *supra* note 28, at 203–04 (quoting Karl Rove).

38. *Id.*

39. *Id.*

40. *See* Kenski et al., *supra* note 31, at 229.

41. Greg Pierce, *Inside Politics: County By County*, WASH. TIMES, Nov. 15, 2000, at 7.

42. *Id.*

43. *Id.*

44. David Jackson, *Trump Seeks Republican Unity, but GOP Critics Remain*, USA TODAY (July 7, 2016, 9:12 AM), http:// www.usatoday.com/story/news/politics/elections/2016/07/07/ donald-trump-house-senate-republicans/86793560.

45. *See, e.g.*, Donald J. Trump (@realDonaldTrump), TWITTER (May 29, 2016, 5:53 PM), https://twitter.com/ realDonaldTrump/status/737054226833149952; Donald J. Trump (@realDonaldTrump), TWITTER (May 9, 2016, 7:15 AM), https://twitter.com/realDonaldTrump/

status/729645861089775616; Donald J. Trump
(@realDonaldTrump), Twitter (June 26, 2016, 6:24 AM),
https://twitter.com/realDonaldTrump/
status/747027629652443136; Donald J. Trump
(@realDonaldTrump), Twitter (May 29, 2016, 6:02 PM),
https://twitter.com/realDonaldTrump/
status/737056428452630528; Donald J. Trump
(@realDonaldTrump), Twitter (May 22, 2016, 9:47 AM),
https://twitter.com/realDonaldTrump/
status/734395329588670465.

46. Donald J. Trump (@realDonaldTrump), Twitter (May 25,
2016, 8:39 AM), https://twitter.com/realDonaldTrump/
status/735465352436408320.

47. Michael Finnegan & Noah Bierman, *Conflict Fuels Rallies
for Trump*, L.A. Times, Mar. 14, 2016, at A1; David Jackson,
*Trump-Cruz Battle Will Shape the Race for GOP
Nomination*, Cin. Enquirer, Feb. 2, 2016, at B1.

48. *E.g.*, Ruth Marcus, *The Igniter of Campaign Violence*, Wash.
Post, Mar. 13, 2016, at A23.

49. Maggie Haberman, *Trump Says His Mocking of Reporter
Was Misread*, N.Y. Times, Nov. 27, 2015, at A25.

50. He didn't actually say the word, but he mouthed it. Calvin
Woodward & Josh Boak, *AP Fact Check: Trump Objects to
Cursing*, Associated Press: U.S. Elections (Feb. 25, 2016,
11:59 PM), http://elections.ap.org/lakeway/content/ap-fact-
check-trump-objects-cursing.

51. *Cf.* Katherine J. Cramer, The Politics of Resentment:
Rural Consciousness in Wisconsin and the Rise of
Scott Walker (2016).

52. Brendan O'Neill, *Trump! How Did This Happen?*,
Spectator: Coffee House (Jan. 20, 2017, 3:33 PM), http://
blogs.spectator.co.uk/2017/01/trump-how-did-this-happen.

53. Mike Rowe (@TheRealMikeRowe), Facebook (Nov. 10, 2016, 3:00 PM), http://www.facebook.com/ TheRealMikeRowe/posts/1330853343591472:0.

54. Dan Merica & Sophie Tatum, *Clinton Expresses Regret for Saying 'Half' of Trump Supporters are 'Deplorables,'* CNN: Politics (Sept. 12, 2016, 7:51 AM), http://www.cnn.com/2016/09/09/politics/hillary-clinton-donald-trump-basket-of-deplorables.

55. Diane Hessan, *Understanding the Undecided Voters*, Bos. Globe (Nov. 21, 2016), https://www.bostonglobe.com/opinion/2016/11/21/understanding-undecided-voters/9EjNHVkt99b4re2VAB8ziI/story.html.

56. Michael Reeb, *I'm a Lifelong Democrat. Here Are 3 Reasons I Pulled the Lever for Trump*, Heritage Found.: Daily Signal (Jan. 3, 2017), http://dailysignal.com/2017/01/03/im-a-lifelong-democrat-here-are-3-reasons-i-pulled-the-lever-for-trump.

57. *Id.*

58. *Id.*

59. Matthew Boyle, *Meet the 'Trumpocrats': Lifelong Democrats Breaking with Party Over Hillary Clinton to Support Donald Trump for President*, Breitbart (Aug. 23, 2016), http://www.breitbart.com/2016-presidential-race/2016/08/23/meet-trumpocrats-lifelong-democrats-breaking-party-hillary-clinton-support-donald-trump-president.

60. A portion of this vote was also driven by the knowledge that a Supreme Court seat was at stake. Twenty-one percent of voters felt that the Supreme Court appointment was the single most important factor in their vote. Of these, 56 percent voted for Trump. This subset of voters was tired of liberal judges who kept replacing the people's policies with their own. Judges who dictate policy are, after all, just another expression of

elitism—another way of telling voters that they don't know enough to vote for their own policies. *Exit Polls*, CNN: POLITICS (Nov. 23, 2016, 11:58 AM), http://www.cnn.com/ election/results/exit-polls.

61. *Id.*

62. Lee Simmons, *What Does Donald Trump Mean for Our Two-Party Political System?*, STAN. GRADUATE SCH. OF BUS.: INSIGHTS (Mar. 17, 2017), https://www.gsb.stanford.edu/ insights/what-does-donald-trump-mean-two-party-political-system.

63. *See* Donald J. Trump (@realDonaldTrump), TWITTER (Oct. 18, 2016, 10:33 AM), https://twitter.com/realDonaldTrump/ status/788402585816276992.

64. For more on 2016 election results, see discussion *supra* note 16 (Introduction).

65. Edward-Isaac Dovere, *How Clinton Lost Michigan—and Blew the Election*, POLITICO (Dec. 14, 2016, 5:08 AM), http:// www.politico.com/story/2016/12/michigan-hillary-clinton-trump-232547.

66. Carl Campanile, *Bill Blames FBI, Russia*, N.Y. POST, Dec. 20, 2016, at 11.

67. *See, e.g.*, Deroy Murdock, *Beyond 'Angry White Men,'* NAT'L REV. (Dec. 30, 2016, 4:00 AM), http://www.nationalreview. com/article/443415/angry-white-men-trump; *see also* Susan A. MacManus, *Voter Participation and Turnout: The Political Generational Divide Among Women Voters*, *in* GENDER AND ELECTIONS: SHAPING THE FUTURE OF AMERICAN POLITICS 80, 82 (Susan J. Carroll & Richard L. Fox eds., 3d ed. 2014) (reporting numbers for the Obama-Romney race).

68. Donald J. Trump (@realDonaldTrump), TWITTER (Nov. 27, 2016, 2:30 PM), https://twitter.com/realDonaldTrump/ status/802972944532209664.

69. Lydia Saad, *Trump and Clinton Finish with Historically Poor Images*, GALLUP (Nov. 8, 2016), http://www.gallup.com/poll/197231/trump-clinton-finish-historically-poor-images.aspx [hereinafter *Trump and Clinton Finish*].

70. Lydia Saad, *Trump Leads Clinton in Historically Bad Image Ratings*, GALLUP (July 1, 2016), http://www.gallup.com/poll/193376/trump-leads-clinton-historically-bad-image-ratings.aspx.

71. *Trump and Clinton Finish, supra* note 69.

72. It's worth noting that this number is probably too low. States have rules governing when they will or won't count write-in candidates. Based on social media commentary in the weeks leading up to the election, it doesn't seem like too much of a stretch to conclude that many people wrote in votes for someone who was not a registered write-in candidate, thus ensuring that their votes were thrown away without ever being counted in an official vote total.

CHAPTER SEVEN

1. Donald J. Trump (@realDonaldTrump), TWITTER (Jan. 25, 2017, 6:10 AM), https://twitter.com/realDonaldTrump/status/824227824903090176; Donald J. Trump (@realDonaldTrump), TWITTER (Jan. 25, 2017, 6:13 AM), https://twitter.com/realdonaldtrump/status/824228768227217408. Vice President Mike Pence was later given responsibility for overseeing an investigatory commission. *See* Ashley Parker, *Trump: Pence Will Head Probe of Voting Issues*, WASH. POST, Feb. 6, 2017, at A7.

2. Jeh Johnson, *Statement by Secretary Jeh Johnson on the Designation of Election Infrastructure as a Critical Infrastructure Subsector*, U.S. DEP'T HOMELAND SECURITY (Jan. 6, 2017), https://www.dhs.gov/news/2017/01/06/

statement-secretary-johnson-designation-election-
infrastructure-critical.

3. *Id.*

4. Christy McCormick, *Statement by Commissioner Christy McCormick*, U.S. ELECTION ASSISTANCE COMMISSION (Jan. 7, 2017), https://www.eac.gov/documents/2017/01/07/statement-by-commissioner-christy-mccormick-mccormick-statements.

5. Tim Starks, *DHS Labels Elections as 'Critical Infrastructure,'* POLITICO (Jan. 6, 2017, 6:39 PM), http://www.politico.com/story/2017/01/elections-critical-infrastructure-homeland-security-233304; *see also* McCormick, *supra* note 4 (discussing the concerns of Secretaries of State and the other commissioners).

6. To the degree that Americans are working to fight fraud, preserving the decentralized nature of the presidential election process actually works *better* than the measures proposed by Johnson and Trump. *See* discussion *supra* notes 33–44 (Ch. 3) and accompanying text.

7. U.S. CONST. art. II, § 1, cl. 4; *id.* amend. XII. Obviously, if a House contingent election is needed, that would become an additional congressional responsibility.

8. *Id.* art. I, § 4, cl. 1; *see also id.* art. I, § 5, cl. 1.

9. *See* discussion *supra* notes 40–44 (Ch. 3) and accompanying text.

10. *Cf.* McCormick, *supra* note 4 (discussing the financial liabilities that states could incur if elections are designated as "critical infrastructure").

11. A discussion of the first several presidential elections can be found in *McPherson v. Blacker*, 146 U.S. 1, 29–32 (1892).

12. The legislatures of Connecticut, Delaware, Georgia, New Jersey, and South Carolina each appointed electors on behalf of their citizens. *Id.* at 29.

13. Virginia created 12 districts specifically for the election of electors and 10 different districts for the election of Congressmen. *Id.*

14. Massachusetts asked voters in each congressional district to vote for two candidates for elector. The state legislature next selected one of the top two candidates from each district to serve as elector. The legislature also selected two "at large" electors. *Id.*

15. Letter from George Washington to James Madison (Nov. 5, 1786), *in* 4 THE PAPERS OF GEORGE WASHINGTON: CONFEDERATION SERIES 331, 332 (W.W. Abbot et al. eds., 1995).

16. JAMES MADISON, NOTES OF DEBATES IN THE FEDERAL CONVENTION OF 1787, at 153 (Adrienne Koch ed., W.W. Norton & Co. 1987) (1966).

17. *Id.* at 56.

18. *Id.* at 151.

19. For a discussion of how those with a stronger commitment to preserving states' rights may have shaped the Constitution during the Committee on Detail, see John C. Hueston, Note, *Altering the Course of the Constitutional Convention: The Role of the Committee of Detail in Establishing the Balance of State and Federal Powers*, 100 YALE L.J. 765 (1990). Importantly, the rest of the Convention accepted most of the compromises that had been proposed by the Committee on Detail. *Id.* at 778.

20. THE FEDERALIST NO. 51, at 319 (James Madison) (Clinton Rossiter ed., Signet Classic 2003) (1961).

21. *Id.*

22. *Id.*

23. *Id.* at 320.

24. THE FEDERALIST NO. 46, *supra* note 20, at 294 (James Madison).

25. U.S. CONST. art. I, § 4, cl. 1.

26. THE FEDERALIST NO. 59, *supra* note 20, at 360–61 (Alexander Hamilton) ("They have submitted the regulation of elections for the federal government, in the first instance, to the local administrations; which, in ordinary cases, and when no improper views prevail, may be both more convenient and more satisfactory; but they have reserved to the national authority a right to interpose, whenever extraordinary circumstances might render that interposition necessary to its safety.").

27. *Id.* at 361 ("Nothing can be more evident than that an exclusive power of regulating elections for the national government, in the hands of the State legislatures, would leave the existence of the Union entirely at their mercy. They could at any moment annihilate it by neglecting to provide for the choice of persons to administer its affairs.").

28. U.S. CONST. art. II, § 1, cl. 2.

29. *Id.* art. II, § 1, cl. 4.

30. *Id.* amend. XII. Obviously, Congress also has more responsibilities if no one receives a majority of electors and a House contingent election is needed. *See id.*

31. *See, e.g.,* Anthony Peacock, *Article I, Section 4: Election Regulations, in* THE HERITAGE GUIDE TO THE CONSTITUTION 71, 72 (David F. Forte & Matthew Spalding eds., 2005) (noting that the constitutional provision "lodged the power to regulate elections in the respective legislative branches of the states and the federal government, not with the executive or judicial").

32. For more information on Katharine Lee Bates and her poem "America the Beautiful," see ACE COLLINS, STORIES BEHIND THE HYMNS THAT INSPIRE AMERICA: SONGS THAT UNITE OUR NATION 20–28 (2003); MARC FERRIS, STAR-SPANGLED BANNER: THE UNLIKELY STORY OF AMERICA'S NATIONAL ANTHEM 108–09 (2014); ROBERT J. MORGAN, THEN SINGS MY SOUL: 150 OF THE WORLD'S GREATEST HYMN STORIES 229 (2011); LYNN SHERR, AMERICA THE BEAUTIFUL: THE STIRRING TRUE STORY BEHIND OUR NATION'S FAVORITE SONG (2001); Sylvester Baxter, *"America the Beautiful,"* 88 J. EDUC. 428–29 (1918).

33. MORGAN, *supra* note 32, at 229; SHERR, *supra* note 32, at 34..

34. There seem to be minor disagreements about the primary factor(s) motivating Colorado's decision that year. In all likelihood, there were a variety of issues that played into the decision. Either way, the state did what it needed to do to be represented in the process, without regard to the fact that popular elections were being held everywhere else. *See* CQ PRESS, PRESIDENTIAL ELECTIONS: 1789–2008, at 192 (2010) (noting that Colorado had joined the Union mere months before the 1876 presidential election and "did not want to go to the trouble and expense of holding a popular vote for the presidential election so soon thereafter"); ROBERT DUDLEY & ERIC SHIRAEV, COUNTING EVERY VOTE: THE MOST CONTENTIOUS ELECTIONS IN AMERICAN HISTORY 49 (2008) (discussing the short timeline as well as the "excessive cost" of holding a presidential election so soon after statewide elections). *But see* EUGENE H. BERWANGER, THE RISE OF THE CENTENNIAL STATE: COLORADO TERRITORY, 1861–76, at 150 (2007) (discussing the practical hurdles to holding an election so quickly and noting political motivations to appoint electors instead).

35. South Carolina remained an exception until 1860. CQ PRESS, *supra* note 34, at 192.

36. *See id.*

37. The Florida House approved a resolution appointing 25 Republican electors for the state on December 12. The Florida Senate was scheduled to meet the next day, but the Supreme Court decision in *Bush v. Gore*, 531 U.S. 98 (2000) (per curiam), made Senate consideration of the bill unnecessary. *See, e.g.*, Steve Miller, *Florida House OKs Bush Electors*, WASH. TIMES, Dec. 13, 2000 at A1.

38. CQ PRESS, *supra* note 34, at 131, 192.

39. *Id.* at 192.

40. GEORGE HARMON KNOLES, THE PRESIDENTIAL CAMPAIGN AND ELECTION OF 1892, at 227–28 (Stanford Univ. Press 1942); CHARLES MUSSER, POLITICKING AND EMERGENT MEDIA: US PRESIDENTIAL ELECTIONS OF THE 1890s, at 10, 24 (2016).

41. Bush v. Gore, 531 U.S. 98, 104 (2000) (per curiam) ("[T]he state legislature's power to select the manner for appointing electors is plenary; it may, if it so chooses, select the electors itself . . . .").

42. Justice Clarence Thomas expressed this principle in *U.S. Term Limits, Inc. v. Thornton*, 514 U.S. 779, 861 (1995) (Thomas, J., dissenting). His comment was made in dissent, but the other justices did not dispute him on this particular point. "States may establish qualifications for their delegates to the electoral college," he noted, "as long as those qualifications pass muster under other constitutional provisions." *Id.*

43. U.S. CONST. amend. XIV ("The right of citizens of the United States to vote shall not be denied or abridged by the United States or by any State on account of sex."). Similarly, the Equal Protection Clause or the First Amendment may curb

state discretion once a state legislature chooses direct popular election as its method of appointing electors. In short, a state legislature does not have to choose direct popular election; however, once it has done so, some federal constitutional rights may be held to attach. *See, e.g.*, Anderson v. Celebrezze, 460 U.S. 780, 794 n.18 (1983); Williams v. Rhodes, 393 U.S. 23, 29 (1968).

44. By the terms of the proposed compact, states holding 270 electoral votes can approve it, putting it into effect. After the 2010 Census, the eleven largest states hold exactly 270 votes among them. The full text of the compact can be found in JOHN R. KOZA ET AL., EVERY VOTE EQUAL: A STATE-BASED PLAN FOR ELECTING THE PRESIDENT BY NATIONAL POPULAR VOTE 258–60 (4th ed. 2013).

45. A more thorough assessment of NPV's plan can be found in Chapters Twelve through Fourteen of TARA ROSS, ENLIGHTENED DEMOCRACY: THE CASE FOR THE ELECTORAL COLLEGE (Colonial Press 2d ed. 2012) (2004); *see also* Tara Ross, *Legal and Logistical Ramifications of the National Popular Vote Plan*, ENGAGE: J. FEDERALIST SOC'Y PRAC. GROUPS, Sept. 2010, at 37; Tara Ross & Robert M. Hardaway, *The Compact Clause and National Popular Vote: Implications for the "Federal Structure,"* 44 N.M. L. REV. 383 (2014).

46. McPherson v. Blacker, 146 U.S. 1, 27, 35 (1892).

47. Bush v. Gore, 531 U.S. 98, 104 (2000) (per curiam).

48. Hall v. Beals, 396 U.S. 45, 52 (1969) (Marshall, J., dissenting) (asserting that the case before the Court was not moot, as held by the majority).

49. WILLIAM E. LEUCHTENBURG, IN THE SHADOW OF FDR: FROM HARRY TRUMAN TO BARACK OBAMA 1–2 (4th ed. 2009); *see also* CQ PRESS, *supra* note 34, at 65.

50. CQ Press, *supra* note 34, at 65.

51. David McCullough, Truman 432 (1992).

52. *Id.* at 436.

53. *See, e.g.*, Richard S. Kirkendall, *Election of 1948, in* 3 History of American Presidential Elections: 1789–2008, at 1157, 1174–77 (Gil Troy et al. eds., 4th ed. 2012); *Candidate Truman Comes out Fighting*, Life, July 26, 1948, at 15, 15–19 [hereinafter *Candidate Truman*].

54. The Federalist No. 51, *supra* note 20, at 319 (James Madison).

55. "The time has arrived in America," he argued, "for the Democratic Party to get out of the shadow of states' rights and to walk forthrightly into the bright sunshine of human rights." Senator Hubert H. Humphrey, Address at the 1948 Democratic National Convention in Philadelphia, PA (July 14, 1948) (audio and transcript available at http://www.americanrhetoric.com/speeches/huberthumphey1948dnc.html).

56. *Candidate Truman, supra* note 53, at 18.

57. *Id.*

58. *Id.* Almost all of the southern delegates who remained behind refused to vote for Truman. Instead, they cast a protest vote for Senator Richard B. Russell of Georgia. Kirkendall, *supra* note 53, at 1176.

59. A discussion of who was or was not on the ballot during these years can be complicated. Until the 1900s, states printed the name of electors (instead of presidential candidates) on their ballots. As early as 1892, other forms of ballots began to be used, and the presidential short ballot developed over time. For purposes of this discussion, it's simply worth noting that a discussion about which candidate is or isn't on the ballot could actually be a reference to which candidate a slate of electors

considered themselves pledged to supporting. For instance, in
1948, official slates of Democratic electors were on the ballot
in four southern states, but they considered themselves pledged
to Strom Thurmond, not to Harry Truman. *See infra* note 60.
For more on the early evolution of the presidential short
ballot, see Spencer D. Albright, *The Presidential Short Ballot*,
34 AM. POL. SCI. REV. 955 (1940).

60. *See* CQ PRESS, *supra* note 34, at 66, 156; *see also* WILLIAM D.
BARNARD, DIXIECRATS AND DEMOCRATS: ALABAMA
POLITICS, 1942–1950, at 120 (1974); Jill M. Budny & J.
Michael Bitzer, *Dixiecrats, in* ENCYCLOPEDIA OF AMERICAN
POLITICAL PARTIES AND ELECTIONS 113, 114 (Larry J. Sabato
& Howard R. Ernst eds., updated ed. 2007).

61. *See, e.g.,* CQ PRESS, *supra* note 34, at 67.

62. *Id.* at 246. Thurmond's victory in four states should have
given him only 38 electors, but one arguably faithless elector
in Tennessee brought his total to 39 instead. *See also infra*
note 2 (app. C) for more on the elector, Preston Parks.

63. The 23 Virginia electors who refused to vote for vice
presidential candidate Richard M. Johnson are often reported
as "faithless electors," and conventional wisdom has long held
that these electors voted contrary to their instructions. *See,
e.g.,* Tony L. Hill, *Elector, Faithless, in* SABATO & ERNST,
supra note 60, at 132, 133; *Faithless Electors*, FAIRVOTE,
http://www.fairvote.org/faithless_electors (last visited Mar. 7,
2017); *see also* ROBERT W. BENNETT, TAMING THE
ELECTORAL COLLEGE 98–99 (2006) (describing the electors as
faithless, but also acknowledging the difficulty of determining
the status of elector pledges during America's early years). This
author wrote at least one editorial labeling the Virginia
electors as "faithless" (per the conventional wisdom on the
subject) before realizing that the evidence is perhaps a bit more

conflicting than generally appreciated. *See* Tara Ross, *What's an Elector to Do? Plumbing the History of the Electoral College for Answers to the Tough Question*, N.Y. DAILY NEWS (Dec. 18, 2016, 5:00 AM), http://www.nydailynews. com/opinion/elector-article-1.2913390. The author is grateful to Professor Derek Muller, who highlighted the conflicting evidence about the Virginia electors when he was reviewing an early draft of this book.

In some regards, the "faithless" label is understandable. The national party probably did believe that those electors should vote for Johnson and doubtless felt that Virginia had betrayed the party when they didn't. However, it doesn't appear that the electors themselves agreed to such a pledge. To the contrary, as discussed in the main text, Virginians had been expressing their discontent with the nomination ever since the national party convention in May 1835. When the political party later held a convention within their own state, Virginians opted to pledge their support to William Smith of Alabama instead of Johnson. At the meetings of the Electoral College later that year, they cast their ballots for Martin Van Buren and William Smith, just as they had said they would. *See* STAN M. HAYNES, THE FIRST AMERICAN POLITICAL CONVENTIONS: TRANSFORMING PRESIDENTIAL NOMINATIONS, 1832–1872, at 47, 50 (2012); Joel H. Silbey, *Election of 1836, in* 1 HISTORY OF AMERICAN PRESIDENTIAL ELECTIONS, *supra* note 53, at 252, 268, 272; Robert Bolt, *Vice President Richard M. Johnson of Kentucky: Hero of the Thames—Or the Great Amalgamator?*, 75 REG. KY. HIST. SOC'Y 191, 202 (1977); *Democratic Ticket: Electors for the State of Virginia*, RICHMOND ENQUIRER, Oct. 18, 1836, at 1 (listing electors for Van Buren and Smith); *Legislative*

Convention, RICHMOND ENQUIRER, Jan. 16, 1836, at 3
(reporting on a vote to support Smith instead of Johnson).

64. Lindsey Apple, *Richard Mentor Johnson (1781–1850), in*
VICE PRESIDENTS: A BIOGRAPHICAL DICTIONARY 86, 91 (L.
Edward Purcell ed., 4th ed. 2010); Bolt, *supra* note 63, at 198.

65. PAUL F. BOLLER, JR., PRESIDENTIAL CAMPAIGNS 60 (rev. ed.
1996); HAYNES, *supra* note 63, at 47.

66. *Presidential Convention*, 48 NILES WKLY. REG. 226, 229
(May 30, 1835).

67. *See* discussion *supra* note 63.

68. Despite Virginia's action, the Senate still selected Johnson to
serve as Vice President. Apple, *supra* note 64, at 92.

69. *See* discussion *supra* note 59 and accompanying text.

70. *See, e.g.*, SABATO & ERNST, *supra* note 60, at 319.

71. *See* WILLIAM GILLETTE, JERSEY BLUE: CIVIL WAR POLITICS
IN NEW JERSEY, 1854–1865, at 99–103 (1995) (discussing the
development of the fusion ticket); *see also Nothing to Brag of,
After All*, N.Y. TIMES, Nov. 16, 1860, at 4.

72. *Nothing to Brag of, After All, supra* note 71, at 4. The
Chicago Tribune also reported these identical numbers, except
it reported William Cook with 63,801 votes instead of 62,801
votes. Given the dynamics of the election, the "3" appears to
be a typo. *See New Jersey*, CHI. TRIB., Nov. 19, 1860, at 2.

73. *See, e.g., New Jersey*, DETROIT FREE PRESS (Detroit,
Michigan), Nov 15, 1860, at 1 ("In some parts of the State the
people voted as though news of the fusion had never reached
them. Take all the vote together there is a majority of from
three to four thousand against Lincoln.").

74. CQ PRESS, *supra* note 34, at 134, 224.

75. LEWIS L. GOULD, WYOMING: A POLITICAL HISTORY, 1868–
1896, at 162–63 (1968); T.A. LARSON, HISTORY OF
WYOMING 284–85 (2d. ed. rev. 1990).

76. *See* CQ PRESS, *supra* note 34, at 142; KNOLES, *supra* note 40, at 245; MUSSER, *supra* note 40, at 24; *see also* discussion *supra* note 59 and accompanying text.

77. *See* CQ PRESS, *supra* note 34, at 142, 232. For a discussion of the issues affecting the campaign, see BOLLER, *supra* note 65, at 162–66; H. Wayne Morgan, *Election of 1892, in* 2 HISTORY OF AMERICAN PRESIDENTIAL ELECTIONS, *supra* note 53, at 712.

78. For a compilation of some of these rules, see *2016 Democratic Delegate Allocation Rules by State*, FRONTLOADING HQ, http://frontloading.blogspot. com/p/2016-democratic-delegate-allocation.html (last visited Mar. 8, 2017); *2016 Republican Delegate Allocation Rules by State*, FRONTLOADING HQ, http://frontloading.blogspot.com/ p/2016-republican-delegate-allocation-by.html (last visited Mar. 8, 2017).

79. Press Release, Senator Brad Hoylman Announces Legislation Requiring the Release of Presidential Candidates' Tax Returns as a Qualification for the Ballot in New York (Dec. 6, 2016), https://www.nysenate.gov/newsroom/press-releases/brad-hoylman/senator-brad-hoylman-announces-legislation-requiring-release.

80. Fenit Nirappil, *Blue-State Lawmakers Want to Keep Trump off 2020 Ballot Unless He Releases Tax Returns*, WASH. POST, Jan. 4, 2017, at B8.

81. *Id.*

82. Harvard Professor Laurence Tribe noted that such a move was likely constitutional because of the states' broad plenary power in elections. *Id.* In the meantime, University of Illinois College of Law Dean Vikram David Amar questioned the legality of such a move, citing *Anderson v. Celebrezze*, 460 U.S. 780 (1983), a Supreme Court decision that struck down

an early ballot deadline in Ohio. Vikram David Amar, *Can and Should States Mandate Tax Return Disclosure as a Condition for Presidential Candidates to Appear on the Ballot?*, JUSTIA: VERDICT (Dec. 30, 2016), https://verdict. justia.com/2016/12/30/can-states-mandate-tax-return-disclosure-condition-presidential-candidates-appear-ballot. In *Anderson*, Justice John Paul Stevens delivered the opinion for a closely divided court, emphasizing the fact that "state-imposed restrictions implicate a uniquely important national interest" and that the "enforcement of more stringent ballot access requirements, including filing deadlines, has an impact beyond its own borders." *Anderson*, 460 U.S. at 794–95. The *Anderson* holding misunderstands the decentralized presidential election system created by the Founders, which Justice William Rehnquist's dissent emphasizes. *Id.* at 808 (Rehnquist, J., dissenting) ("But the Constitution does not require that a State allow any particular Presidential candidate to be on its ballot, and so long as the Ohio ballot access laws are rational and allow nonparty candidates reasonable access to the general election ballot, this Court should not interfere with Ohio's exercise of its Art. II, § 1, cl. 2, power."). The more recent case of *Bush v. Gore* seems to be moving back toward the more accurate understanding of the state's broad discretion in this area. 531 U.S. 98, 104 (2000) (per curiam).

83. Many voters in the Midwest were upset about Cleveland's position on the free coinage of silver. On the other hand, in a state such as Colorado, some members of the Democratic Party may also have felt that endorsing the third-party ticket would be the best way to defeat Republicans in the state. *See, e.g., Believes in Fusion: Candidate Cleveland Indorses the Scheme in Colorado*, CHI. TRIB., July 24, 1892, at 3 (quoting a Colorado operative who concluded that "alone we have no

reason to expect to carry the hitherto strong Republican State of Colorado, but if we conclude to nominate no ticket of our own but to indorse the candidates of the People's Party, the defeat of the Republicans in Colorado is certainly assured").

84. U.S. CONST. art. VI, cl. 3 ("The Senators and Representatives before mentioned, and the Members of the several State Legislatures, and all executive and judicial Officers, both of the United States and of the several States, shall be bound by Oath or Affirmation, to support this Constitution; but no religious Test shall ever be required as a Qualification to any Office or public Trust under the United States.").

85. Some questions might arise about the extent of the state's authority if it tries to cancel an election once early voting has already started. Are Equal Protection or other constitutional concerns created by the attempt to change the process midstream? The Supreme Court has held that "the State may not, by later arbitrary and disparate treatment, value one person's vote over that of another," *Bush*, 531 U.S. at 104–05. But early voters are not being treated unfairly compared to other voters. Instead, all voters are on an equal playing field: Each lost an opportunity to vote during that single election year. Moreover, the state wouldn't be changing the rules midstream so much as it would simply be canceling an election, altogether, because of a change in circumstances. The bigger question is the policy one: What are the state's priorities in any given circumstance?

86. Letter from James Madison to W.T. Barry (Aug. 4, 1822), *in* 9 THE WRITINGS OF JAMES MADISON 103, 103 (Gaillard Hunt ed., 1910); *see also* Centinel, *III: To the People of Pennsylvania* (Nov. 5, 1787), *in* 2 THE COMPLETE ANTI-FEDERALIST 154, 159 (Herbert J. Storing ed., 1981) ("Liberty only flourishes where reason and knowledge are encouraged;

and wherever the latter are stifled, the former is extinguished.").

87. Address from George Washington to the United States Senate and House of Representatives (Jan. 8, 1790), *in* 4 THE PAPERS OF GEORGE WASHINGTON: PRESIDENTIAL SERIES 543, 545 (W.W. Abbot et al. eds., 1993).

CHAPTER EIGHT

1. Christopher Suprun, Op-ed, *Why Electors Should Reject Trump*, N.Y. TIMES, Dec. 6, 2016, at A27.

2. *Id.*

3. Art Sisneros, *Conflicted Elector in a Corrupt College*, BLESSED PATH (Nov. 26, 2016), https://theblessedpath.com/2016/11/26/conflicted-elector-in-a-corrupt-college.

4. *Id.*

5. Michael Hardy, *An Exit Interview with Art Sisneros, The Texas Elector Who Resigned Rather Than Vote for Trump*, TEX. MONTHLY: BURKABLOG (Dec. 13, 2016), http://www.texasmonthly.com/burka-blog/522780.

6. Robert Wilonsky, *Texas Elector Chris Suprun Talks About Becoming an 'A-Word' Just Because He Won't Vote for Trump*, DALL. MORNING NEWS (Dec. 6, 2016), http://www.dallasnews.com/opinion/commentary/2016/12/06/chris-suprun-talks-becoming-word-just-vote-trump.

7. HAMILTON ELECTORS, http://www.hamiltonelectors.com (last visited Mar. 1, 2017).

8. LAWRENCE D. LONGLEY & NEAL R. PEIRCE, THE ELECTORAL COLLEGE PRIMER 2000, at 104 (1999); *see also, e.g.,* JUDITH A. BEST, THE CHOICE OF THE PEOPLE? DEBATING THE ELECTORAL COLLEGE 43–45 (1996); ROBERT W. BENNETT, TAMING THE ELECTORAL COLLEGE 14–17, 196–98 n.23 (2006); GEORGE C. EDWARDS III, WHY THE ELECTORAL

College Is Bad for America 49–51 (2d ed. 2011); Norman R. Williams, *Reforming the Electoral College: Federalism, Majoritarianism, and the Perils of Subconstitutional Change,* 100 Geo. L.J. 173, 182 (2011). In *McPherson v. Blacker,* 146 U. S. 1 (1892), the Supreme Court adopted this view. "Doubtless it was supposed that the electors would exercise a reasonable independence and fair judgment in the selection of the chief executive," Chief Justice Fuller wrote for the Court, "but experience soon demonstrated that, whether chosen by the legislatures or by popular suffrage . . . , they were so chosen simply to register the will of the appointing power in respect of a particular candidate." *Id.* at 36. "[T]he original expectation may be said to have been frustrated," he concluded. *Id.*

9. *See* Robert M. Hardaway, The Electoral College and the Constitution: The Case for Preserving Federalism 85–87 (1994); *see also* Luis Fuentes-Rohwer & Guy-Uriel Charles, *The Electoral College, the Right to Vote, and Our Federalism: A Comment on a Lasting Institution,* 29 Fla. St. U. L. Rev. 879, 896 & n.102 (2001); Walter Dellinger, *Popularity Contest: In Defense of the Electoral College,* Slate (Nov. 1, 2004, 3:30 PM), http://www.slate.com/articles/news_and_politics/politics/2004/11/popularity_contest.html.

10. The Federalist No. 68, at 412 (Alexander Hamilton) (Clinton Rossiter ed., Signet Classic 2003) (1961).

11. *Id.* at 410.

12. *Id.* at 412.

13. *Federalist No. 68* was published in mid-March. At that point, six states had ratified the Constitution: Delaware, Pennsylvania, New Jersey, Georgia, Connecticut, and

Massachusetts. New York would finally ratify the document much later, in July 1788.

14. 2 The Documentary History of the Ratification of the Constitution 566 (Merrill Jensen ed., 1976) [hereinafter Documentary History]; *see also* Pauline Maier, Ratification: The People Debate the Constitution, 1787–1788, at 114 (2010).

15. Wilson took a position in favor of popular election almost immediately after the convention opened, and he continued to express that view in the weeks that followed. *See, e.g.*, James Madison, Notes of Debates in the Federal Convention of 1787, at 48–49, 307, 362 (Adrienne Koch ed., W.W. Norton & Co. 1987) (1966).

16. "[I]f gentlemen object, that an 8th part of our country forms a district too large for elections," he asked, "how much more would they object, if it was extended to the whole Union?" Documentary History, *supra* note 14, at 567.

17. *Id.*

18. *Id.*

19. The concept of electors had been proposed in various ways during the course of the summer, but the mechanics of the system were finally nailed down in the Committee on Postponed Matters. For a discussion of the committee, see Carol Berkin, A Brilliant Solution: Inventing the American Constitution 137–40 (1st Harvest ed. 2003); Richard J. Ellis, *Constitutional Convention, in* Encyclopedia of the American Presidency 113, 115 (Michael A. Genovese ed., rev. ed. 2010).

20. John Dickinson to George Logan (Jan. 16, 1802), *in* Supplement to Max Farrand's the Records of the Federal Convention of 1787, at 300, 301 (James H. Hutson ed., 1987). Dickinson took credit for pushing the

committee to reconsider legislative selection of the Executive, but at least one scholar questions whether he fairly took credit for the committee's work. BERKIN, *supra* note 19, at 140.

21. MADISON, *supra* note 15, at 574.
22. *Id.* at 576.
23. *Id.* at 577.
24. *Id.*
25. An alternative perspective is that the states' power to bind electors could avert the possibility of corruption and cabal. *See* Note, *State Power to Bind Presidential Electors*, 65 COLUM. L. REV. 696, 709 (1965). This seems inconsistent with the delegates' comments at the Constitutional Convention, however. They were more likely to allude to the fact that electors couldn't be influenced very easily because they would be scattered across the country when they were casting their votes.
26. MADISON, *supra* note 15, at 578.
27. *See, e.g.*, Lucius Wilmerding, Jr., *Reform of the Electoral System*, 64 POL. SCI. Q. 1, 14–15 (1949) ("[I]t is very doubtful that these electors were ever intended to act a part wholly independent of the people. The electoral system was not the invention of that part of the Federal Convention which distrusted the people but of that part which trusted them. First proposed by James Wilson, it seems to have been regarded by him as an equivalent to an election by the people."); *see also* BEST, *supra* note 8, at 43–44.
28. BENNETT, *supra* note 8, at 102; Tony L. Hill, *Elector, Faithless, in* ENCYCLOPEDIA OF AMERICAN POLITICAL PARTIES AND ELECTIONS 132, 132 (Larry J. Sabato & Howard R. Ernst eds., updated ed. 2007).
29. U.S. CONST. art. II, § 1, cl. 2.
30. *See* Ray v. Blair, 343 U.S. 214 (1952).

31. This issue is sometimes raised in the context of an Article V
     Convention for proposing Amendments. When a state
     appoints delegates to that Convention, can it also bind those
     delegates and restrict them from discussing certain topics?
     Advocates for the Convention argue that, yes, states can limit
     the authority of their delegates. *See generally* Robert G.
     Natelson, *Founding-Era Conventions and the Meaning of the
     Constitution's "Convention for Proposing Amendments,"* 65
     FLA. L. REV. 615 (2013) (discussing the history of conventions
     among the colonies and the states). If delegates to an Article V
     convention can be restricted in some ways, then why wouldn't
     the same principle hold true for presidential electors? It's
     important to note that the two processes differ. Presidential
     electors are constitutional officials with their own duties to
     perform under the Constitution. They are specifically
     mentioned in the constitutional text and are assigned duties,
     whereas delegates to an Article V convention are not. The
     state cannot invade the constitutional sphere. *Cf.* Opinion of
     the Justices, 34 So. 2d 598, 600 (Ala. 1948) ("When the
     legislature has provided for the appointment of electors its
     powers and functions have ended. If and when it attempts to
     go further and dictate to the electors the choice which they
     must make for president and vice-president, it has invaded the
     field set apart to the electors by the Constitution of the United
     States, and such action cannot stand."). *But see* Michael B.
     Rappaport, *Reforming Article V: The Problems Created by
     the National Convention Amendment Method and How to
     Fix Them*, 96 VA. L. REV. 1509, 1575–78 (2010) (comparing
     and contrasting Article V delegates and presidential electors
     and suggesting that any attempt to bind either could be
     illegal).

32. *Ray*, 343 U.S. at 230 ("However, even if such promises of candidates for the electoral college are legally unenforceable because violative of an assumed constitutional freedom of the elector under the Constitution, Art. II, § 1, to vote as he may choose in the electoral college, it would not follow that the requirement of a pledge in the primary is unconstitutional.").

33. A truth that is perhaps reinforced by the fact that electors take an oath of office, just as senators and representatives do. In Texas, for instance, presidential electors are administered an oath by the Chief Justice of the Texas Supreme Court. Texas electors are asked to swear or affirm that they "will to the best of my ability preserve, protect, and defend the Constitution and laws of the United States and of this State, so help me God." TEX. SEC. ST., FORM 2204-OATH OF OFFICE (last updated Oct. 2011), http://sos.state.tx.us/statdoc/forms/2204. pdf. They are also to make a "statement of officer," in which they swear or affirm that they "have not directly or indirectly paid, offered, promised to pay, contributed, or promised to contribute any money or thing of value, or promised any public office or employment for the giving or withholding of a vote at the election at which I was elected or as a reward to secure my appointment or confirmation . . . ." TEX. SEC. ST., FORM 2201-OATH OF OFFICE (last updated Jan. 2015), http:// sos.state.tx.us/statdoc/forms/2201.pdf. The statement seems somewhat at odds with any attempt to bind Texas electors to the outcome of the statewide popular vote. Why wouldn't a vote for President be a "thing of value" within the meaning of the statement?

34. *Opinion of the Justices*, 34 So. 2d at 600. The Supreme Court of Alabama later adopted this opinion in *Ray v. Blair*, 57 So. 2d 395, 398 (Ala. 1952). That decision was overruled by the Supreme Court a few weeks later in *Ray v. Blair*, 343 U.S. 214

(1952), but the Supreme Court specifically declined to decide whether pledges could or could not be enforced, as the state court had.

35. *See, e.g.,* Derek T. Muller, *Faithless Electors: Now It's Up to Congress,* WALL STREET J. (Dec. 20, 2016, 6:34 PM), https://www.wsj.com/articles/faithless-electors-now-its-up-to-congress-1482276847 ("Whatever Congress does will set a major precedent. If it counts the votes in Minnesota and Colorado, for instance, it will ratify the power of the states to remove faithless electors for breaking state pledges.").

36. *See, e.g.,* Richard Winger, *Colorado and Minnesota State Governments Try to Short-Circuit Lawsuits Filed by Certain Presidential Electors,* BALLOT ACCESS NEWS (Feb. 25, 2017, 9:01 AM), http://ballot-access.org/2017/02/25/colorado-and-minnesota-state-governments-try-to-short-circuit-court-opinions-on-rights-of-presidential-elector-candidates (discussing the status of presidential elector lawsuits that were still ongoing in early 2017); *see also* Richard Winger, *Washington State Electors Who Refused to Vote for Hillary Clinton Appeal Their Fine, Using a State Administrative Process,* BALLOT ACCESS NEWS (Feb. 24, 2017, 4:49 PM), http://ballot-access.org/2017/02/24/washington-state-electors-who-refused-to-vote-for-hillary-clinton-in-electoral-college-appeal-their-fine-in-state-administrative-process (discussing Washington electors who are appealing fines levied upon them).

37. Tom Hamburger & Kathy Chen, *GOP Electors Feel Heat, And It Annoys Them,* WALL STREET J. (Dec. 1, 2000, 1:42 AM), https://www.wsj.com/articles/SB975631336953411236.

38. *E.g.,* Frank J. Murray, *Bush Electors Ignore Pleas to Defect,* WASH. TIMES, Dec. 15, 2000, at A16. Some even mentioned the possibility before Gore conceded. *See* Edward Walsh, *A*

Quixotic Effort to Rally the 'Faithless'?: Electors Almost Never Defect, WASH. POST, Nov. 17, 2000, at A26.

39. Mary Beth Schneider, *Faithful Electors Are Being Courted*, INDIANAPOLIS STAR, Nov. 30, 2000, at A1.

40. Tom Hamburger, *Some Die-Hard Democrats Try to Sway GOP Electors for Gore*, WALL STREET J. (Dec. 14, 2000, 12:01 AM), https://www.wsj.com/articles/ SB976754325875463874.

41. *Id.*

42. *See* Mike DeBonis, *Barbara Lett Simmons, 'Faithless Elector,' is Dead at 85*, WASH. POST: DISTRICT OF DEBONIS (Dec. 27, 2012), https://www.washingtonpost.com/blogs/mike-debonis/ wp/2012/12/27/barbara-lett-simmons-faithless-elector-has-died ("'I think that it is an opportunity for us to make blatantly clear our colonial status and the fact that we've been under an oligarchy,' she said at the time.").

43. Timothy Noah, *Faithless Elector Watch: Post-Game Wrap-Up*, SLATE: CHATTERBOX (Dec. 19, 2000, 11:55 AM), http://www.slate.com/articles/news_and_politics/ chatterbox/2000/12/faithless_elector_watch_postgame_ wrapup.html.

44. LONGLEY & PEIRCE, *supra* note 8, at 104 (quoting an 1826 Senate report). The history of faithless electors is also discussed in Chapter Eight of TARA ROSS, ENLIGHTENED DEMOCRACY: THE CASE FOR THE ELECTORAL COLLEGE (Colonial Press 2d ed. 2012) (2004).

45. *See* AFTER THE PEOPLE VOTE: A GUIDE TO THE ELECTORAL COLLEGE 83 app. C (John C. Fortier ed., 3d ed. 2004) (listing the method of nomination in each state).

46. LONGLEY & PEIRCE, *supra* note 8, at 113.

47. One elector was elected to Congress and thus did not cast his ballot. His replacement defected from the expected vote,

voting for Adams instead. One of the other electors voted for William Crawford. The other voted for Andrew Jackson. *Id.* at 111–12.

48. Plumer is commonly included in lists of faithless electors, but at least one academic disputes his inclusion. He agrees that citizens in the state probably expected Plumer to cast a ballot for Monroe, but disagrees that Plumer ever felt personally bound to that expectation. *See* Lynn W. Turner, *The Electoral Vote against Monroe in 1820—An American Legend*, 42 MISS. VALLEY HIST. REV. 250, 252 (1955). It seems likely, though, that Plumer was aware that people expected him to vote for Monroe. The Concord *New Hampshire Patriot* featured a notice on October 31: "The universal sentiment of the people of this state is in favor of the re-election of MONROE and TOMPKINS, and the Electors of course will represent that sentiment." *Id.* (citing the newspaper article). For further discussion, see BENNETT, *supra* note 8, at 228–29 n.6.

49. Charles O. Paullin, *The Electoral Vote for John Quincy Adams in 1820*, 21 AM. HIST. REV. 318, 318 (1916) (quoting William Plumer's letter of January 8, 1821). Another variation of this quote leaves out the phrase "and economy" and inserts the word "had" before "grossly." *See* GEORGE MORGAN, THE LIFE OF JAMES MONROE 384 (1921). A final variation reads: "I was compelled, not only from a sense of duty, but respect to my own character, to withhold my vote from Monroe & Tompkins; from the first because he had discovered a want of foresight & economy; & from the second, because he grossly neglected his duty." *E.g.*, Turner, *supra* note 48, at 266.

50. See L. PAIGE WHITAKER & THOMAS H. NEALE, CONG. RESEARCH SERV., RL30804, THE ELECTORAL COLLEGE: AN OVERVIEW AND ANALYSIS OF REFORM PROPOSALS 12 (2004);

see also AFTER THE PEOPLE VOTE, *supra* note 45, at 90 app. G
(listing faithless electors); CQ PRESS, PRESIDENTIAL
ELECTIONS: 1789–2008, at 189 (2010) (same); LONGLEY &
PEIRCE, *supra* note 8, at 111–13 (same).

51. Balloting in Minnesota is secret, so the identity of the elector
is not known. BENNETT, *supra* note 8, at 224 n.38.

52. One anti-Electoral College group agrees: "In summary,
faithless electors are a historical curiosity associated with the
Electoral College, but they never have had any practical effect
on any presidential election." JOHN R. KOZA ET AL., EVERY
VOTE EQUAL: A STATE-BASED PLAN FOR ELECTING THE
PRESIDENT BY NATIONAL POPULAR VOTE 118 (4th ed. 2013).

53. David B. Rivkin, Jr. & Andrew M. Grossman, *Let the
Electoral College Do Its Duty*, WALL STREET J. (Sept. 7, 2016,
7:25 PM), http://www.wsj.com/articles/let-the-electoral-
college-do-its-duty-1473290734.

54. Daniel Brezenoff, *Electoral College: Make Hillary Clinton
President*, CHANGE.ORG (Nov. 9, 2016), http://www.change.
org/p/electoral-college-make-hillary-clinton-president-on-
december-19-4a78160a-023c-4ff0-9069-53cee2a095a8?.

55. *See, e.g.*, Valerie Richardson, *Republicans Call on Clinton,
Obama to Reel in Soros-Linked 'Professional' Anti-Trump
Protesters*, WASH. TIMES (Nov. 14, 2016), http://www.
washingtontimes.com/news/2016/nov/14/republicans-call-
clinton-obama-reel-professional-a; *see also* Sapna
Maheshwari, *How Fake News Goes Viral: A Case Study*,
N.Y. TIMES: MEDIA (Nov. 20, 2016), https://www.nytimes.
com/2016/11/20/business/media/how-fake-news-spreads.html.

56. In an interview with this author, Bill Greene reported that the
pressure came both from the Republican Party and from the
Trump campaign itself. Greene also estimates that he received

Notes

more than 90,000 emails urging him to vote for Hillary
Clinton.

57. Patrick Svitek, *Rogue Texas Elector Explains Decision to
Back Ron Paul*, Tex. Trib. (Jan. 9, 2017), https://www.
texastribune.org/2017/01/09/rogue-texas-elector-explains-
decision-back-ron-pau.

58. He also spoke to a journalist at the Mises Institute about his
reasons for believing that Ron Paul was best-suited for the job.
*See Ron Paul's "Faithless" Elector: A Conversation with Bill
Greene*, Austrian, Mar.-Apr. 2017, at 8.

59. *See* 163 Cong. Rec. H189 (daily ed. Jan. 6, 2017); *see also*
discussion *supra* note 16 (Introduction) for a discussion of
electoral vote totals and available sources. As a side note,
many news stories disagreed on whether Ron Paul was a
Libertarian or a Republican in December 2016. This author
decided to stick with Republican, since Paul served as a
Republican congressman.

60. *See, e.g.,* Kyle Cheney, *2 Presidential Electors Encourage
Colleagues to Sideline Trump*, Politico (Nov. 14, 2016, 2:33
PM), http://www.politico.com/story/2016/11/electoral-college-
effort-stop-trump-231350; Walker Orenstein, *Four
Washington Electors Defect, Make History, as Electoral
College Goes to Trump*, News Tribune (Tacoma, Wash.)
(Dec. 19, 2016, 5:41 PM), http://www.thenewstribune.com/
news/politics-government/article121794643.
html#storylink=cpy.

61. Unite for America, *A Message for Electors to Unite for
America*, YouTube (Dec. 14, 2016), https://www.youtube.
com/watch?v=0z0iuWh3sek.

62. *See, e.g.,* Orenstein, *supra* note 60; Jeff Stein, *Could 2 Electors
in Washington State Throw the Election to Donald Trump?*,
Vox (Nov. 6, 2016, 2:20 PM), http://www.vox.

com/2016/11/6/13540504/electors-electoral-college-washington.

63. Orenstein, *supra* note 60 (discussing Washington elector Bret Chiafalo and his satisfaction that the faithless votes "brought attention to the Electoral College system as a whole" because he hopes to "abandon[ ] the Electoral College and elect[ ] presidents by popular vote").

64. *See* Wilmerding, *supra* note 27, at 17.

65. *See, e.g., New Mexico Seeks Safeguards Against Faithless Electors*, U.S. NEWS & WORLD REP. (Feb. 21, 2017, 9:03 PM), https://www.usnews.com/news/new-mexico/articles/2017-02-21/new-mexico-seeks-safeguards-against-faithless-electors; Patrick Svitek, *Patrick: Rogue Texas Elector Could Lead to Binding Law*, TEX. TRIB. (Dec. 7, 2016), https://www.texastribune.org/2016/12/07/patrick-rogue-texas-elector-could-lead-binding-law.

66. *See, e.g.,* Jennifer Calfas, *More Electors Join Call for Russia Interference Briefing Before Vote*, THE HILL (Dec. 13, 2016, 8:02 AM), http://thehill.com/blogs/blog-briefing-room/news/310108-more-electors-join-call-for-russia-interference-briefing-before; Jennifer Steinhauer, *G.O.P. Feud Looms as Leaders Back Russia Inquiries*, N.Y. TIMES, Dec. 13, 2016, at A1.

67. *See, e.g.,* BENNETT, *supra* note 8, at 40 (discussing the 1960 Alabama ballot); EDWARDS, *supra* note 8, at 67–70 (same); *see also* Peter Robinson, *What We Really Know About Who Really Won in 1960*, NAT'L REV: THE CORNER (Dec. 14, 2004, 1:33 PM), http://www.nationalreview.com/corner/92080/what-we-really-know-about-who-really-won-1960-peter-robinson.

68. JOSEPH CUMMINS, ANYTHING FOR A VOTE: DIRTY TRICKS, CHEAP SHOTS, AND OCTOBER SURPRISES IN U.S.

PRESIDENTIAL CAMPAIGNS 113 (2007). Greeley had some religious views that were out of the mainstream. These views were used against him during the campaign, but he was not actually an atheist. He was a Universalist. According to one of his biographers, his reported last words were "I know that my Redeemer liveth" and "It is Done." ROBERT C. WILLIAMS, HORACE GREELEY: CHAMPION OF AMERICAN FREEDOM xv, xviii, 193 (2006) (quoting his last words and discussing his Universalist faith).

69. CHIP BISHOP, THE LION AND THE JOURNALIST: THE UNLIKELY FRIENDSHIP OF THEODORE ROOSEVELT AND JOSEPH BUCKLIN BISHOP 16 (2012); *see also* PAUL F. BOLLER, JR., PRESIDENTIAL CAMPAIGNS 130 (rev. ed. 1996); HY B. TURNER, WHEN GIANTS RULED: THE STORY OF PARK ROW, NEW YORK'S GREAT NEWSPAPER STREET 80 (1999).

70. Fourteen electoral votes from Louisiana and Arkansas are not included in these numbers; they were not counted by Congress due to difficulties caused by Reconstruction and uncertainty about the vote. *See* CONG. GLOBE, 42d Cong., 3rd Sess. 1301–05 (1873); *see also* CQ PRESS, *supra* note 50, at 227; William Gillette, *Election of 1872, in* 2 HISTORY OF AMERICAN PRESIDENTIAL ELECTIONS: 1789–2008, at 543, 549 (Gil Troy et al. eds., 4th ed. 2012).

71. WILLIAMS, *supra* note 68, at 305. The quote is sometimes reprinted slightly differently as: "I was the worst beaten man who ever ran for high office." BOLLER, *supra* note 69, at 130; CUMMINS, *supra* note 68, at 113.

72. BISHOP, *supra* note 69, at 16; BOLLER, *supra* note 69, at 130; CUMMINS, *supra* note 68, at 113.

73. Gillette, *supra* note 70, at 549, 571.

74. *See* CQ PRESS, *supra* note 50, at 227; *see also* Akhil Reed Amar, *Presidents, Vice Presidents, and Death: Closing the*

Constitution's Succession Gap, 48 ARK. L. REV. 215, 218–19
(1995) (discussing the choice confronting the Greeley electors);
John C. Fortier & Norman J. Ornstein, *If Terrorists Attacked
Our Presidential Elections*, 3 ELECTION L.J. 597, 606 (2004)
(same); Beverly J. Ross & William Josephson, *The Electoral
College and the Popular Vote*, 12 J.L. & POL. 665, 706–07
(1996) (same).

75. Several elections later, in 1912, electors nearly faced the same
situation again. President Taft's running mate, James S.
Sherman, passed away on October 30, mere days before the
election. Voters cast their ballots on Election Day, knowing
that the Republican Party would need to select a replacement
candidate. *See* Michael Nelson, *Biographies of the Vice
Presidents*, *in* 2 GUIDE TO THE PRESIDENCY AND THE
EXECUTIVE BRANCH 1757, 1779 (Michael Nelson ed., 5th ed.
2013).

76. CONG. GLOBE, 42d Cong., 3rd Sess. 1285 (1873).

77. The House voted on the resolution: "[The votes] cast by the
electors of the State of Georgia for Horace Greeley, of New
York, for President of the United States, ought not to be
counted, the said Horace Greeley having died before the said
votes were cast." *Id.* at 1297. The results were close: 101
(yeas), 99 (nays), 40 (not voting). *Id.* The Senate reversed the
question and voted on the resolution: "*Resolved*, That the
electoral vote of Georgia cast for Horace Greeley be counted."
Id. at 1287. The Senators were less divided, and the outcome
was 44 (yeas) to 19 (nays). *Id.*

78. *Id.* at 1285–86.

79. U.S. CONST. art. I, § 3, cl. 7.

80. *See, e.g.,* Andrew C. McCarthy, *Impeach Clinton to Bar Her
from Holding Federal Office. It's Constitutional*, NAT'L REV.
(Sept. 6, 2016, 4:00 AM), http://www.nationalreview.com/

article/439715/impeach-hillary-clinton-congress-has-power-
do-it.

81. U.S. CONST. art. I, § 3, cl. 7.

82. *Id.* art. II, § 1, cl. 5.

83. For more information regarding the problems caused by the
death of a candidate, see BEST, *supra* note 8, at 46–49; Amar,
supra note 74; Fortier & Ornstein, *supra* note 74.

84. If there is no Vice President-elect on January 20, Section 3 of
the 20th Amendment arguably can't be applied immediately.
See William Josephson, *Senate Election of the Vice President
and House of Representatives Election of the President*, 11 U.
PA. J. CONST. L. 597, 615–17 (2009). A contrary position is
taken by the Congressional Research Service, which equates
"qualifies" with "elected." *See* THOMAS H. NEALE, CONG.
RESEARCH SERV., RS20300, ELECTION OF THE PRESIDENT
AND VICE PRESIDENT BY CONGRESS: CONTINGENT ELECTION
5 (2001). Robert Bennett also assumes that the congressionally
provided line of succession in 3 U.S.C. § 19 (2006) would be
used if there were no President-elect and no Vice President-
elect. *See* BENNETT, *supra* note 8, at 81. These timing issues
are also discussed in Chapter Eight of Ross, *supra* note 44.

85. U.S. CONST. amend. XX, § 3. In the event that a Vice
President-elect was inaugurated as President through
operation of the 20th Amendment, the 25th Amendment
would then allow him to designate a new Vice President
following his inauguration. *See* U.S. CONST. amend. XXV, §
2.

86. There is perhaps some disagreement about whether a
candidate can be formally declared the President-elect before
Congress has counted the votes. Akhil Reed Amar notes that
the "legislative history of the Twentieth Amendment suggests
that the electoral college winner is 'President elect' the moment

the electoral college votes are cast, and before they are counted in Congress." Amar, *supra* note 74, at 217–18. However, "the text of the Amendment fails to say this explicitly," *id.* at 218, and "[b]oth Article II and the Twelfth Amendment seem to focus on the formal counting of votes in the Congress as the magic, formal moment of vesting in which the winning candidate is elected as 'President.'" *Id.* at 217. On the other hand, Robert Bennett states that a candidate can be President-elect before the votes are counted by Congress. BENNETT, *supra* note 8, at 119 & 239 n.100. Such a position seems to ignore the fact that Congress at least claims the authority to reject slates of electors and to decide certain election disputes. How can the outcome be known with certainty until Congress has acted? In the case of a candidate who has passed away, Congress could decide not to accept these votes cast for a deceased candidate, as it did in 1873 when Horace Greeley died. The most rational point at which to formally designate a candidate "President-elect" is after Congress has decided which votes to count and accept as valid on January 6.

87. Naturally, this solution will not work well when the results of the presidential election are very close, as they were in 1876 and 2000.

88. *See, e.g.,* Wilmerding, *supra* note 27, at 13–14 (discussing the constitutional amendment that was proposed).

89. 2 REG. DEB. app. 121 (1826). The report also noted that it "was the intention of the Constitution that these electors should be an independent body of men, chosen by the People from among themselves, on account of their superior discernment, virtue, and information; and that this select body should be left to make the election according to their own will, without the slightest control from the body of the People. That this intention has failed of its object in every

election, is a fact of such universal notoriety, that no one can dispute it." *Id*.

90. Letter from James Madison to Robert Taylor (Jan. 30, 1826), in 9 THE WRITINGS OF JAMES MADISON 149 n, 150 n (Gaillard Hunt ed., 1910).

91. MADISON, *supra* note 15, at 578.

92. THE FEDERALIST NO. 68, *supra* note 10, at 410 (Alexander Hamilton).

93. *Id*.

94. *Id*. at 412.

CHAPTER NINE

1. Benjamin Morris, *How Evan McMullin Could Win Utah and the Presidency*, FIVETHIRTYEIGHT (Oct. 13, 2016, 5:20 PM), http://fivethirtyeight.com/features/how-evan-mcmullin-could-win-utah-and-the-presidency.

2. McMullin was on the ballot in Arkansas (6 electoral votes), Colorado (9), Idaho (4), Iowa (6), Kentucky (8), Louisiana (8), Minnesota (10), New Mexico (5), South Carolina (9), Utah (6), and Virginia (13). *See, e.g.*, Rebecca Kheel, *Independent May Make History in Utah*, THE HILL (Oct. 15, 2016, 4:23 PM), http://thehill.com/policy/defense/301062-independent-may-make-history-in-utah.

3. For example, one prominent McMullin supporter posted on Facebook: "Nearly all of the [Representatives] know and respect Evan McMullin. . . . Evan would win a contingent election (HOUSE VOTE) by a landslide." Becky Turley Rasmussen (@becky.t.rasmussen), FACEBOOK (Oct. 4, 2016, 1:12 PM), http://www.facebook.com/becky.t.rasmussen/posts/10210775488289199. Her post was shared several thousand times and ended up earning her local media attention. *See, e.g.*, Amanda Beal, *Does Evan McMullin*

Really Have a Chance at the White House?, Rexburg
Standard J. (Oct 14, 2016), http://www.
rexburgstandardjournal.com/news/local/does-evan-mcmullin-
really-have-a-chance-at-the-white/article_17620096-9194-
11e6-9f83-cf51fa6f8c92.html.

4. *See* Dennis Romboy, *Poll: Trump Falls into Tie with Clinton
Among Utah Voters*, Desert News (Oct. 11, 2016 11:25
PM), http://www.deseretnews.com/article/865664606/Poll-
Trump-falls-into-tie-with-Clinton-among-Utah-voters.
html?pg=all; *Utah President: Trump 32%, McMullin 29%,
Clinton 28%*, Rasmussen Reports (Oct. 26, 2016), http://
www.rasmussenreports.com/public_content/archive/
election_2016_state_survey_archive/utah/utah_president_
trump_32_mcmullin_29_clinton_28.

5. Writing for *The Hill*, one commentator put forth a scenario
that would result in an electoral split of 263 (Clinton), 269
(Trump), and 6 (McMullin). Jonathan Walczak, *A Totally
Plausible Path for Evan McMullin to Become President*, The
Hill (Nov. 1, 2016, 1:55 PM), http://thehill.com/blogs/
pundits-blog/presidential-campaign/303792-a-totally-
plausible-path-for-independent-evan.

6. Robert Gehrke, *Mike Pence to Make Campaign Visit in Bid
to Shore up Utah Support*, Salt Lake Trib. (Oct. 24, 2016,
8:42 PM), http://www.sltrib.com/home/4502782-155/mike-
pence-to-make-campaign-visit.

7. Martin Diamond, Am. Enter. Inst., Testimony in
Support of the Electoral College 7 (1977); *see also*
George C. Edwards III, Why the Electoral College Is
Bad for America 74 (2d ed. 2011) (calling the contingent
election "the most egregious violation of democratic principles
in the American political system").

8.   He made this prediction when delegates were still considering a contingent election in the Senate, instead of the House. Mason felt that the Senate shouldn't choose the President so often. JAMES MADISON, NOTES OF DEBATES IN THE FEDERAL CONVENTION OF 1787, at 577 (Adrienne Koch ed., W.W. Norton & Co. 1987) (1966).

9.   This isn't to suggest that similar ideas weren't discussed earlier in the Convention. On July 17, for instance, James Wilson defended the possibility of a national popular election, noting the possibility of using a back-up procedure if no candidate obtained a majority of individual votes. The process, he noted, could look like that "used in Masts. where the Legislature by majority of voices, decide in case a majority of people do not concur in favor of one of the candidates." *Id.* at 307.

10. John Dickinson to George Logan (Jan. 16, 1802), *in* SUPPLEMENT TO MAX FARRAND'S THE RECORDS OF THE FEDERAL CONVENTION OF 1787, at 300, 301 (James H. Hutson ed., 1987).

11. MADISON, *supra* note 8, at 574.

12. *Id.*

13. *Id.* at 577.

14. *Id.*

15. *Id.*

16. *See id.*

17. *Id.* at 578.

18. *Id.*

19. CAROL BERKIN, A BRILLIANT SOLUTION: INVENTING THE AMERICAN CONSTITUTION 143 (1st Harvest ed. 2003).

20. MADISON, *supra* note 8, at 587, 592.

21. James Wilson expressed his concern on this point. "According to the plan as it now stands," he remarked, "the President will

not be the man of the people as he ought to be, but the Minion of the Senate." *Id.* at 588.

22. Only one day earlier, Sherman had observed that large and small states each had an advantage at different points in the Senate contingent election process then being considered: "[I]f the small states had the advantage in the Senate's deciding among the five highest candidates, the large States would have in fact the nomination of these candidates." *Id.* at 584. Rufus King of Massachusetts soon echoed this sentiment, noting that "the influence of the Small States in the Senate was somewhat balanced by the influence of the large States in bringing forward the candidates . . . ." *Id.* at 585. Sherman's proposal for a state-by-state vote in the House preserved this balance. *See id.* at 592.

23. Letter from James Madison to Henry Lee (Jan. 14, 1825), *in* 9 THE WRITINGS OF JAMES MADISON 215, 217 (Gaillard Hunt ed., 1910).

24. U.S. CONST. art. II, § 1, cl. 3.

25. *Id.*

26. *Id.* amend. XII.

27. *Id.* amend. XX, § 3.

28. 3 U.S.C. § 19 (2012); *see also* THOMAS H. NEALE, CONG. RESEARCH SERV., R40504, CONTINGENT ELECTION OF THE PRESIDENT AND VICE PRESIDENT BY CONGRESS: PERSPECTIVES AND CONTEMPORARY ANALYSIS 10 (2016). *But see* discussion *supra* note 84 (Ch. 8).

29. *The Statistics Are Against Him, But Wallace's Drive Surges Ahead*, LIFE, Sept. 20, 1968, at 40B.

30. A description of the 1968 election can be found at CQ PRESS, PRESIDENTIAL ELECTIONS: 1789–2008, at 75–77 (2010); David S. Broder, *Election of 1968*, *in* 3 HISTORY OF AMERICAN PRESIDENTIAL ELECTIONS: 1789–2008, at 1317,

1317–59 (Gil Troy et al. eds., 4th ed. 2012); Lawrence D.
Longley & Neal R. Peirce, The Electoral College
Primer 2000, at 59–69 (1999).

31. *E.g.*, Broder, *supra* note 30, at 1350.

32. Although some historians wonder if he wasn't beginning to
believe that he could pull off a victory after all, given the size
of the crowds that came to see him and the number of
contributions that he was receiving. *See id.*

33. *See id.* at 1350–51; *see also* Jody Carlson, George C.
Wallace and the Politics of Powerlessness: The
Wallace Campaigns for the Presidency, 1964–1976, at
79–80 (1981) (discussing Wallace's intent to obtain
concessions).

34. Broder, *supra* note 30, at 1351; Carlson, *supra* note 33, at
80.

35. Broder, *supra* note 30, at 1350.

36. *Id.* at 1351.

37. *See* CQ Press, *supra* note 30, at 161, 251. He would later get
one additional vote from a faithless elector, for a final total of
46 electoral votes. *See id.* at 189.

38. *See* discussion *supra* notes 9–13 (Ch. 5) and accompanying
text.

39. Letter from Thomas Jefferson to George Hay (Aug. 17, 1823),
in 12 The Works of Thomas Jefferson 302, 303 (Paul
Leicester Ford ed., 1905).

40. *See* discussion *supra* notes 5–9 (Ch. 2) and accompanying
text.

41. *See* Letter from James Madison to George Hay (Aug. 23,
1823), *in* 9 The Writings of James Madison, *supra* note
23, at 147, 151 ("But with all possible abatements, the present
rule of voting for President by the H. of Reps. is so great a
departure from the Republican principle of numerical equality,

and even from the federal rule which qualifies the numerical by a State equality, and is so pregnant also with a mischievous tendency in practice, that an amendment of the Constitution on this point is justly called for by all its considerate & best friends.").

42. To be fair, even at the Constitutional Convention, Madison seemed concerned with making sure that most elections did not end up in the secondary election procedure—or, at least, he expressed this concern before the "one state, one vote" rule had been proposed for the House. *See* MADISON, *supra* note 8, at 584 ("Mr. MADISON considered it as a primary object to render an eventual resort to any part of the Legislature improbable. He was apprehensive that the proposed alteration would turn the attention of the large States too much to the appointment of candidates, instead of aiming at an effectual appointment of the officer, as the large States would predominate in the Legislature which would have the final choice out of the Candidates. Whereas if the Senate in which the small States predominate should have this final choice, the concerted effort of the large States would be to make the appointment in the first instance conclusive.").

43. Letter from James Madison, *supra* note 23, at 217.

44. These issues are also discussed in Chapter Nine of TARA ROSS, ENLIGHTENED DEMOCRACY: THE CASE FOR THE ELECTORAL COLLEGE (Colonial Press 2d ed. 2012) (2004).

45. *See, e.g.,* JUDITH A. BEST, THE CHOICE OF THE PEOPLE? DEBATING THE ELECTORAL COLLEGE 13–15 (1996) (relating the primary complaints made about the contingent election procedure); *see also* ROBERT W. BENNETT, TAMING THE ELECTORAL COLLEGE 78–85 (2006) (noting the additional complaint that D.C. has no representation in the House

contingent election); LONGLEY & PEIRCE, *supra* note 30, at 169–75.

46. Such a Vice President would doubtless work to frustrate the President's agenda in the Senate—although maybe some would consider that a good thing.

47. DAVID MCCULLOUGH, JOHN ADAMS 475 (2001). Although some might argue that no great harm comes from having Presidents and Vice Presidents of different parties. The President does not have to assign duties to Vice Presidents, although they sometimes do so. As a constitutional matter, the most important task of a Vice President is to be available to serve as President in the event that a President passes away. Moreover, as a historical matter, many Vice Presidents have found themselves in the same situation as Jefferson, even when they were members of the same political party as the President. For instance, Theodore Roosevelt served briefly as Vice President prior to his presidency. He had few responsibilities and was reportedly bored and frustrated with his role. See NATHAN MILLER, THEODORE ROOSEVELT: A LIFE 346 (1992) (describing Vice President Roosevelt as "[f]rustrated," "feeling unused," and looking for ways to fill his time).

48. Walczak, *supra* note 5.

49. BENNETT, *supra* note 45, at 76.

50. Professor Bennett's numbers rely upon the 1990 and 2000 censuses. *Id.*

51. *See* BEST, *supra* note 45, at 13–15 (arguing that the contingent election procedure is not usually needed and the solutions that have been proposed will simply make matters worse); *see also* ROBERT M. HARDAWAY, THE ELECTORAL COLLEGE AND THE CONSTITUTION: THE CASE FOR PRESERVING FEDERALISM

153–55, 166–68 (1994) (arguing that the contingent election procedure should not be changed).

52. Legal questions might arise regarding how far a state can go in redirecting its electors at this point in the election process, particularly in those states that have enacted statutes purporting to bind their electors to the winner of the popular vote. However, if electors truly are "distinguished citizens" with a constitutional right to make independent decisions, then the opportunity for states to redirect them grows. If nothing else, they could approve a resolution asking their electors to consider a new course of action. The electors could cast their vote accordingly and would be likely to do so if they agree that the states' voters approve of such a change.

53. MADISON, *supra* note 8, at 578.

CONCLUSION

1. Donald J. Trump (@realDonaldTrump), TWITTER (Nov. 15, 2016, 7:40 AM), https://twitter.com/realDonaldTrump/status/798521053551140864.

2. Donald J. Trump (@realDonaldTrump), TWITTER (Nov. 27, 2016, 2:34 PM), https://twitter.com/realDonaldTrump/status/802973848022847489; Donald J. Trump (@realDonaldTrump), TWITTER (Nov. 27, 2016, 2:41 PM), https://twitter.com/realDonaldTrump/status/802975667197386752.

3. Donald J. Trump (@realDonaldTrump), TWITTER (Dec. 21, 2016, 7:15 AM), https://twitter.com/realDonaldTrump/status/811560662853939200.

4. Donald J. Trump (@realDonaldTrump), TWITTER (Nov. 6, 2012, 10:45 PM) https://twitter.com/realdonaldtrump/status/266038556504494082.

5. First Inaugural Address: Final Version (Apr. 30, 1789), *in* 2 THE PAPERS OF GEORGE WASHINGTON: PRESIDENTIAL SERIES 173, 175 (W.W. Abbot et al. eds., 1987).
6. A point that this author made at the time. *See* Tara Ross (@TaraRoss), TWITTER (Oct 19, 2016, 8:15 PM), https://twitter.com/TaraRoss/status/788911597959852032 ("This #debate continues to pretend this is a nat'l election b/w two nat'l candidates. But doesn't reflect reality of #ElectoralCollege); Tara Ross (@TaraRoss), TWITTER (Oct 19, 2016, 8:16 PM), https://twitter.com/TaraRoss/status/788911776297422850 ("#ElectoralCollege is,at its heart, series of state-by-state actions. 4 candidates competitive in state races. 2 missing from #debate stage").
7. *See, e.g.,* JUDITH BEST, THE CASE AGAINST DIRECT ELECTION OF THE PRESIDENT: A DEFENSE OF THE ELECTORAL COLLEGE 67 (1975).
8. THE FEDERALIST NO. 68 at 410 (Alexander Hamilton) (Clinton Rossiter ed., Signet Classic 2003) (1961).

APPENDIX B

1. The figures in this chart were obtained from CQ PRESS, PRESIDENTIAL ELECTIONS: 1789–2008 (2010).
2. No record of the popular vote was kept until 1824.
3. A list of faithless electors can be found in Appendix D.
4. Percentages may not add up to 100 percent because of rounding. Due to the combined voting procedure for President and Vice President, this figure is not useful until after adoption of the 12th Amendment in 1804.
5. The total number of available elector votes was 176; however, only 175 votes were cast because one Kentucky elector did not vote.

6. The total number of available elector votes was 218; however, only 217 votes were cast because one Ohio elector did not vote.

7. The total number of available elector votes was 221; however, only 217 votes were cast because one Delaware elector and three Maryland electors did not vote.

8. The total number of available elector votes was 235; however, only 232 votes were cast because three electors—from Mississippi, Pennsylvania, and Tennessee—did not vote.

9. The election of 1824 was decided in the House contingent election, since no presidential candidate received a majority of electoral votes. John Quincy Adams received the votes of 13 state delegations; Jackson, 7; and Crawford, 4.

10. The total number of available elector votes was 288; however, only 286 votes were cast because two Maryland electors did not vote.

11. The total number of available elector votes was 234; however, only 233 votes were cast because one Nevada elector did not vote. Eleven southern states did not vote because they had seceded from the Union.

12. The total number of available elector votes was 366; however, only 349 votes were cast and counted. The Democratic candidate, Horace Greeley, died between the time of the popular vote and the meeting of the presidential electors. Sixty-three of his electors voted for alternative candidates, but three electors cast their votes for Greeley despite his death. Congress refused to count these last three votes, since they had been cast for a deceased candidate. In addition, Congress refused to accept votes from Arkansas and Louisiana due to problems resulting from Reconstruction.

13. An anonymous elector in Minnesota voted for John Edwards instead of John Kerry.

14. Election results as of May 25, 2017. For a discussion of the faithless electors in 2016, see Chapters Six and Eight.

APPENDIX C

1.   *See* L. Paige Whitaker & Thomas H. Neale, Cong. Research Serv., RL30804, The Electoral College: An Overview and Analysis of Reform Proposals 12 (2004); *see also* After the People Vote: A Guide to the Electoral College 90 app. G (John C. Fortier ed., 3d ed. 2004) (listing faithless electors); CQ Press, Presidential Elections: 1789–2008, at 189 (2010) (same); Lawrence D. Longley & Neal R. Peirce, The Electoral College Primer 2000 at 111–13 (1999) (same).

2.   There is a reasonable argument for excluding Preston Parks from this list. He was nominated to (and pledged to vote for) two different slates of electors: the Democratic slate (Truman) and the States' Rights slate (Thurmond). Although he'd originally pledged to vote for Truman, he changed his mind and campaigned for Thurmond. His vote for Thurmond could not have been a surprise. *See, e.g.*, George C. Edwards III, Why the Electoral College Is Bad for America 55 (2d ed. 2011); Longley & Peirce, *supra* note 1, at 112.

APPENDIX D

1.   The right to remove an elector is not explicitly spelled out in the state's election code. Neither does the code explicitly provide for punishment of an elector. However, recent events suggest that any of these actions may be considered against an elector. In 2016, Colorado's Secretary of State removed an

elector who tried to vote independently. The removal was
based on last-minute election regulations that required electors
to take an oath that "I will vote for the presidential candidate
and vice-presidential candidate who received the highest
number of votes at the preceding general election in this state,"
combined with a section of the statutory text that references a
"refusal to act" by the elector. COLO. REV. STAT. § 1-4-304(1);
see also Wayne W. Williams, Sec'y State Colo., *Notice of
Temporary Adoption: Amendments to 2 CCR 1505-l* (Dec.
19, 2016), https://www.sos.state.co.us/pubs/rule_making/
files/2016/20161219_Election_NoticeTempAdoption.pdf. Of
course, an elector who takes an oath but then breaks it is not
engaging in a "refusal to act." That elector is taking action,
but he is acting in a way that state officials do not want. As
this book goes to press, the state's Attorney General is
reportedly investigating the Colorado elector who was
removed. Prosecution of the act as a misdemeanor warranting
up to one year in jail or a $1,000 fine is still being considered.
See, e.g., John Frank, *Denver Judge Rules Against "Faithless"
Colorado Electors Trying to Block Donald Trump*, DENVER
POST (Dec. 13, 2016; 4:56 PM), http://www.denverpost.
com/2016/12/13/denver-judge-orders-faithless-colorado-
electors-vote-clinton; Corey Hutchins, *Colorado Secretary of
State on 2016 Electoral College Vote: 'They're Investigating,'*
COLO. INDEP. (Apr. 25, 2017), http://www.colorado
independent.com/165059/colorado-electoral-college-
investigation-hamilton-electors.

2. Maine's statutes require presidential electors to vote in
accordance with the popular vote in the state or in a
congressional district. No provision appears to authorize the
removal of an elector who fails to abide by this requirement.

Nor does any provision address the possibility of invalidating an "incorrect" vote. *See* ME. STAT. tit. 21-A, § 805(2). Nevertheless, Maine elector David Bright attempted to vote for Bernie Sanders in 2016. That vote was rejected. Bright then cast a second ballot for Hillary Clinton. The second vote was accepted. Scott Thistle, *Maine Electors Cast Votes for Clinton, Trump—After Protests Inside and Outside State House*, PORTLAND PRESS HERALD (Dec. 19, 2016), http://www.pressherald.com/2016/12/19/maine-electoral-college-elector-says-he-will-cast-his-ballot-for-sanders.

3. Oregon law does not explicitly provide for the removal of an elector who votes independently; however, it does contain a "refusal to act" provision, similar to the one used in Colorado in 2016. OR. REV. STAT. § 248.370; *see also supra* note 1.

4. The law distinguishes between situations in which a presidential versus a vice presidential candidate has passed away. In the event of the former, electors may vote "as they see fit" for both offices. TENN. CODE ANN. § 2-15-104(c)(2). If the vice presidential candidate has passed away, but the presidential candidate is still alive, then they are expected to vote "for the presidential candidate of the political party which nominated them," but they can vote for vice president "as they see fit." TENN. CODE ANN. § 2-15-104(c)(3).

5. Vermont law does not explicitly provide for the removal of an elector who votes independently; however, it does contain a "refusal to act" provision, similar to the one used in Colorado in 2016. VT. STAT. ANN. tit. 17, § 2732; *see also supra* note 1.

6. Virginia law does not explicitly provide for the removal of an elector who votes independently; however, it does contain a "refusal to act" provision, similar to the one used in Colorado in 2016. VA. CODE ANN. § 24.2-203; *see also supra* note 1.

7.   Washington law does not explicitly provide for the removal of an elector who votes independently; however, it does contain a "refusal to act" provision, similar to the one used in Colorado in 2016. WASH. REV. CODE § 29A.56.320; *see also supra* note 1. Nevertheless, no attempt was made to replace the four Washington electors who cast independent votes in 2016. Instead, the state levied $1,000 fines on each elector, as provided for in WASH. REV. CODE § 29A.56.340.

8.   Wisconsin law does not explicitly provide for the removal of an elector who votes independently; however, it does contain a "refusal to act" provision, similar to the one used in Colorado in 2016. WIS. STAT. § 7.75(1); *see also supra* note 1.

APPENDIX E

1.   10 ANNALS OF CONGRESS 1009–11 (1801).
2.   1 REG. DEB. 509–15 (1825).

INDEX